D1207938

The
Rocky
Mountain
Bench

THE TERRITORIAL SUPREME COURTS OF COLORADO,

MONTANA, AND WYOMING, 1861–1890

by
John D. W. Guice

NEW HAVEN AND LONDON, YALE UNIVERSITY PRESS, 1972

Published with assistance from
the Louis Stern Memorial Fund.

Library of Congress catalog card number: 72-75195
International standard book number: 0-300-01479-1
Designed by Sally Sullivan
and set in Linotype Baskerville type.
Printed in the United States of America by
The Vail-Ballou Press, Inc., Binghamton, New York
Published in Great Britain, Europe, and Africa by
Yale University Press, Ltd., London.
Distributed in Canada by McGill-Queen's University
Press, Montreal; in Latin America by Kaiman & Polon,
Inc., New York City; in Australasia and Southeast
Asia by John Wiley & Sons Australasia Pty. Ltd.,
Sydney; in India by UBS Publishers' Distributors Pvt.,
Ltd., Delhi; in Japan by John Weatherhill, Inc., Tokyo.

For Carol

Contents

Preface

In the light of recent pleas for a new type of scholarship in western history, a reassessment of the contributions of territorial supreme courts—indeed, of all territorial officials—is overdue. Accepting the challenge to replace narrative with analysis, this study deals with a major but neglected institution which played a significant role in the development of the American West.

Those historians who have not completely ignored the territorial bench have examined the judiciary from a moralistic rather than from a functional view. Consequently, the carpet-bagger theme dominates accounts of territorial jurists. This constrictive approach accents the negative features of the supreme courts, and it fails to assess objectively their contributions to territorial growth and to the jurisprudence of the region. The moralistic view also aids in the perpetuation of an interpretation of territorial history which is locally and environmentally oriented, to the neglect of the impact of the federal government and national political parties.

To understand the mechanics of the territorial process, new questions must be posed. Rather than asking whence and why the officials—the justices, in this case—came, the historian should ask what they did. The following study is the application of this question to the territorial supreme courts of Colorado, Montana, and Wyoming. Once the smoke screen of political denigration is penetrated and the hard record is examined, it becomes evident that the territorial judiciary accomplished far more than has been suspected. And much of the story is found either in very unappealing places such as court opinions, legislative journals, and territorial codes, or in records of the National Archives which have not been micro-filmed. Those who question the relevance to other territories of the following conclusions must, in order to allay their doubts, apply similar yardsticks to the territories they have in mind.

Recognition is due the scores of helpful people, from the Continental Divide to the eastern seaboard, who assisted me in more ways than I can list. My indebtedness to them is as sincere as it is great, and it is most earnestly hoped that each of them, from head librarians and archivists to those often unappre-ciated heavers of boxes and pushers of carts, will accept this thanks which must be delivered en masse. Special apprecia-tion, nevertheless, must be extended to the tireless and pleasant staffs of the Colorado State Historical Society Library, the Montana Historical Society, the Wyoming State Archives and Historical Department, and the Denver Public Library West-ern History Department.

Professors Howard R. Lamar and Clark C. Spence were kind enough to share with me their assessment of the merits of my investigation in its formative stages. Without the guidance, confidence, and generosity of Professors Clifford P. Wester-meier and Robert G. Athearn of the University of Colorado, this study would have never been begun, much less completed. It is hoped that this volume will in some way bring them a fraction of the reward to which they are entitled.

Professor Elliott West graciously read the manuscript and offered valuable comments. And I am particularly indebted to the editorial staff of Yale University Press—especially to Patri-cia Woodruff for her many useful suggestions. The final stages of research and preparation of the manuscript were done with grants from the American Philosophical Society and from the University of Southern Mississippi through funds adminis-tered by Dean of the University, Charles W. Moorman. The initial research was partially financed by the University of Colorado.

My greatest support, however, has come from my family in the form of understanding and love from my wife, Carol, and from Soni Jo and Johnny.

I

"Yesterday's
Villains"

For too long lecturers and writers have described the more entertaining and visible frontier personalities while ignoring deeper questions of interpretation. Now that the emphasis has changed, historians are attempting to reconstruct the underpinnings of frontier America, and they are acknowledging the impact of the less glamorous types on the trans-Mississippi West. Entrepreneurs, industrialists, technologists, railroaders, and farmers are receiving long overdue attention. Not only do historians' assessments shift, but the "villains of yesterday's texts have a way of becoming the heroes of today's books." [1] Territorial justices are now candidates for a similar transformation.

Though scant attention has been directed toward territorial supreme courts, the carpetbagger theme dominates most accounts. Consequently, too many authors classify the judiciary as the weakest branch of an administration rife with corruption and incompetence.[2] The bench has been caricatured as a virtual haven for judicial derelicts—party hacks who were unschooled, unskilled fortune seekers, serving without personal involvement or sincere interest in the destiny of their territories. However, rejection of this simplistic carpetbagger characterization of territorial judges is appropriate in view of recent calls for a fresh examination of Reconstruction politicians. Richard N. Current warns that the carpetbagger stereotype cannot be uncritically accepted, and he questions whether so-called carpetbag officials differed in decency and ability

1

from other politicians of the same time and place.[3] Similarly, the validity of applying the carpetbagger label so frequently to the territorial supreme court justices of the Reconstruction, as well as those of later periods, must be challenged.

The semantic controversy, however, is not as critical to a reevaluation of the judiciary's work as is the question of functionalism raised by Howard Lamar. Calling for an abandonment of moralistic criteria in the assessment of territorial officials, he argues that their achievements must be measured in a functional way.[4] Only in this manner can it be determined who made positive contributions to territorial development. Lamar correctly rejects the prevailing view of territorial officials as a parasitic group whose "contributions were negative rather than positive." [5] Historians have devoted entirely too much attention to moralistic criticism while the objective analysis of territorial growth and operation, particularly in the postwar era, has been virtually neglected.[6] The following study of the territorial judiciary illustrates the pertinence of these observations.

Because they ignore one of the most significant activities of the period—the politics of development—moralistic interpretations of territorial history are particularly constrictive. Glamorous only at times, territorial development was literally a "nuts and bolts" process. Someone had to "tend the store," and at the same time, the gears of the economy had to be set in motion. Territorial judges were at the center of both activities. They established a jurisprudence that facilitated growth in the mining industry and permitted the evolution of an orderly system of agricultural irrigation.

Historians of the trans-Mississippi West have too often examined the territories apart from, rather than as an integral part of, our political system; this localizing tendency has given rise to several pleas for a reorientation of western history. In 1955 Earl S. Pomeroy called for scholarship of greater "breadth and flexibility of mind" and for the extrication of scholarship from the "old radical-environmental bias." [7]

"In the field of government and politics, most clearly of all, it is evident that western history has been constricted by a local framework that has slighted similarities, antecedents, and outside influences generally."[8] Ray A. Billington has also urged a synthesis of western scholarship which would abandon provincialism, antiquarianism, and popularization as well as the continual semantic gymnastics of definition.[9] In essence Billington's advice is to stop quibbling and start testing so that an understanding of the frontier's role in the evolution of today's social order can be reached. Conveying a sense of urgency in the inaugural issue of *The Western Historical Quarterly*, Billington emphasized the necessity of recognizing the national implications of our western heritage.[10]

A new scholarship of the West is becoming apparent, a scholarship in which the frontier and, specifically, the territories are being reexamined with an eye toward the influence of national institutions on their political and economic configuration. This is a most welcome development. In *Exploration and Empire*, William H. Goetzmann describes the West as "a theater in which American patterns of culture could be endlessly mirrored" (p. xiii). As if determined to prove the validity of Billington and Pomeroy's counsel, Goetzmann insists that western men engaged in an endless Americanization process as "prisoners of an emulative society." His explorers fulfilled "national images and plans."

Reflecting our computer-oriented, space-age society, Goetzmann writes that explorers are programmed for the extension of their cultures. If this concept is valid, it is imperative that the role of the judiciary be closely studied since, by training and tradition, lawyers tend to be more highly programmed than settlers or explorers. Of all the legacies transplanted first on the eastern seaboard and later in the West, the common law was perhaps the most deeply rooted. Strained and even broken at times by the demands of the mountains and plains, it nevertheless was as much a part of the program as any institution. So much a part of the American, this legal

heritage did not draw as much attention as other less ingrained institutions.

There are other parallels between Goetzmann's explorers
and the judiciary. Exploration, he feels, is an activity; its
missionlike qualities distinguish it from simple acts of dis-
covery (p. xi). The program of this activity includes virtually
all facets of the civilization of the explorers. In like manner,
the justices were engaged in an activity of great moment to
both the transmission of a culture and the welfare of the
people in general.

More directly concerned with territorial history, Lewis L.
Gould's *Wyoming: A Political History, 1868–1896* reexamines
the role of the federal government and national parties in the
political and economic development of Wyoming's territorial
and early statehood periods. How much federal-local interplay
there was has not been established, but Gould at least shows
that it was considerable. Two of the major figures in Gould's
study, Joseph M. Carey and Willis Van Devanter, served on
the Wyoming Territorial Supreme Court.

As agents of acculturation, the territorial courts were by no
means exempt from the boisterous conduct which often
characterized the people of the frontier. To ignore the more
sensational incidents in their history would indeed deprive the
reader of both pleasure and truth. But a study of these courts
clearly illustrates that both the federal government and the
East were major influences in the territories, influences which
affected the entire territorial administration. Relying mainly
on informal sources, historians have overlooked the interplay
of East and West, thereby perpetuating the semilegendary Roy
Bean image of western justice. Their preference for dealing
with the dramatic issues of law and order and their reluctance
to investigate rather burdensome sources—codes, reports, and
other legal records—is understandable. Though pioneer judges
enjoyed their share of excitement and danger, their primary
duties were laborious and far from romantic. It was in less

spectacular roles that they served as links between the old and new sections of the nation.

Usually from the East and often unpopular, the frontier judges and lawyers carried west from "the states" the familiar codes and texts in which they had been trained. The federalizing or nationalizing effect of this was reinforced by the fact that the justices worked under the rather close supervision of the attorney general of the United States. His office watched over them much as it did the district judges of the United States itself.[11] Another unifying or standardizing factor was the subordination of territorial supreme courts to the United States Supreme Court.

If the courts were transmitters of American institutions, they were also innovators, and their decisions are strong testimony to the fact that environment modifies a people's heritage. Walter Prescott Webb's classic, *The Great Plains,* immediately comes to mind. Webb was neither the first nor the last to comment on the strain and rupture of institutions, including the law, west of the Mississippi, but his prose has indelibly imprinted itself on the minds of historians. An evaluation of territorial supreme court justices as innovators is long overdue.

The glaring inadequacies of the judicial system have so attracted the attention of territorial historians that they have ignored the contributions of the court as an institution as well as those of individual members of the bench.[12] Despite its role in both acculturation and innovation, the judiciary has been almost completely expunged from history; only its most notorious aspects are remembered. A survey of territorial bibliography graphically reflects this. Environmental and local themes are clearly dominant, and most accounts of the frontier bench and bar are of the "grandfather practiced here" variety.[13]

Textbooks and social histories invariably pay tribute to mountain men, soldiers, Indians, cowboys, miners, farmers, freighters, et cetera. Hardly a sentence, however, is devoted to the courts which upheld or redefined the rules by which many of these people operated. Monographs and periodical literature also tend to ignore the judiciary. A survey of the Index to the first ten volumes of *Montana the Magazine of Western History* reveals, for example, no direct references to the Montana Territorial Supreme Court. Equally curious is the fact that W. Turrentine Jackson wrote only one sentence about the supreme court in his extremely helpful analysis of the territorial papers in the National Archives.[14] The role of territorial justices, individually and as a body, in the economic development of their respective territories is ignored. It is doubtful that the potential of either mining or agriculture would have been realized without the territorial bench's formalization of mineral and water law. In addition, some of the judges contributed to economic growth as investors or brokers of eastern capital.

This neglect of the judiciary reflects a narrow view and has helped to produce what is perhaps an overemphasis on the more visible responsibilities of the governor (for example, his duties as Superintendant of Indian Affairs). Laws and institutional values are inseparable, and though governors were entrusted with more dashing responsibilities, the judges were equally involved in the transmission of national institutions to the frontier. The governor's impact on territorial society was no greater than that of the justice. Another key to his prominence in accounts of the period is the fact that sources dealing with him are more readily available. As titular head of territorial administration, the governor left a trail easily followed by the historian.[15]

The demands of contemporary scholarship are clear. The nostalgic narrative must be superseded by an explanation of the place of the territorial system within the governmental, economic, and social framework of the nation as a whole. The role of the court in its dual capacity as acculturator and innovator merits an integral part in the attempt to view territorial development in its proper perspective. And, finally, the contributions of individual judges to the general growth and welfare of territorial society must be acknowledged, as must those of the court as an official agency. The challenge is to accomplish these goals without becoming bogged down by codes, reports, and scholarly apparatus. Aided by a careful search of court records, I have tried to meet this challenge in the present study through an analysis of themes, problems, and personalities.

Wilbur Fisk Stone, historian and Colorado Supreme Court justice, has accented the relevance of biographical material. "Every court takes its quality and complexion from the judge," Stone observed, "and its influence and effects are measured by the structure of the man and not the machine." [16] Indeed, a history of the courts involves a history of their judges. As the Rocky Mountain territories matured during and after the Civil War, opportunity for contributions by members of the bench abounded, and Stone's maxim is most apropos in reference to them. What these men accomplished is of more consequence than whence and why they came!

Practical considerations dictate the form of any work. Thus, the diversity, inaccessibility, and uninviting nature of the sources probably explain the reticence of historians to analyze the role of the judiciary. Codes, statutes, reports, and other legal sources, though invaluable in such research, do not by themselves provide enough material to weave a whole cloth. Among other sources the richest are official correspondence, territorial newspapers, and the various records preserved in national and state archives and private manuscript collections. Even with all these sources, biographical information for a number of justices proved exceedingly difficult to extract. In reviewing this material, however, a number of recurrent themes and problems emerged. An examination of these themes and problems reveals the contributions of the justices, and thus the general historian can make his evaluations as readily as the legal specialist. In addition, a valuable by-product of the historian's research is new knowledge about the economic and social activities of litigants—men and women who were representative of territorial society. For this reason, the often tedious and forbidding court records become virtual "mines of social history." [17]

The fact that the governmental and political affairs of the territories have been generally neglected does not entirely explain the selection of the Colorado, Montana, and Wyoming territories as the basis of this study. Little attention has been directed toward the area beyond the first tier of states west of the Mississippi.[18] Historians have come to realize that the political history of most western states has been affected by their territorial origins, and they now recognize the serious-ness of their oversight.[19] The consequences of scholarly neglect are magnified for the area beyond the Mississippi because the territorial system had its longest and most extensive applica-tion there. In addition, it was in the far western territories that the system was most harshly criticized and challenged by the populace.[20]

The Colorado, Montana, and Wyoming territories shared not only these general conditions but also specific problems of mining, water, and range law. Each of the three territories is traversed by the Rocky Mountains, and each has large, flat plains in its eastern region. Mining posed new problems of jurisprudence which demanded speedy settlement and involved unusually large sums of money. Both the extraction of minerals and the irrigation of the parched plains neces-sitated a departure from the common law principle of riparian rights. Furthermore, all three (but especially Colorado and Montana) became territories as the result of sudden influxes of population. Finally, Colorado and Montana weathered many problems stemming from the Civil War, and all three suffered from the discordant postwar political climate.

In all three territories the character and contributions of the early bench are distinct from those of the later judiciary. The earlier courts, for instance, were greatly concerned with the pragmatic demands of organization and the establishment of order. A hardy, adventurous breed of men served on these courts. But it was during the later territorial periods that the justices made the most significant contributions to the body of the law as conditions became more settled and the peculiar demands of the environment more thoroughly understood. Of the many effects the railroads had on the West, one virtually ignored thus far was that they indirectly improved the quality of the courts. The tribulations, distractions, and dangers faced by the justices, once the courts were organized, were minor compared with those of their predecessors. In addition to these changes, an expanding economy of far greater complexity accounts for a contrast in the complexion of the courts of the formative and the mature territorial periods.

The general design of the territorial system and the method by which the judges were appointed generated partisanship, and the judiciary was under constant political bombardment. Job security was nonexistent and politically inspired attacks incessant. I have evaluated information gleaned from newspapers and correspondence with these facts in mind, and have tried to distinguish between partisan outcries and the true judgment of the citizenry.

Though the following study is not intended as an in-depth political history, politics, of course, cannot be omitted. In occasional, isolated incidents more detailed analysis may have been possible, but the insertion of more political minutiae would not have altered the basic conclusions. It might, however, have made the work unmanageable for some readers. My objective is neither to exculpate carpetbagger judges nor to replace old shibboleths with new. Rather, this study is an acceptance of the challenges of Billington, Lamar, Pomeroy, and others. I have tried to determine the functional role of the supreme courts of the territories of Colorado, Montana, and Wyoming, thereby placing American territorial history in a new and, I hope, proper perspective.

2

"For Want
of Judicial
Organization"

One of the strongest demands in the trans-Mississippi West was for a system of laws to protect new found treasures and to restore and maintain the social order, a task achieved largely through the labors of territorial supreme courts. Subsequent chapters deal in some depth with the major challenges that faced the courts and with their more outstanding contributions. However, it is necessary first to describe the organizational scheme within which the judges worked and the environment in which their activities took place.

Like the Organic Acts which established all trans-Mississippi territories, those which created the territories of Colorado, Montana, and Wyoming were patterned after the Wisconsin Act of 1836.[1] Based on the Ordinance of 1787, the Wisconsin Act incorporated the results of the experimentation of nearly a half-century, a period during which the Organic Acts took many different forms.[2]

During the post-1836 era, Congress attempted to enact general laws affecting all territories equally. However, territorial legislation did not become uniform until after the settlement of the slavery question. Abolition of slavery destroyed the last barrier, allowing Congress to legislate for the territories as a whole. Of even greater significance was the establishment of absolute congressional control between 1836 and 1867.[3] Though the process was under way by mid-century, the resolution of the slavery question by the Civil War and the drive for civil rights in the early postwar period erased all doubts of congressional domination.

Bitterly contested by territorial residents, Washington's tight control was a hard-won prerogative not to be easily wrested from the federal lawmakers. Legislators from the newer states tended to be more sympathetic toward territorial sentiment, but the majority remained adamant on the retention of a tight rein. Territories were clearly considered agents of the federal legislature,[4] and challenges by the westerners often raised the question "whether Congress shall surrender to the Territory or whether the Territory shall conform." [5]

The Organic Acts establishing the Colorado, Montana, and Wyoming territories provided for rather simple judicial systems.[6] In each territory three judges—one designated chief justice—were appointed by the president with the advice and consent of the Senate. Serving four-year terms, they presided individually as district judges and in a body as the supreme court. Their jurisdiction in both capacities included cases under United States and territorial law, and appeals from the territorial supreme court went directly to the Supreme Court of the United States. The justices had chancery as well as common law jurisdiction, a situation which made their responsibilities even more complex.[7] The acts also provided for subordinate probate and justice-of-the-peace courts. When sitting as United States courts, the district courts were empowered with the same jurisdiction as United States District Courts in organized states. At the time of their creation, assemblies in each of the three territories defined and assigned districts and set the calendar of terms.[8]

While the courts cannot be evaluated apart from the judges who served on them, the weaknesses of the court structure must not be glossed over. Undoubtedly the system's imperfections strained to the utmost the human frailties of the men on the bench.[9] The most prevalent and serious objection to the territorial judiciary was that it had both original and appellate jurisdiction in the same cases. Attorneys, litigants, and the press were all vociferous in their condemnation of the dual powers of territorial supreme court justices. Even the judges involved surely had, at times, serious qualms about the system. It must have been embarrassing indeed for the associate who was asked to retire so that his colleagues could conspire to reverse one of his district court decisions. No doubt the two associates would suggest with deft diplomacy that the third member of the bench step out—perhaps to take advantage of one of the frequent offers of hospitality—while they gleefully reversed one of their chief's proudest decisions.

The loudest condemnation of this defect, however, came from the people who saw themselves as victims of an insidious plot by Congress to deprive them of justice. The editor of the *Helena Daily Independent* voiced their grievance well.

> From such decisions there is virtually no redress. If the litigant appeals to the Supreme Court, he finds the same Judge upon the bench, omnipotent for evil, as in the court below. The appellant [*sic*] usually pays his cost, submits to the inevitable, and retires from the court, poor in purse but rich in his experience of Montana justice.[10]

Regardless of who was on the bench at any given time, it would have been difficult to persuade territorial litigants that the justices ever did anything but affirm one another's errors. An analysis of the territorial courts' opinions indicates, however, that affirmation of district court decisions was not automatic (see table 1). In its entire history of record, the Colorado court affirmed only five cases more than it reversed; at several of its sessions, reversals greatly outnumbered affirmations. While the record in Montana and Wyoming was not so balanced, a study of the opinions points toward a better performance than one would expect from accounts of partisan outcries. The territorial system generated intense political acrimony (see chap. 5 below), and exacerbation was an effective technique.

Table 1

Reviews of District Court Decisions by
Territorial Supreme Courts

	Affirmed	Reversed	Dismissed	Modified
Colorado	125	120	7	2
Montana	356	194	16	20
Wyoming	108	51	16	5
Total:	589	365	39	27

Note: A court's tendency to either affirm or reverse depended on the men who served it. Moses Hallett sat on the Colorado court for ten years, and both Hiram Knowles and Decius S. Wade served the Montana court for the better part of a decade—these courts were definitely not of the "rubber stamp" variety. The figures above are the result of a case by case analysis of the reports of the three courts. Administrative actions and procedural matters were ignored in the tabulation. Hence, the totals above do not indicate the exact number of matters considered.

Suggestions for rectifying this grievance were as frequent and varied as they were futile. Intermediate appellate courts were rejected; so were various schemes utilizing supreme courts in contiguous territories on a reciprocal basis. Legislative assemblies offered many other remedies, begging Congress to accept any one of them.[11] Of the Colorado, Montana, and Wyoming territories, this weakness was corrected only in Montana, and even there relief hardly preceded statehood. When the total number of justices in Montana was increased to four, Congress specifically provided that no judge could sit on an appeal from his own decision.[12] John D. Hicks in *The Constitutions of the Northwestern States* heavily stressed this defect of the appellate structure of the territorial courts; separate and independent supreme courts were provided for in the constitutions of all the northwestern states (p. 64).

The second most widespread criticism concerned the small number of justices relative to the vastness of the territories.

Particularly in Montana and Wyoming, coverage on horseback or by stage was an inhuman task, and all three territories
experienced exasperating as well as costly delays in litigation
as a result. Grand Docket No. 5 in the First District Court of
Colorado Territory provides a good illustration. This suit,
which involved one lot of potatoes, was decided December 18,
1861, in Denver; final dismissal by the Colorado Territorial
Supreme Court did not occur until September 26, 1867.[13] On
occasion, judges lived over four hundred miles from some of
the county seats where their district courts were scheduled to
hold terms, and backlogs of civil cases were at times estimated
as high as three hundred.[14] A perennial complaint during
expansion to the West, an insufficient number of judges had
also been a problem in the territories of the Mississippi
Valley.[15]

The Organic Acts applicable here empowered the legislative assemblies to define judicial districts, assign them, and
schedule the places and times of court terms. Governors
and judges quickly recognized the dangers inherent in this
power.[16] The legislative threat of "sagebrushing" was always
in the air, and its actual practice interfered in a number of
instances with the freedom and independence of the judiciary.[17] On the other hand, territorial politicians sometimes
viewed this device as their only effective weapon against tyrannical carpetbag regimes. While territorial policies were usually
general in application, peculiar circumstances sometimes
fostered specific legislation. An example of such congressional
action was the 1867 law which deprived the Montana Territorial Legislative Assembly of this power over the judiciary.
It extended to the judges the right to define and assign districts
and to fix times and places of court terms.[18] Colorado and
Wyoming were not affected and the threat of sagebrushing
persisted in those territories.

Criticism of the territorial judicial system can be well summarized in terms of its rigidity. "The most damning indictment," wrote Clark Spence concerning Montana's territorial

judicial structure, was "the basic inflexibility of the system which kept it from keeping pace with the development of the territory over a quarter of a century." [19] Spence's comment is an excellent distillation, but the clamor of the pioneers was usually directed at the specific maladies just discussed.

Despite their awareness of the defects of territorial administration, the early settlers of the Rocky Mountains quickly begged for organization. This fact in itself points to the prime importance of the functional evaluation which so many historians have neglected. Passage of the Organic Acts was only the first tantalizing step in the establishment of formal government. Guaranteeing "nothing else but the fact of political existence," the Organic Acts, in the narrow view, provoked perhaps more frustration than they dispelled. [20]

It is to this early frustration rather than to the frequent cries for the establishment of courts that most accounts of territorial periods refer. While Miners' Courts and their initial effectiveness have received ample attention, [21] it is generally overlooked that pioneers soon recognized the necessity for legally established tribunals. Correspondence during the first months after the enactment of the Organic Acts clearly reveals great concern about the need for traditional courts, particularly for the protection of property. There is abundant evidence in the files of the National Archives to indicate that these pleas were urgent. Colorado Territory's first governor, William Gilpin, in lengthy and frequent letters described the establishment of the courts as a "peremptory necessity." Gilpin wrote: "Such is the amount of valuable property in mills and imported machinery, that millions of dollars are perishing and industry ruined for want of judicial organization." [22] Secretary Lewis Ledyard Weld added strength to the governor's case by stressing to Secretary of State William H. Seward the urgency of organizing the courts. [23] Not alone in their pleas, territorial officials received the support of numerous petitions explicitly seeking "security to life and property" through the establishment of courts. [24]

In contrast to Colorado and Montana where mining was the

source of the most pressing legal problems, Wyoming had its
own peculiar motivating force. The first territorial governor of
Wyoming, John A. Campbell, expressed the uniqueness of
his territory's situation rather well in his address to the first
Wyoming legislative assembly.

> In one particular our situation as a territory is entirely new
> and somewhat anomalous for pioneers. For the first time in
> the history of our country, the organization of a territorial
> government was rendered necessary by the building of a
> railroad. Heretofore, the railroad has been the follower
> instead of the pioneer of civilization.[25]

Though delay in organization was not confined to Wyoming,
its settlers did experience one of the longest and most agonizing delays of any territory. More than three years elapsed between the introduction of the Organic Act and its passage; the
Johnson-congressional feud was costly indeed to Wyoming's
pioneers. All her territorial officials were not qualified nor
were courts established until May 19, 1869, some ten months
after Congress created the territory.[26]

Prognostications were disappointing and frustration intense
as the early-day Wyomingites struggled for government. "On
the whole," predicted the editor of the *Cheyenne Daily
Leader,* "we may look for a speedy organization and an abun-
dance of officials to ride Wyoming and her revenue safely and
expeditiously out of the wilderness." [27] In effect, these settlers
were in organizational limbo. "The Judges of Dacotah [*sic*]
refuse to hold Court here now and we are worse off than if we
were not organized." A fellow sufferer described the situation
as "worse than useless" and as having "materially injured our
interests." Others were quick to recognize the danger of slow
organization because of the need for protecting the "property
of vast value" carried by the Union Pacific.[28]

Newspapers reflected the eagerness with which the people
awaited organization of the courts. The arrival of each judge
was usually noted, and, as in the case of Colorado Territorial
Chief Justice Benjamin F. Hall, considerable importance was

placed on the judiciary. The editor of Denver's *Rocky Mountain News* pointed out that "his [Hall's] presence was necessary before the wheels of Government could be fairly set in motion." In addition to editorial comment, the public's keen interest was evidenced by surprisingly detailed coverage of all activities of the court.[29] Territorial residents were of course unhappy about some of the court's decisions, but this fact does not detract from the importance of an organized court system and the establishment of judicial order.

The immediate objective of the territorial justices, aside from the rudimentary organization of their courts, was the establishment of law and order, a process in which the judges were inextricably involved. And as the early judges worked toward this goal, they were not loath to disparage a large segment of the territorial population. Chief Justice John H. Howe of Wyoming observed a year after his arrival that "reckless, roving adventurers who have no settled well defined notions of the rights and obligations of society" were in the majority. Howe found the "intelligent, steady, law-loving and abiding people" who brought with them "ideals of well settled and regulated communities" outnumbered by less savory characters.[30]

In describing the unruly element which he found in Montana, Chief Justice Hezekiah L. Hosmer, who organized its court, displayed a sense of history as well as a flamboyant style.

> Had the convicts liberated on the approach of Napoleon, on the condition that they burn Moscow, been thrown en masse into the new settlements east of the mountains, it could not have been worse than it was with the crowd that entered and undertook to control Bannack and Virginia City in the years 1862 and 1863.[31]

Admitting that territorial officials may have adorned the truth to enhance their own achievements, it is still true that the kinds of people who went west to settle increased the need for law and order.

With missionary zeal Wyoming's Chief Justice Howe advocated a "firm, inflexible and vigorous administration of the law" to confront crime and immorality "which everywhere prevailed and was *predominant.*" [32] Howe also directed his crusading efforts at attorneys. Tardiness particularly irritated His Honor, and the *Cheyenne Daily Leader* concurred with his lack of sympathy with lawyers' oversleeping "on account of *spiritual manifestations* the previous evening." The chief justice kept a sharp eye out for other irregularities and early in his tenure fined four lawyers for practicing without licenses. Like many justices in this era following the Civil War, Howe was a former army officer, which may partly explain his stern disposition. Other judges followed Howe's hard line. On occasion courtroom demeanor reflected the general behavioral patterns of everyday life; fights at the bar of justice were not unknown. [33]

Though vigilantes may have deterred some criminal acts, these extralegal groups complicated the task of establishing law and order. [34] At times their activities hindered the territorial bench's efforts to introduce a formal judicial system, and more than one pioneer judge must have harbored mixed emotions about vigilantes' role in the campaign to administer the law with fairness and justice. One of the most celebrated clashes between territorial courts and the vigilantes in the trans-Mississippi West involved James Daniels who had been convicted of manslaughter in Montana. Acting Governor Thomas Francis Meagher pardoned Daniels against the advice of Associate Justice Lyman E. Munson. [35] The judge asserted the supremacy of the courts, but before the marshal could comply with Munson's order for the reconfinement of Daniels, "the vigilantes or some one else hung him that evening with the Governor's pardon in his pocket."

During their tenure, as well as in their reminiscences in later years, the justices took great pride in having contributed to the development of an orderly society. Toward the end of his service, Chief Justice Howe of Wyoming professed that by 1871 Laramie had a worldwide reputation of "peace, sobriety, and good order." The accuracy of his claim may be debatable, but his estimate of the achievements of the judiciary is clear. After decades of law practice in New Haven, Connecticut, Lyman E. Munson, who had served on Montana's first territorial supreme court, saw the bench as an important contributor to peace and prosperity. Having mellowed somewhat, Munson displayed greater charity toward the less desirable settlers whom he now described as "refractory elements." [36]

The response of the people to the judicial assault on lawlessness indicates that perhaps conditions were not as dreadful as they appeared. On his return from a leave of absence, Howe was praised by the *Leader* which noted that everyone welcomed him except the criminals. The next spring Howe himself admitted that he and his colleagues had been "well sustained" and that generally even the "bad" had "submitted with good grace to the new order of things." [37]

Though newspapers at times reflected a "chamber of commerce" spirit in hopes of encouraging immigration, editorials are, nevertheless, a measure of attitudes toward the courts. The *Laramie Daily Sentinel* was generous in its assessment. "The Laws are respected, the Courts are in perfect operation; and morality, religion and justice give the tone and character to society." [38] As the territory grew, so did efforts to advertise its law-abiding nature. According to Wyoming's governor, in 1878 law and order existed "to a degree that would do honor to New England communities." Nineteenth-century historians also tended to be highly complimentary in their evaluation of the effectiveness of the courts.[39]

Response to the judiciary's attempts to impose law and order was generally positive, but not unanimously so. Though interference by the vigilantes was most prevalent in Montana, courts in other territories also met resistance in the enforcement of criminal law. The vigilantes welcomed the bench's attention to civil matters, but they made their position clear with regard to the punishment of outlaws. The combination of interference by extra legal groups and the apathy of many citizens explains to a large extent the difficulty experienced by many territorial judges in the enforcement of criminal law. "One man is dead, what do you want to kill another for?" [40] This was the attitude of more than a few prospective jurors toward trials.

During the very earliest stages of the Colorado, Montana, and Wyoming territories, the judiciary's improvisation of civil law was neither as romantic nor as noticeable as its attempts at controlling the criminal element. In all three areas, litigation and commercial transactions were in progress under the statutes of the "parent" territories. The equitable and orderly carrying on of such activities under the supervision of the supreme courts was an accomplishment of no mean proportions. Because the situation demanded a great deal of ingenuity, a number of justices enjoyed their finest hours during this interim period.

As far as the courts are concerned, there is certainly no inaccuracy in the statement that the Organic Acts provided "hardly more than a right to exist." [41] Congress devoted but few words to matters other than structure, and it made no mention of codes or practice, except in regard to rights of litigants under the Constitution and United States statutes. The jurisdiction of territorial supreme courts was described in the broadest of terms—"appellate and original," "chancery as well as common law," and "authority for redress of all wrongs committed against the Constitution as laws of the United States, or of the Territory." [42]

Even when the president and Congress promptly established territorial administrations, considerable time elapsed before legislatures could be elected and laws enacted. Without exception, the supreme courts of the Colorado, Montana, and Wyoming territories displayed commendable initiative in coping with this situation. The experiences in Colorado and Montana again followed remarkably similar paterns; both were mining areas and had been organized within roughly three years. Wyoming differed in that it suffered an unusually long delay in organization.

Though the Rocky Mountain territories shared many common experiences and eventually acquired similar systems of jurisprudence, the resourcefulness of each court was tested during its organizational stage. As the oldest, Colorado's bench had fewer precedents to follow than the courts of Montana and Wyoming, and it immediately found itself in a jurisdictional entanglement.[43] Because Colorado had been carved out of Kansas Territory, Kansas statutes were technically in force when Colorado's new judges arrived. But Kansas' laws had been publicly repudiated in anticipation of an extralegal provisional government, Jefferson Territory, which had never functioned. The questionable status of millions of dollars' worth of commercial and real estate transactions in this new Rocky Mountain territory was of the utmost gravity to Colorado Territorial Chief Justice Hall. Speculators and adventurers were poised to take advantage of any temporary lapse in the law. The *Weekly Commonwealth and Republican* lavished praise upon Hall for upholding the laws of Kansas while the enactment of Colorado statutes was pending. "It was certainly bad for lawyers who had expected to upset matters," the editor philosophized, "but it was salvation to the people who had property." Colorado Territory subsequently based many of its original codes on the Kansas statutes.[44]

In Montana the judiciary encountered conditions akin to those experienced by Colorado's first bench. Months prior to the meeting of Montana's first territorial legislative assembly, the organization of the district courts began. Under the leadership of Chief Justice Hosmer, rules and statutes were improvised using the common law and Idaho statutes as guides.[45] Hosmer wisely enlisted the assistance of members of the bar in this work. In its first session in January, 1865, the legislative assembly formally adopted the common law "so far as the

same is applicable and of a general nature, and not in conflict
with special enactments of this territory." While Montana's
civil, criminal, and probate codes were founded on the common law, the Idaho statutes served as a model. Accordingly,
one of the council's first orders of business was to authorize
the purchase of three copies of the Idaho codes.[46]

Montana's legislators continued to look to their older and
more experienced neighbors for more appropriate codes.
Citing the similarity of the two areas, Governor Green Clay
Smith urged the adoption of the California civil code in 1866.
After delaying a year the legislative assembly accepted Smith's
counsel, and an extensive Civil Practices Act, modeled on
California's, was enacted.[47]

Improvisation of codes and practices taxed the professional
resources of the pioneer justices, but they faced mundane
problems as well. Of these the most crucial was arranging for
appropriate court facilities. At least temporarily, and in many
towns for years, makeshift courts sufficed. Consequently, the
sanctity of procedures depended more on the conduct of men
than on an atmosphere created by appointments and trappings.
Voluminous correspondence about the provision of adequate
buildings and furnishings clearly attests the desperate need for
suitable courtrooms.[48] The sites of the first district courts were
as varied and rustic as the settlements themselves. The residents usually outdid themselves in a show of hospitality
during a judge's first term, and more often than not a bar or
dining room was the scene of the improvised courtroom. When
he wore out his welcome in one place, the judge moved to
another establishment until permanent courtrooms could at
last be obtained. Judge Hall was indeed fortunate to have
relatively commodious quarters for his exclusive use when he
opened court in Denver.[49]

The judiciary labored under considerable handicaps, one
of the most imposing being a lack of proper facilities. It is to
emphasize the obstacles overcome, rather than to indulge in
sensationalism, that their privations must be considered. Un-

fortunately, in the past the accent has been on the crude and humorous aspects of western justice. Frontier courtroom scenes made particularly good copy for journalists anxious to take advantage of eastern snobbery.[50]

Proper accommodations for themselves also posed a problem for the judges. Not only did the public expect a judge to maintain certain standards, but his pride and position also demanded it. Prestige was apparently more important in the railroad towns of Wyoming than it was in the mining areas. Correspondence from Judge J. W. Kingman, for example, indicates that he was unwilling to board with the laborers.[51] That the judges in the mining regions were also concerned with maintaining a respectable standard of living was indicated, however, in their struggle for better salaries.[52] The extremely high cost of living was perhaps their best argument.

Ignorant of Rocky Mountain conditions and limited by bureaucratic mentalities, Washington officials must have felt that organizing the judicial system was a major headache. Hiring space by the day only during court terms appeared sound practice in the capital. Federal officials were not aware that the unsettled conditions of the West required the transaction of a greater than normal portion of business in chambers between sessions.[53] As a result, conscientious justices on numerous occasions rented their own offices.

As the administrative arm of the court, the United States marshal was responsible for cutting through enough red tape so that facilities could be found for the supreme court and the district courts when they sat on federal cases. The enormous piles of paperwork stacked in the marshals' offices would disillusion the modern television viewer. Nevertheless, as government real-estate men, the marshals outdid themselves to acquire buildings in a market where prices were exorbitant at best, particularly by eastern standards.[54]

It is understandable that eyebrows were lifted when the 1866 leases for courtrooms in the three districts of Montana were compared. Fifteen hundred dollars became a magic figure. All three leases were for that amount, and one William Thompson held two of the three, one at Deer Lodge and the other at Virginia City. There was no reason why Montana should have been spared postwar opportunism and corruption, and by 1870 the Comptroller's Office smelled a rat, charging that the federal government was paying a total of $4,500 per year for the courtroom, jail, and custom house in a building valued at only $3,500.[55] Montana's fourth governor, Benjamin F. Potts, recommended an investigation of these conditions, boasting he would "clean the *Augean Stable.*" By 1875 rents had leveled off at $400 to $700 per year for court facilities. In Wyoming the federal government called on the quartermaster from Fort D. A. Russell to check the reliability of the marshal's proposals. This suspicious attitude worked a hardship on judges and litigants alike.[56]

In addition to the problems the judges faced in establishing codes and practices, finding suitable courtroom and personal facilities, and enforcing law and order, they encountered many other obstacles of lesser importance. One of their most obvious frustrations was the difficulty of actually assembling territorial officials and keeping them at their posts. Judges often had to cover for delinquent colleagues who either had been delayed or were away on leaves of absence, and in Colorado the repercussions of this problem assumed sizable proportions.[57]

The vastness of the frontier and absenteeism made it necessary for all federal officers to "double in brass," and in order to expedite litigation, justices exercised initiative in appointing special United States attorneys.[58] The ineffectiveness of some of their colleagues certainly imposed a hardship on all territorial appointees at one time or another, and an additional source of tribulation was the incompetence of some of the attorneys appointed in Washington to serve in the territories.[59] The bureaucratic quagmire in the nation's capital demoralized conscientious members of the bench. Theoretically the secretary of state was responsible for territorial

347.78035 G94lr
c.1

administration (after 1873, the secretary of interior), but in reality supervision came from seemingly innumerable offices. Colorado's Judge Hall had hardly arrived when he suggested that reporting to one department would "obviate a great deal of vexatious trouble." [60]

Of the hindrances which severely tested the ability, ingenuity, and patience of territorial justices, among the most exasperating were the delays they experienced in getting territorial statutes printed and the scarcity of law books in general. For want of funds and facilities, Montana experienced the most difficulty in publishing its first statutes. Passed by the first legislative assembly, Montana's laws were printed in Maine and were not distributed until nearly two years after their enactment. Fortunately, territorial newspapers often printed certified copies of the legislation of most interest. This practice was of great value to attorneys and judges and, in the case of mining laws, to prospectors and investors.[61] Reports of supreme court decisions were also published only after much delay.[62]

Law libraries were as scarce in the territories as most other accouterments of civilization, and more practical items, like picks and shovels, were of course supplied first. The small collections of law books which did exist usually contained basic texts and not the pertinent statues and codes. By the end of 1860, the library purported to be the largest in Denver contained some fourteen volumes. The judge who arrived expecting to find a government-furnished library was in for a gross disappointment; even the United States statutes were scarce items. And when Congress finally responded to memorials for law libraries, the books, like those sent to Montana, sometimes fell prey to the hazards of the journey and mysteriously disappeared.[63]

In 1871 law libraries were belatedly received in the Montana and Wyoming territories; the delay had been caused at least partly by the government's lengthy purchasing procedures. Libraries for five territories were acquired at one time after maneuvers in Washington to drive the price down. Bought for $2,500, Wyoming's library was inventoried at 706 volumes and placed under the care of the clerk of the supreme court. The importance of these books is indicated by the care they were given. At first either the clerk of the courts or the territorial secretary was responsible for them, but librarians were soon hired. In 1879 Wyoming's legislature instructed the librarian to insure its collection at not less than $6,000, and 300 copies of a catalog of its holdings were ordered printed and distributed among other territories and states.[64] By 1885 the governor could boast about the growth of this collection to 10,000 volumes, and the following year $5,150 was appropriated for rent and operational expenses.[65] After nearly two decades the Wyoming law library had "arrived."

The men appointed to the territorial bench could scarcely have anticipated the many frusrations they were to face. Armed with little more than their titles, the judges traveled west to impose the order of American society on the rugged settlements of the Rocky Mountains. Intelligence, ingenuity, and courage were needed to forge solutions to novel problems. Not everyone had these requirements, but those who did have long awaited acknowledgment.

3
"The Juggle
of Habeas Corpus"

Upon their arrival in Denver some three months after the firing on Fort Sumter, Colorado's first territorial justices discovered that division and bitterness were not confined to the organized states of the East. The booming supply town already had experienced its tense moments when the "rag of treason" was ripped from the pole atop Wallingford and Murphy's store. Though Northern sympathizers predominated, Southerners were very much in evidence. Georgians, with an important mining heritage, had led considerable numbers of prospectors from below the Mason-Dixon Line to the gold fields of Colorado and Montana. The Civil War added significantly to the responsibilities of the judiciary, and it afforded some justices an opportunity to contribute more notably to the development of the territories, particularly Colorado, than otherwise might have been possible. Scars of the war were left in Montana and Wyoming, but it was in Colorado that the judiciary became most directly involved.

Spared by their remoteness from the worst tragedies of the fighting, Coloradans nevertheless experienced many of the same general problems confronting fellow Americans to the east. Fears of rebel invasion or infiltration were not merely figments of fired-up imaginations. Though Governor William Gilpin has been chided for his zealous defense preparations, his reports to Washington offered a strong case for "the value which attaches to the possession of these mountains." [1] A need for specie and dreams of a western empire were not the sole

motivations of the Confederacy. Gilpin alluded to the value
of controlling communications to the West and to the psychological impact of Southern occupation of the Rockies both
on the Indians and abroad.

Despite the divided loyalties of the court, a major role in
the effort to thwart rebel designs was played by Colorado's
Chief Justice Benjamin F. Hall. The absence of his associates
during the most trying period of organization was agonizing.
Justice S. Newton Pettis, who had arrived prior to Hall, departed Denver less than a month after taking his oath; his
replacement was not named until June 1862.[2] Finally appearing on the scene in late October 1861, the second associate,
Charles Lee Armour, could not have diminished Hall's
anxiety by delaying departure to his Central City post until
the following February.[3]

Joining Hall in his concern over the effects of such derelic-
tion of responsibility, Governor Gilpin termed the prolonged
absence of Hall's associates a "severe calamity." Gilpin attributed to their conduct the creation of an "element of insurrection and terror," and he charged them with complicating
the "difficulty of handling treason." [4]

The delinquency of his associates imposed considerable
personal hardship upon the chief justice who had to temporarily fill the empty benches as best he could. While
Gilpin and Hall were equally annoyed and anxious about
their dilemma, the governor did not hesitate to assign the
chief justice the Herculean task of covering all the judicial
districts.[5] Neither was Hall reluctant to seek alleviation from
his superiors. He complained to Lincoln, availing himself at
the same time of an opportunity to boast of his own deeds.
First District Court civil-case records indicate he did handle
an exceedingly heavy docket.[6] Perhaps Hall was justified in
informing the president he had succeeded "in keeping a
Judiciary alive in their [Armour and Pettis's] districts" while
completing two terms in his own. He further elaborated upon
his difficulties to the secretary of state. Some seven months

passed with little improvement, and Hall sent another barrage of letters to the capital.[7]

Despite braggadocian tendencies, the first chief justice of Colorado did exert every effort he could muster in behalf of the Union. Hall, who had delayed his departure for Colorado to recruit troops, was known for his resoundingly patriotic charges to the jury. His spirit was infectious. Charged merely with "treasonable acts and utterances" or with being "rank secessionists," many suspected rebel supporters felt the arresting hand of the United States marshal.[8] Because existing records are incomplete, it is not possible to ascertain the exact number of suspect rebels arrested. However, judging from the use of printed indictment forms, the total might be surprisingly high. During the December 1861 term of the First District Court in Denver, for instance, forty-three men were indicted for treason. They were later discharged without a trial.[9]

Generous in his praise of Hall's ability and loyalty, Gilpin wrote Seward that he had been "constantly sustained by the loyal, brave and wise judicial conduct of Chief Justice Hall." To the president, Gilpin singled out Hall as the "only Judge who has remembered that he has a country and owes to it devotion." The chief justice himself displayed little reticence in writing to Gilpin, "but for me this territory would have been lost." [10] The following summer he assured the attorney general that "no territory was ever in better order" and "the supremacy of the law here is established." Denying himself a leave of absence for two years, Hall worked long hours for the security of his country solving problems which ranged from the immigration of draft dodgers to the deployment of troops. He was also responsible for the care and disposition of prisoners of war.[11]

Of Hall's innumerable wartime activities, however, he is widely known for only one—the denial of a writ of habeas corpus to Captain Joel McKee. McKee was arrested on order of Governor Gilpin for recruiting troops in Colorado for "unlawful purposes," i.e. raising a rebel army.[12] Hall subsequently wrote a fifteen-page decision entitled "The Privilege of the Writ of Habeas Corpus under the Constitution," justifying abridgement of that privilege at the discretion of the judiciary in cases of rebellion or invasion.[13] No rigid policy had been announced by the attorney general's office concerning the suspension of the writ of habeas corpus prior to this decision. Correspondence indicated that the discretion of federal officials would be trusted, and it was pointed out that the president was required by the Constitution and statutes to suppress insurrection. Establishing a clear precedent in Colorado, the McKee decision received wide publicity, and the proud author sent more than one copy to Washington.[14]

Because of this "bold and timely decision," Hall was later credited by the *Weekly Commonwealth and Republican* with disrupting a plot to burn Denver and with being instrumental in maintaining Colorado in the Union camp.[15] At the time, however, dissension raged even among the judiciary. In the Denver area Justice Armour became the hub of resistance. Gilpin labeled Armour a man of "narrow heart and a peddling politician," and he assessed the McKee affair as follows.

> He [Armour] is relied upon by sixty Texan assassins, lately captured in arms, to reverse the loyal judicial acts of Judge Hall, to play for them the juggle of Habeas Corpus and send them to rally and bring in an army of invasion, recruited from the Indians who threatened us to the number of more than 50,000.[16]

It was not until one Benjamin Franklin was ordered held by Acting Governor Lewis L. Weld that Armour publicly objected to the suspension of the writ of habeas corpus.[17] Franklin apparently was arrested during a fracas following an attempt of a member of the First Colorado Volunteers to crash a social affair of rebel sympathizers. When his order to release the prisoner was ignored, Armour objected, to no avail, to the United States attorney general.[18]

The habeas corpus question only brought to a head the antagonisms on the Colorado Supreme Court. From the beginning of their association, Hall who was originally from Auburn, New York, must have been suspect of Armour, a Virginian. Armour's habitual tardiness intensified Hall's animosity toward him, and his association with Southerners was more than Hall could stomach. The chief justice informed William Seward that his associate "hangs around the tents of the rebels here apparently affording them aid and comfort." [19] The patriotic endeavors of Gilpin and Hall and the aggravations they suffered in organizing the territory taxed their emotions to the limit. After asking Lincoln for Armour's removal, Hall warned the president not to appoint any applicant from Colorado because of the possibility of disloyalty. To the secretary of state he wrote with still greater feeling that Armour's conduct had "neutralized" Hall's own efforts to save the territory for the Union. Hall passionately repeated to Seward his warning against placing territorial residents on the bench: "There is not one republican Lawyer in Denver who can be trusted to perform any duty at this time." [20]

Though the chief justice allowed his emotions to prevail, he nevertheless properly assessed the general incompetency of Judge Armour, and Hall enjoyed the last laugh on the *Rocky Mountain News* which defended Armour on the grounds that "Abe Lincoln knew what he was doing." [21] In announcing the judge's impending departure for Central City, the editor had also congratulated his friends there on the enviable addition to their community. During the balance of his tenure, Armour was embroiled in one of the most notorious squabbles in the history of the territorial bench. Before leaving Colorado, he was denounced in a widely circulated poster as a man incapable of dealing in the truth.[22]

The chaotic wartime conditions, rather than incompetence or disloyalty, marked the judicial career of Justice Pettis. The first to arrive and the first to leave, Pettis was the only territorial justice in Colorado who never heard a single case, although he remained on the payroll for fifteen months.[23] It is clear from the letters he wrote to the territory after returning East, and from his subsequent recruiting record for the Union, that his rapid departure was motivated at least in part by emotional and political involvement in Civil War mobilization.[24] In 1864 he recruited some eighteen hundred men for the Union Army from the rebel prisoners at Rock Island, Illinois. However, personal ambition may have also been a motivating factor. In his letter of resignation, Pettis gave "unfinished professional business" as his reason. Perhaps he recognized that the tumultuous atmosphere in Colorado was politically treacherous and elected to escape before he too became engulfed.[25]

It was not only from his colleague, Armour, that Hall's overzealous patriotism came under attack. Exception was voiced to his use of the bench as a podium from which to lecture on treason. An irate Coloradan compared one of his charges to a jury with a "self-issued license for tyranny." [26] It took one and a half columns of fine print to record the ire of this complainant.

Hall's general castigations of Colorado's populace soon caught up with him. In the spring of 1862 a letter Hall had written the previous fall to friends in the East reached the editor of the *Rocky Mountain News*. Hall had cast aspersions on Colorado's rebel tinge, and the *Rocky Mountain News*, which had previously been complimentary to Hall, published a scathing editorial—the first in a series of attacks on the judge.[27] Bemoaning the fact that he was in constant personal danger, Hall had suggested to his Auburn confidants that the Colorado population hailed chiefly from "the most demoralized Slave States" and "the debauched Free State of Pennsylvania" and that it also included "border ruffians who fought for slavers in Kansas." In the same letter he disclosed his policy of giving no lawyer a license who would not take "an oath of allegiance," a procedure Hall admitted was meaningless. Two weeks later William Byers, editor of the

Rocky Mountain News, heartily endorsed the denunciations of Hall by a correspondent from Idaho who described the "learned" chief justice as a "vain, bloated, egotistical, self-complacent, bombastic, ignorant old ass." [28] The writer showed no restraint, claiming that the judge was "trying to cover himself with the lion skin of a judicial authority, which though large, could not be made to cover so great an ass without the distinctive mark of the species being at all times visible."

With the removal of any serious rebel threat by the victory at Glorieta Pass in the spring of 1862, the Colorado pioneers again turned their primary attention to the tasks of developing their territory. The war was still constantly before them, as were the Indians, but excitement subsided. Colorado had its own return to normalcy, and this meant, at least for the time being, a heightened interest in gold mining. Judge Hall had no knowledge of mining and had alienated many residents early in the war; perhaps he had served his usefulness in the West. In the summer of 1863, in the face of serious pressure from mining interests for his removal, Hall resigned and returned to Auburn to practice law until his death in 1891.[29]

In addition to the problems it caused in Colorado, the Civil War was the source of several practices and policies which adversely affected all territories. Salaries, financial support, appointments, and tenure felt the impact of the war and its aftermath.[30] An immediate financial pinch as well as prolonged deprivation is directly attributable to the Union's financial crises. During the war the effectiveness of the courts was reduced,[31] and Congress now had an excellent rationale for its continued niggardly attitude toward operation of the territories.

The complexity of the political situation only added to the difficulties confronting Lincoln on the question of patronage. Later, in the postwar era, military contributions became such a standard qualification for any patronage position that the appointment files took on the complexion of service records. Two decades after Lee's surrender questionable judicial conduct was still tolerated because of the individual's war record. Another by-product of the conflict which remained on the scene for years was the "Iron Clad Oath." This statement of loyalty was required in addition to the regular oath of office before a territorial official was considered to have qualified, and the documents were the subject of endless rounds of interpretation.[32]

The Civil War's most lasting and detrimental effects on the territories were often indirectly felt. Of these, the most significant was the election of General U. S. Grant to the presidency. The capriciousness of his appointments and removals diverted the attention of territorial officials from their responsibilities and involved them in a constant process of political fence-mending. Lewis L. Gould attributes much of the disorder of Wyoming's early territorial administration to the absence of a clear presidential policy toward western patronage.[33] Closely akin was the widespread acceptance of corruption also characteristic of the period. A stain-free territorial administration would have indeed been incongruous with the generally scandalous deportment of many national and state officials during the Reconstruction.

Colorado's Civil War episodes tend to overshadow the sectional antagonisms harbored by the settlers of Montana and Wyoming. While Coloradans had an opportunity to thrash out their differences in the first stages of the war, immigrants to Montana and Wyoming brought with them hatreds intensified by the fighting, sentiments which seemed to linger longer in those territories.

Radicals of one disposition or another were prevalent in Montana during its organizational years.[34] Settlers arrived from all over the nation, and moderation was not part of their baggage. Governors, judges, legislators—indeed all persons of influence—felt strongly about their divergent political views. Most of the pioneers fell into one of three basic categories. First, there was an active and aggressive Republican minority from Union states who regarded all others as rebels of a sort. Second, there were Northern Democrats, supporters of the Union, who refused to unite with the Republicans who had dubbed them traitors. And finally, there were former Southerners, many of whom were Confederate veterans, and all of whom were thoroughly Democratic. Territorial leaders were in a most precarious position. Support of the national administration resulted in loud outcries from Democrats; on the other hand, attempts to accommodate the territorial Democrats sparked reverberations among both local and national Republicans.[35]

The extent of pro-Southern sentiment in Montana is sometimes overlooked. A primary frustration of this territory's early governors was a legislature controlled by men whose attitudes were Southern, anti-Negro, and Democratic.[36] The journalist Alexander K. McClure was vexed by the anomalous situation wherein Confederate veterans were actively participating in the democratic process in Montana. "In the South," McClure observed, "rebel officers of certain grades cannot vote or hold office. In Montana," he continued, "they vote, and control and fill most of the important public trusts."[37] McClure then quipped that the "Iron Clad Oath" only multiplied perjury.

Montana's first territorial governor was so concerned with the political complexities spawned by the war that he discussed the situation at length in his message to the first legislative assembly. The feared repercussions were not long in developing. On a technicality the Montana Territorial Supreme Court declared null and void the enactments of the legislative session of 1866, and Congress sustained the judges by disapproving the legislature's acts.[38] This feud, which involved a Democratic territorial legislature, Republican judges, and a Republican Congress, may have been more of an expression of Civil War prejudices than an effort to assert the supremacy of the judiciary.[39] The confrontation produced a bitterness which affected Montana politics for years.

While no head-on collision occurred in Wyoming, the first justices found a populace at odds with their own staunch Republican backgrounds. Justice John W. Kingman recalled: "Apparently the worst men and women from the border states and many who had fled from the relentless draft among the rebels seemed to dominate society." Similarly, five years after the war's end Governor James A. Campbell sought prospective appointees who "think General Grant fully as good a man as Jeff Davis." The antagonisms were not quick to disappear. As late as 1890, just prior to Wyoming's becoming a state, Civil War veterans were pressuring President Benjamin Harrison to remove Judge Micah Chrisman Saufley who had bragged of his exploits as one of Morgan's guerillas.[40] Saufley had not restricted his comments to his own past, but had accused Union veterans of discovering war-related disabilities to qualify for pensions. It is not surprising that a loud clamor was raised for the replacement of the "irrepentant guerilla."

The *Frontier Index,* whose presses moved westward with the tracks of the Union Pacific, provides an excellent barometer of the hostility which greeted Wyoming's original bench or anyone bearing the Republican label. The editor castigated "Useless Slaughter" Grant for his role in the delay of Wyoming's organization, and the procrastination of Congress was described as a Grant-inspired subterfuge "for bayonet rule" in a design to prevent Wyoming from being settled by "conservative white men." [41] The *Index*'s rantings were incessant, and it outlined its position clearly.

This community will not be run, or represented by any one cent, pettifogging, cloaked, black Republican and all aspirants of that stamp had better pack their carpet bags, and put out for Thad Stevens' Hell, at the head of the Yellowstone river. That is the only part of Dakota that the Devil has set apart for the domicile of such mongrels. Your store clothes do not encase the gizzard foot sambo smell, sufficiently secure to make your presence agreeable among honest white men.[42]

The *Index* was surely not representative of all Wyoming, but it enjoyed a wide circulation and illustrates the welcome one segment of the population gave the judges.

From this appraisal of the role of the courts during the Civil War, it is clear that the judiciary was a major force in saving Colorado from rebel infiltration, particularly as a result of the McKee ruling. In all three territories the war compounded already adverse conditions, and the climate in which the courts subsequently functioned during the development of the Far West was in many ways a sequel to the war.

4

"Making Bricks without Straw"

At the core of most territorial administrative deficiencies was the want of funds.[1] Neither the rigors of frontier existence nor the pressures for judicial innovation were as debilitating as the numerous problems which arose from inadequate appropriations. Because Congress and the territorial legislatures could have substantially remedied this malady, the situation was particularly galling. It is hardly surprising that an early Colorado judge vented his exasperation by charging that the national administration expected territorial officers "to make bricks without straw." [2] Considering the vast implications of insolvency, His Honor's summation was precise.

The justices' pitifully meager salaries, established for each territory by the Organic Acts, were paramount among financial irritations.[3] The annual salary for a Colorado justice was set in 1861 at $1,800, payable quarterly; it was finally increased to $2,500 six years later. In 1870 the salary became $3,000, and it remained at this figure until the Centennial State was admitted to the Union. In creating Montana Territory in 1864, Congress was a trifle more generous, paying each of the justices $2,500. When Congress nullified the acts of Montana's controversial 1866 legislature in 1867, it also adjusted the income of the members of the victorious court to $3,500 each, only to standardize the pay of all territorial justices at $3,000 in 1870.[4] Theoretically, this level was maintained for the remainder of the territorial period.

The prevailing salary of territorial justices in all but

Montana and Idaho was $2,500 when Wyoming was formally organized in 1868, and that figure was adopted in her Organic Act. However, because of a prolonged congressional hassle over Wyoming appointments, Congress departed from its customary practice of payment from date of commission, stipulating that salaries would not commence until justices were "commissioned and qualified." [5] Consequently, Wyoming's supreme court judges were not placed on the payroll until they were on the job in the territory. From 1870 until statehood, Wyoming's justices had their salaries pegged at the standard $3,000 figure. [6]

The territorial bench was aggravated not only by its impecunious state but also by frequent clerical delays and denials of appropriations. Acting Governor Thomas F. Meagher complained to President Andrew Johnson that not "a single dollar" had been paid toward the salaries of territorial officers. Meagher evidently overstated his case, but encumbrances were routine. [7] Although control of leaves of absence was necessary, at times clerks in the comptroller's office were unduly officious, and occasionally a most conscientious judge found his pittance withheld. Such tactics, in the long run, were successful from a bureaucratic point of view—later officials flooded files with reports of leaves of absence. Nevertheless, there seemed to be no end to clerical entanglements in which pay checks could become ensnared. [8] Perhaps even more upsetting was the deliberate failure of Congress to appropriate the full remuneration to which the justices were entitled. Congress deprived them of $400 annually from 1877 to 1880, appropriating only $2,600 apiece. [9]

The inadequacy of judicial salaries was recognized by everyone concerned except the United States Congress, and its was the only voice that mattered. Arguments for higher pay were continually submitted by the territorial legislatures, delegates, and press. The Colorado, Montana, and Wyoming legislative assemblies all passed resolutions at their first sessions urging Congress to remedy the deficiencies, and in subsequent sessions

it was routine to memorialize in behalf of appropriate compensation.[10] These frequent pleas were transmitted to the territorial delegates who faithfully and vigorously, but in vain,
tried to convince Congress of the error of its miserly attitude.
In the territories, newspapers were generally enthusiastic in
support of efforts to rectify "this invidious and unfair distinction." [11]

Virtually every plea for financial relief contained a statement of the high cost of living in the Far West. Some of the
resolutions amount to basic lessons in frontier economics,
spelling out in detail the effects of supply and demand and
ruinous freight rates.[12] While conditions varied from one
territory to another, prices fluctuated constantly, and it is
amazing that any of the judges could subsist on their salaries.

Colorado's Chief Justice Hall could hardly have been
exaggerating in 1862 when he complained to his superiors that
his $1,800 stipend "merely defrayed" personal expenses, "leav-
ing me to labor for nothing in effect, and to support my
family from other income." Hall had earlier estimated
$5,000 to be a fair annual salary for the first two years with
$3,500 thereafter. Even with $3,500, only a small family could
be maintained in the same style expected of an $1,800-a-year
clerk in Washington.[13]

Pitiful references to financial embarrassment also came
from Montana and Wyoming. Montana's Chief Justice
Hezekiah L. Hosmer implored Attorney Wilbur F. Sanders
to work hard for higher salaries. Using the plainest language,
Hosmer explained he was "really poor" and concerned about
"bread and butter." [14] In addition to the normal costs of
living, justices had to bear the extra expenses of frequent
trips.

Though booms were often temporary and price levels
lowered as activity settled into a pattern, the financial lot of
territorial officials did not substantially change during the
later period. Only three years prior to Wyoming's becoming a
state, Governor Thomas Moonlight suggested to Secretary of

the Interior L. Q. C. Lamar that Cheyenne was the most
expensive place to live that he had ever seen, indeed perhaps
the most expensive in the United States.

> We keep but one servant—a cook, my family doing the
> house work. The cost of keeping a horse is more than my
> pay will warrant, and so we go on foot. . . . Calls are made
> continually upon my purse for charitable, benevolent, and
> other public purposes. There is no escaping many of the
> demands.[15]

Moonlight fired a parting shot, reminding Lamar that "leading county officers" would laugh at the governor's salary.

The discrepancy between the face value of greenbacks and
their value in gold added considerably to the quandary of
the justices. Salaries were paid in greenbacks, but on the
frontier most cash transactions were in gold.[16] As a result,
salaries were discounted by at least 15 to 25 percent even
before the greenbacks reached the judges' pocketbooks. Net
salaries were calculated at $1,950 by a Montana editor who
deducted $75 for income tax from $2,500 and then translated
the balance from treasury notes into gold dust at the going
rate.[17]

Next to the cost of living, the most prevalent argument for
better remuneration for the justices was a comparison of their
salaries with the incomes of the better lawyers and a consideration of the value of properties under litigation. Montana's delegate in 1870 went so far as to argue that "any
lawyer in Montana" could make twice the $3,000 salary about
to be enacted.[18] Nearly two decades later, Montana Justice
J. H. McLeary explained to President Grover Cleveland that
income from his practice when he accepted the appointment
exceeded his judicial salary by "nearly three hundred percent." [19] The frequency with which "cards" of law firms appeared in newspapers indicates that the profession was
enjoying considerable activity. Many lawyers advertised special
competence in mining law in Colorado and Montana, and in

land law in Wyoming. Another indirect sign of an active legal practice was the constant advertisement of legal blanks.[20] Against this prosperous background, judicial salaries had to be a source of deep and daily frustration.

At one time or another, all three territories supplemented the incomes of their supreme court justices. Legislative assemblies ostensibly voted "increased compensation" or, as it was sometimes called, "extra compensation," to attract and keep competent judges. In some instances enactment of increased compensation was honorably motivated. Too often, however, legislators evaluated competency in terms of docility.

Montana's first legislative assembly appropriated $2,500 per year for the governor and each justice, but it clearly stipulated that this additional income would not be paid for any quarter during which the official was absent from the territory the entire time. Disenchanted with the judiciary, the second session repealed increased compensation.[21] At least at first, extra compensation appears to have been a ruse for control of officials.[22] Congressman David P. Dyer of Missouri flatly accused territorial politicians of using extra compensation not as an inducement to good men, but as a weapon of control.[23] While Wyoming's initial enactment of extra compensation fits into this coercive pattern, in the later period her legislature did attempt to be equitable and to alleviate some of the financial hardships of the members of the bench. Judges were partially reimbursed for travel expenses and extra terms. But extra compensation was expensive and could be ill afforded by the territories. Montana's Governor Potts warned the legislature that the costs of such a practice were too high, and he privately attributed the territorial debt of $104,000 to the nearly $175,000 spent for increased compensation from 1865 to 1871.[24]

As early as 1812, Congress wisely forbade territorial justices to practice law.[25] But when it failed to give the judges a salary commensurate with the responsibilities and expenses of their office, Congress opened the door to mediocrity, corruption, rapid turnover, and the official neglect which comes with outside economic interests. While the reasons for every resignation cannot be authenticated, an inadequate salary was the cause most often cited by resigning judges. Colorado's William H. Gale is typical of the well-respected judges who left the bench because of the "entire inadequacy of the salary either to defray the expenses of living or to remunerate for the labor required." [26] Francisco G. Servis wasted few words in resigning, simply writing, "Owing to my financial embarrassment I am compelled to tender my resignation." [27]

While inequitable salaries were the most salient financial handicap of the territorial supreme courts, the entire judicial system was grossly underfinanced. It was not uncommon for the system to collapse temporarily for want of funds to defray the costs of routine operations; when this happened, all cases were continued to a future term. Perhaps an anonymous clerk has most appropriately summarized the situation when he scrawled on the jacket of a letter "Conditions of courts: no funds; no juries; the new marshal not there." [28]

Since all three territories were sparsely populated and encompassed enormous areas, the insolvency of their courts was a common fate. Each suffered from the intransigence of Washington bureaus and the poor tax bases which made underwriting their share of court expenses difficult.[29] In a recent study of early Wyoming, Lewis L. Gould discusses that territory's unfavorable economic conditions and its leaders' consequent struggle for the infusion of federal funds into the area.[30] Subsequent investigation should prove that a similar situation existed in neighboring territories.

As in the case of salaries, the court's general financial problems were the result of either the bureaucratic maze in the capital or intentional congressional limitations on appropriations. References to fiscal matters are most prolific in the Justice Department's Source-Chronological files in the National Archives, and an examination of those records leads one to sympathize with the frustrations of the men who tried to

bring a system of jurisprudence to the Rockies. After reports
and requests for money were repeatedly sent in duplicate to
various agencies, to no avail, Chief Justice Hall of Colorado
brazenly suggested that the attorney general should send one
of his clerks out to clear the paperwork to their satisfaction.
Governor Sidney Edgerton of Montana learned a hard lesson
about the federal government's fiscal operation; he paid the
expenses of the first legislature in 1864–65 out of his own
pocket and was not reimbursed for two years.[31]

On the other hand, perhaps administrators in Washington
were also inconvenienced by financial restrictions. Since their
accommodations were considerably more commodious, however, it is likely that their frustrations were not as demoraliz-
ing. Regardless of who shared which feelings, the ultimate
result was the frequent incapacitation of territorial courts.
Marshals were too often instructed to "keep the expenses
within the narrowest limits possible," and warned not to call
unnecessary witnesses or otherwise use court funds unless the
business was urgent.[32] More serious, of course, were notices
that funds were entirely exhausted, a situation which sometimes occurred by the middle of the fiscal year.[33]

The contributions of the territorial courts loom even larger
when viewed in the context of the farcical structure within
which the judges performed. Indeed, a playwright would find
Justice Department files fertile ground for inspiration. Marshals received expressions of appreciation rather than reim-
bursements of their expenses in capturing criminals, law books
could not be delivered for lack of express money, animals
seized by the government ate at a marshal's personal expense,
and all manner of other ludicrous capers were cut.[34]

The miserly attitude of Congress and the distrust of agency
officials may be partially explained by their nearly total lack
of knowledge about frontier conditions. Easterners were particularly ignorant about the free flow of gold when the mines
were booming. Territorial purchases were often made in an
inflated market by men swept along in a current of fast

spending. As a result, it was not unusual for contracts to be challenged as wasteful and exorbitant. The comptroller's office was stunned at the $90 price tag approved in Montana for large, leather-bound court journals. The marshal, on the other hand, ridiculed the eastern mentality, explaining that even county officials paid as much as $100 for such volumes.[35] In the mining country, he quipped, businesses bought the best and it was not unusual for the supplier to stock those books.

It was not just the plush items that caught clerical eyes. Judges and marshals were indignant at having to justify travel expenses, frequently itemizing the high-priced food and lodging for both man and beast. In 1878 Montana prices were reported as follows: Meals, 75¢ to $1.00; lodging, 50¢ to 75¢ per night; horse feed, $1.50 to $2.00 per night; and noon grain, 50¢ to 75¢.[36]

Congress made a travesty of territorial justice and further manacled the supreme court by insisting on totally unrealistic travel and per diem allowances for witnesses and jurors. An 1853 statute established per diem expenses at $2.00 for a juror and $1.50 for a witness; both received 5¢ per mile for travel. These rates were in effect until 1870 when a juror's allowance was raised to $3.00 per day. In 1879 this amount was returned to $2.00, and per diem and travel allowances remained unchanged until statehood was granted in all three territories.[37]

Expressions of outrage and indignation from everyone involved—attorneys, judges, grand juries, marshals, federal attorneys, delegates, and other officials—arrived in the capital by the ream.[38] Grand juries frequently reported on the absurdities of the per diem and travel allowances, and they delved into every facet of travel expenses. Perhaps the most graphic report itemized a $26 reimbursement for one witness's $140 trip.[39] The failure of Congress to react to these appeals made the dispensation of justice a virtual impossibility in cases which involved considerable travel for witnesses; in

many instances they would appear only if arrested. As a
result, reliable witnesses in such cases seldom appeared,
forcing the courts to rely on the questionable testimony of
"blow-hards," and prompting experienced lawyers to label the
judicial structure a "sublime farce." [40] As combatants of a
parsimoniously inclined Congress, the territorial justices identified themselves with local residents. Thus, much of the
blame for the defects of the judicial system was placed on
Congress—where it rightfully belonged.

Some of the contemporary criticism of the federal legislature, however, brings to mind the old adage about the pot
calling the kettle black. Territorial legislatures were responsible for the financial support of district courts when they
heard cases under the jurisdiction of territorial statutes.[41] Yet
local legislators were as cost conscious as their counterparts
in Washington, and, in some instances, the counties were
even more reluctant to raise necessary funds. To overcome
this reticence, the Montana legislature provided for jail terms
for county commissioners who failed to provide for the territorial courts in the prescribed manner.[42] Not even the
governors were free from frugal tendencies. In 1873 Governor
John A. Campbell of Wyoming recommended several reduc-
tions in expenditures for court operations; he was addressing
a legislature that needed little encouragement in that direction. At least some territorial officials and residents were objective enough to cast part of the blame on local government.[43]

The constant surveillance of printing contracts was not, according to Earl Pomeroy, "mere bureaucratic officiousness." [44]
The accessibility of government printing tempted underpaid
—and at times opportunistic—officials to award contracts to
newspaper publishers who clearly intended to advance political and personal interests. Territorial legislatures also suc-
cumbed on occasion to similar temptations, and logrolling
was not unknown when codification contracts were passed. In
his veto message, one governor wryly suggested that the returned bill would be more appropriately entitled a bill for

the relief of the proposed codifier, and the governor did not hesitate to name the man.[45]

In fairness to both territorial and federal legislatures, it must be admitted that the financial strain of the Civil War and the psychological impact of the long-lived Panic of 1873 created a national mood of fiscal restraint which affected the way those bodies operated. Thus, the prevailing economic and political climate of the last third of the nineteenth century may excuse, to a degree, their failure to recognize territorial needs. The worst economic disaster, the Panic of 1873, touched off a five-year depression in the middle of the territorial periods of Montana and Wyoming. In addition, the sparsely settled territories were hindered by an inadequate tax base. The fact remains that the territorial supreme courts were severely impeded by insufficient financial support, and this distressing circumstance tends to further magnify the significance of the judiciary's achievements.

5

"Meanness, Political Chicanery, & Rotten Machinations"

Ideally, the judiciary should be divorced from the corruptive influences of politics. In the hope of achieving this goal, the framers of the United States Constitution specified that the tenure of federal judges would be for life. Territorial supreme court justices, however, were not given this guarantee, and the courts were subsequently thrust into perhaps the wildest political scramble in American history. The justices were appointed to four-year terms by the president with the advice and consent of the Senate,[1] but with no assurance of tenure even for four years, they could be dismissed at any time.

Maintaining their positions, therefore, demanded a high degree of political savoir faire, and in this fluid situation some judges were unable to conduct their affairs within the bounds of propriety. Considering the complexity of the political system in which they worked, it is not surprising that indiscretions occurred. The justices were caught between national and territorial pressures, and they also had to cope with a variety of personal challenges. Those who rose to the occasion were in a position to contribute substantially to the development of their respective territories and the strengthening of national institutions. Though the infamous escapades of the judges have usually received attention, recent scholarship tends to include the justices' involvement in territorial politics. Of the territories discussed here, Wyoming was the scene of the greatest amount of political participation by the bench, and Lewis L. Gould, in his political history of that territory, gives much attention to the role of the judiciary in politics.[2]

Aspiring judicial candidates first practiced their political skills in the contest for appointment. This was especially true in the early territorial periods when most appointees were outsiders. Virtually every letter of recommendation refers to the candidate's unrelenting support of the incumbent national administration, and many judges were nominated as payment for specific services rendered during a campaign.[3] An example is President Lincoln's appointment of S. Newton Pettis to the first Colorado territorial supreme court as a reward for his work in behalf of Lincoln's nomination.[4]

In addition to campaign workers, those considered first were other political associates, friends, and relatives—a practice which still prevails. Montana's first territorial chief justice was secretary of the House's committee on territories which drafted the Organic Act under which he was appointed. His counterpart in Colorado was a law partner of Secretary of State William H. Seward.[5] Christian Eyster, who served in Colorado, made no effort to camouflage his point of view when he sought a judgeship. "You can fill this appointment—with your friend—you have promised it to me . . . but if you do not look after it—some other one will, and there will be no one nominated so grateful and true to you as your friend."[6] Eyster also conformed to the practice of securing many supporting letters, however. Another common approach in the postwar decade, mentioned in chapter 3, was the comrade-in-arms routine.[7] The number of job seekers was extraordinary, and the wrangling of a position on the bench was indeed often an indication of political inclinations.

Upon his arrival in the territory the typical justice discovered that he was ensnared in a web of political hazards—

a web spun and supported by the tenuousness of his position.
Decius S. Wade, Montana's chief justice from 1871 to 1887,
wrote with the authority of experience that the fact that
tenure was not assured invited attacks on the judiciary. Such
was their vulnerability that, ironically enough, territorial officers were as often "attacked for being too good, upright, and
just, as for being bad, dishonest, and corrupt." [8] As a result,
judges fell prey to local rivalries and ambitions, and the
many governmental agencies which oversaw the territories
increased the possible sources or directions of attack.

Many assaults upon members of the bench were blatantly
political in origin. A good example was the removal of Justice
John Coburn of Montana whose most serious offense appears
to have been campaigning for the unsuccessful Republican
presidential candidate in Coburn's home state of Indiana.
Justice Department files indicate a great deal of support for
Coburn within his district which could not have been generated if the charges against him were true. It is evident that
Coburn, as he asserted in self-defense, was attacked only to
"make a vacancy." [9]

As political appointees open to attack, the justices seem,
on first glance, to have unnecessarily exposed themselves to
criticism through their active canvassing, often in their home
states, during presidential elections.[10] On the other hand,
however, it is likely that they were under considerable pressure from administration and party leaders, men who could
not easily have been ignored.[11] The judges were called in
from their territorial posts and drafted as campaign squads
in areas where their influence would be most effective. Such
trips obviously caused reverberations in the territories, and in
some instances, the consequences for the participants bring
to mind the biblical admonition that he who lives by the
sword dies by the sword.

The judges' exposure to the hazards of national politics has
been the source of many amusing anecdotes, for example, the
story about the greatest faux pas of Wyoming's Justice Jacob

B. Blair.[12] On election eve, 1884, Blair had adjourned his court "until the morning after James G. Blaine is elected President." Soon after Cleveland's inauguration, His Honor paid his respects to the president, soliciting the continuance of his position on the bench. After some appropriate joshing, Cleveland assured Blair that he would not be removed, barring the appearance of serious charges against him. According to the lore of the profession, Blair blurted, "Mr. President, the most serious charge that I have heard is that I bet on Blaine!" Blair was allowed to complete the term, his third.

Concern over possible removal was expressed at one time or another in the correspondence of almost every judge; even those justices most highly regarded by historians, past and present, were not immune. Of the entire territorial bench in Montana, Hiram K. Knowles has been one of the most highly praised.[13] Yet he was subjected to vicious attack, an example of the adversity which confronted supreme court justices and which might have undone men of lesser stature.

Anson Bangs, a mine operator against whom Knowles had ruled, charged the judge with malfeasance, political infidelity, and incompetence.[14] In particular, Bangs accused Knowles of deliberately rushing the trial of a suit in which his Mineral Land and Mining Company was a defendant. In filing these charges, Bangs was carrying out his threat to have Knowles removed if the judge dared decide against him.[15] So brazen was this disappointed litigant in spreading the word about his planned retaliation that the whole community turned out to witness the showdown. Knowles's description of the reaction in Bannack City bears repeating. "So great an excitement did they [the threats] create that about every man in that little dilapidated village assembled in their little dilapidated court room as I afterward learned 'to see if the Judge would weaken to this wealthy, distinguished and experienced Washington lobbyist.' "[16]

The spurious nature of Bangs's charges soon came to light. Not only was the Mineral Land and Mining Company case the oldest on the docket, but all parties had received ample notice of the trial date.[17] The case was heard late in February 1869, on two months' notice, after the attorneys for all litigants had agreed to be ready the previous January first. Defense of Knowles came from many quarters; one statement regarding his character is of interest here primarily for the order in which his merits were cited. Congressman George W. McCrary of Iowa (later secretary of war) described Knowles as "a sound Republican, a good judge, and an honest man." [18]

Four years later Knowles weathered another assault, spearheaded this time by Montana's Governor Benjamin F. Potts. Certain of his influence within Republican circles, Potts sought to have Knowles chastised for his alleged criticism of the administration in Washington. Prevalent political attitudes are revealed in the governor's conclusion, "I think it bad enough to be abused by our political enemies but when men who live by the favor of the administration abuse us, they should be compelled to draw their sustenance from some other quarter." [19] Actually, Potts was incensed because Helena had been chosen as the site of the capital after the Supreme Court of Montana Territory ruled on technicalities which affected the official canvass of the vote. Despite the governor's efforts, the bar and the people of both parties in Knowles's district sustained the judge and he was reappointed in 1876.[20] A truly distinguished career of eleven years on the territorial supreme court and fourteen years as Montana's first United States district judge vindicated those who had supported Knowles in both major attacks on his integrity and ability.[21]

Many of Knowles's colleagues, however, were not as fortunate, nor perhaps as adept, and they fell victim to similar attacks. An appropriate example is the successful effort of Governor Potts to unseat Justice John L. Murphy who sat on the court with Knowles and Wade, a panel about whose honesty the people could boast.[22] Though Judge Murphy was unable to thwart the designs of Governor Potts, voluminous Justice Department records accent the vulnerability of the justices to political interference and the caprice with which President Grant handled patronage. The Murphy file does not reveal unanimous endorsement of the judge, but it contains ample evidence of extremely wide support for him as well as clear signs of unsavory and even fraudulent machinations on the part of his attackers.[23] Their charges were vague, and the evidence lends support to the opinion of newspaperman James L. Fisk who concluded that "the whole thing originated among a few disaffected shysters, who cannot bend the sterling integrity of the man, or make him subservient to their will." [24]

While the ability and performance of some judges may not have been beyond reproach, the insults to which they were occasionally subjected were extreme, to say the very least. Chief Justice Joseph W. Fisher of Wyoming was relentlessly attacked by P. S. Wilson, a Cheyenne banker, who maintained a steady flow of vicious letters to Washington over a period of several years.[25] Outraged over Fisher's leniency toward an accused embezzler and humiliated by a contempt of court punishment, Wilson recognized no limits to propriety in his open assaults on the judge.[26] The following is an excerpt from a letter he wrote to an Omaha newspaper.

> The basilisk is hatched from the male bird's egg. It is a creature passing all others in its hideousness and venom. The way to kill it, is to hold before it a mirror, when it dies from terror. If our judicial basilisk will examine himself in this mirror of his deeds, he cannot live.[27]

An entire chapter could be composed from the offerings of this critic; they are all as bitter though not as colorful as the basilisk analogy.

Territorial politics followed a pattern which affected the volatile atmosphere in which the judges performed their duties. Perhaps the most embarrassing part of this pattern was the tendency of newly organized territories to vote Democratic. The classic observation of this condition by a contemporary was made by Albert D. Richardson in *Beyond the Mississippi* (1867):

> Our new Territories in their early history show wonderful uniformity. At its first election each invariably votes the democratic ticket. As time passes each has its fevers of speculation, its wild inflations and penalizing reactions, its bitter contests about locating the capital. [p. 502]

During the war and the succeding decade, an increasingly radical attitude toward ex-Confederates added to the justices' difficulties. They found themselves in a highly uncomfortable position, frequently caught between a Republican Congress and the Democratic territorial legislatures in which former rebels abounded even in leadership posts.[28]

The judiciary's involvement in the internal politics of all territories—to varying degrees—was part of the survival process. In Wyoming, however, the early territorial justices became extraordinarily embroiled in such affairs, and out of the factional warfare, one of the greatest leaders in the entire history of Wyoming, Joseph Maull Carey, emerged.[29] Though the Colorado and Montana territories also had their "rings" (as administration factions were usually designated), the story of the "Campbell clique" illustrates perhaps most dramatically the involvement of the judiciary in intraparty as well as partisan rivalries.

The diaries of Wyoming's first governor, John A. Campbell, reveal not only his intimate and constant association with the entire supreme court, but also the control he exercised over their political careers. While he squelched the aspirations of Chief Justice John H. Howe who sought the Republican nomination for delegate, Campbell was instrumental in securing the nomination of two other members of the bench for that post.[30] Justice William T. Jones of Indiana, a Union Army veteran, was the successful Republican nominee in 1870, handpicked by the governor.[31] In 1874, however, Carey (who had been elevated to the supreme court from the post of United States attorney) was an unsuccessful candidate for delegate, despite Campbell's strong sponsorship.[32]

Animosity toward the Campbell clique was quick to appear, and a deep schism soon developed within the Wyoming Republican Party. Since a central figure within the opposing faction was Church Howe, the United States marshal, the ramifications of the hostilities for the judiciary were numerous and serious.[33] Marshal Howe objected at once to the fact that Jones was campaigning while still on the bench, and he demanded the judge's resignation. Jones's later defeat for reelection ushered in hard feelings between him and Judge J. W. Kingman, his former associate on the bench. Jones accused Kingman of working against him, and Kingman became apprehensive about retaliation in Washington by his former colleague.[34]

The polarization of the warring factions continued. By 1871 it appeared to the Campbell group that working for the removal of Marshal Howe was the most expedient course to pursue, and their efforts seemed successful when he was dismissed by President Grant on May 15, 1871. The *Cheyenne Daily Leader* blamed Howe's removal on the "meanness, political chicanery, and rotten machinations of the Campbell clique of political prostitutes and drunkards." [35] The Campbell victory was temporary, however, for Howe was reinstated. A year later the marshal was dismissed again, this time permanently. The undoing of Howe proved to be a hollow victory for the Campbell faction; it set off a chain of events leading to disaster for the Republicans in 1872 and 1874 at the Wyoming polls.[36] It is difficult to explain the "promotion" of the governor to third assistant secretary of state without taking into account these setbacks for his party. With the appointment of John M. Thayer to succeed Campbell, the justices soon realized the folly of their brief foray into politics for the new governor sought a clean sweep of the judiciary.[37]

Fortunately for them, his own tenure was brief, but the legacy of their association with the Campbell clique haunted even their successors.

Masonic ties were very strong in Colorado, Wyoming, and Montana, and herein lies still another complication of territorial politics. Masonic associations are consistently mentioned in biographies of supreme court justices, and many judges served in leadership capacities within Freemasonry, A nineteenth-century history of Montana contains the observation that "a Masonical fraternity rules among" members of the legal profession, and private papers also indicate the deep involvement of the bench and bar in these fraternal activities.[38] The role of Masonry in political developments affecting the judiciary was also quite strong in Wyoming. Of the first territorial administration, for example, the governor, secretary, United States attorney, and Justice Jones were active participants, and throughout the territorial period key political figures were highly involved in Freemasonry.[39] This group also included newspaper editors whose influence the judiciary had to heed. Thus the justices, Masons and non-Masons alike, had to contend with the power struggles common to fraternal and religious associations.

While the justices were not always in agreement with the territorial governors, they were an integral part of the understaffed territorial administration. The strange assortment of their peripheral tasks is outlined in chapter 10, but it is appropriate to mention here the somewhat uncomfortable position of the judge as a third party in executive-legislative clashes. Especially in the early periods characterized by Democratic legislatures, the supreme court often sided with the governor in disputes. Hoping for a supplementary income from the legislatures, dependent on their appropriations, and afflicted by weak tenure, the judges must have found the feuds painful as well as a strain on their integrity.

In both Wyoming and Montana the legislative assemblies challenged the appointive powers of the governors, and in both instances, the judiciary upheld the authority of the governor. In 1869 the first legislative assembly in Wyoming appointed its own slate of county officials over the veto of Governor Campbell. He appealed to the territorial supreme court—arguing that the assembly had violated the Organic Act—and was sustained.[40] The Montana court also sustained the appointive power of the governor, but it ruled that appointments had to be made with the advice and consent of the territorial council. The effect of this decision, which infuriated Governor Potts, was to nullify interim appointments.[41] Since one of the appointments nullified for want of confirmation by the council was the auditor's post, the financial machinery of the territory was brought to a standstill, and Potts apparently never forgave the court for its part in the affair.[42]

The territorial supreme courts had their own clashes with the legislators and the most significant of these conflicts, in terms of its impact on the entire territory, resulted from the court's nullification of Montana's second and third legislatures. According to Montana's Organic Act, the first and all succeeding legislatures were to prescribe the "time, place, and manner of holding all elections" as well as the apportionment of representation.[43] It was also the responsibility of the legislature to set the date on which the next session would begin. Considering the apportionment to be inequitable, Governor Sidney Edgerton vetoed the bill intended to fulfill the above requirements, and the legislature adjourned without enacting another. Regardless of its motivation, which probably was to spite the radically inclined Republican governor, the Democratic assembly had committed legislative suicide.

Life could have been restored to the legislature by an enabling act of the United States Congress. However, while Edgerton was in the East, Acting Governor Thomas Francis Meagher (whose career was brilliant but checkered) allowed himself to be swept up in a wave of defiant Democratic enthusiasm; he convened the legislators who had been elected to

serve in the first legislative assembly.[44] The legitimacy of the
two sessions held by this body was challenged in the territorial
courts, and Justices Munson and Hosmer ruled that since
both sessions were conducted in violation of the Organic Act,
the laws therein enacted were invalid, null, and void.[45] Though
Munson and Hosmer were subjected to "threats of compul-
sion, ridicule, and ribald jest," they held their ground, and
the following spring Congress disapproved the acts of the
extralegal sessions and authorized the governor to call for
another election.[46]

The dispute became a purely partisan matter at both territorial and national levels. At the local level, the independence of the judiciary was at stake, as were economic
advantages for the controlling party. Meagher openly challenged the justices, and the Republicans did not conceal their
objection to the franchises which the Democrats had voted
themselves in a session known disparagingly as the "Toll
Road Assembly." [47] Outrage was most openly expressed in the
territory. Hosmer privately referred to the legislators as "re-
bellious disorganizers," and the Democratic press called for
the removal of the judges, accusing them of nullifying the
laws merely because they included the repeal of extra compensation. The nullification controversy was interpreted by
many territorial residents as a symbol of Congress's determination to flaunt its policy of federal supremacy before citizens
bent on autonomy.[48]

The cost of squabbles with the legislatures was usually high
for the justices. Not only was added compensation involved,
but the legislatures, under the terms of the Organic Acts,
assigned districts and set the dates and places of court terms.
Retaliation was achieved legislatively by the assignment of
recalcitrant judges to uninhabited, uncivilized districts. This
process was known as sagebrushing, a term fully appreciated
only by one who has driven through the area. At any rate, the
third session of the Montana legislature practiced the art of
sagebrushing on Munson and asked both him and Hosmer to

resign.[49] Munson obliged the assembly, but Hosmer served out his term. The Montana legislature, however, was never again able to indulge in the sport of sagebrushing. When Congress nullified the 1866 sessions, it authorized the justices to define and assign the districts and also to set the court calendars.[50] The Montana Supreme Court was the only territorial court which enjoyed this privilege. In Colorado and Wyoming the legislatures also resorted to sagebrushing with varying degrees of effectiveness.[51]

Such was the environment in which the territorial supreme courts performed their duties. The collision of national and local pressures created forces which crushed weak men but formed justices of stature from those of more substance. By congressional design, the territorial supreme courts were political entities, and an assessment of the role of the justices must be made in light of this reality.

6

Judicial Derelicts?

What manner of man would accept, or, for that matter, seek appointment to a territorial supreme court in view of insufficient compensation, a perennial dearth of operating funds, vast districts, and political intrigue, in addition to the general adversities of the frontier? Considering the entire territorial periods of Colorado, Montana, and Wyoming, one of the most surprising characteristics of the courts is the number of capable justices, not ne'er-do-wells or political derelicts, who served on them.

It is misleading to assess the performance of the judiciary within the territorial administrations of this period from a purely statistical point of view for two reasons. First, the judiciary experienced a lower rate of turnover than that of the combined administrations.[1] Secondly, the character of the judiciary during the Civil War and the immediate postwar era was not the same as that of later judiciaries.[2] The supreme courts of all three territories were stabilized by the lengthy tenures of one or more judges—in most instances, judges of quality.[3] In Colorado, Chief Justice Moses Hallett, whose career is detailed in chapter 8, set high standards for the bench from 1866 through 1876, the year statehood was granted. Montana was fortunate in the extended service of her two most distinguished jurists, Justices Hiram Knowles and Decius S. Wade, who, between them, served a total of some twenty-seven years. Justice Jacob B. Blair completed three terms in Wyoming. Though examining statistics alone can provide only an incomplete picture, the judiciaries of Colorado, Montana, and Wyoming are analyzed in terms of tenure in table 2.

Just as it is inaccurate to describe the judiciary solely by means of statistics, it is equally wrong to attempt to rigidly categorize the justices according to motivation. While a few of the jurists may fit into simple patterns, it is exceedingly difficult to construct neat pigeonholes into which most of them can be conveniently filed. Perhaps future historians, well-funded and employing highly sophisticated data-processing devices, will be able to construct a model of a typical territorial supreme court justice. They may even be able to chart variants from the norm. Meanwhile, the most appropriate course is to recognize the tendencies or traits usually exhibited by members of the bench. While one of the tendencies may be dominant in a given individual, it must be acknowledged that other characteristics may also be clearly in evidence.

Since the term *carpetbagger* is too simplistic and categorical, other delineations must be made. A number of the justices fell into one or more of the following categories: classic carpetbagger (ruthless and selfish), opportunist (exploitive but constructive), and patriot or missionary (well-meaning, but often ineffectual). Some of them came west because of personal needs (health, proximity of relatives, etc.). But my objective here is to emphasize function and performance, rather than motivation and origin, and to discuss the scope of judicial contributions within both territorial and national frameworks.

Despite the contributions of the early territorial justices in efforts for the Union cause, in the orderly transition of legal systems, and in the establishment of order, there is little doubt that the carpetbagger image does have some basis in fact. Accentuation of this image has distorted the role of the judiciary, but when the color and notoriety of some of the early jurists is considered, and especially when their correspondence is examined, it is not difficult to understand how

Table 2

Turnover on Territorial Supreme Courts

Judges

	Commissioned	Served at least one full term	Served two terms	Served three terms or more	Resigned	Suspended or removed	Years as territory
Colorado	14	6	1	—	4	1	15
Montana *	19	7	1	2	7	2	25
Wyoming	17	8	1	1	3	1	22

Source: Abstracted primarily from Earl S. Pomeroy, *The Territories and the United States, 1861–1890,* appendix.

Note: One judge in Colorado and another in Wyoming resigned to become delegates. In Wyoming, one justice died before completing his term.

* Henry N. Blake served on two separate occasions, 1876–80, and March through November, 1889.

perspective was lost. The letter quoted below, which began
with a description of the candidate's desperate condition and
his strong desire to head west, is an example of the kind of
letter which substantiates the carpetbagger image.

> . . . where I can serve my party and friends, as well as
> myself—*better* than I can hope to do here. My means do
> not warrant the risk of my going there to wait for business.
> I am in need of a position that will guarantee me a living
> for some time. . . . I am willing to accept some other
> position—not inconsistent with my profession. And if neces-
> sary I will go to some other Territory.[4]

More deserving of the carpetbagger epithet than such letters,
perhaps, were the careers of men like Colorado's Justices
Charles Lee Armour, Stephen S. Harding, and Charles F.
Holly.

Charles Lee Armour has the distinction of being the only
territorial justice known to have been publicly labeled a "Liar
and a Coward" on a 22-by-16-inch handbill.[5] Posted September
22, 1863, at Central City by Attorney James M. Cavanaugh,
the handbill described Armour as a "Judicial vagabond" who
pretended to be a judge and was guilty of "infamously tyrannical" conduct. Unfortunately, Cavanaugh (later Montana
Territory's second delegate) had portrayed the judge's character quite well.[6] Notoriety and tumult accompanied Armour's
four years on the Colorado bench, and his judicial career is
a good example of the effects of political dominance by the
administration, local rebellion, judicial incompetence, and
the animosities of the Civil War.

Justice Armour had hardly settled at his post in Central City
before he became the center of a storm of protest. Though
his association with alleged rebels was one cause of criticism,[7]
his tyrannical courtroom antics were the major source of his
unpopularity. Everyone taking an oath, for example, had to
"swear on an old, musty Bible and kiss the begrimed book
regardless of the labial transfusion of prehistoric microbes." [8]

At times, under the pretext of preserving the court's dignity, Armour jailed his bailiff for chanting too few or too many "hear ye's" at its opening.[9] Considering the many protests of Armour's incompetence, the perservation of dignity in his court was a ludicrous idea in itself. Lawyers, in jest, bragged about quoting His Honor the Bible for Blackstone, and, in gambling cases, Hoyle for the statutes.[10]

The battle of petitions began, and Armour's appointment file in the Justice Department overflowed with requests for his removal—most had been signed by anywhere from sixty-five to two hundred people.[11] The lower house of the territorial assembly passed a resolution demanding his ouster. It contained nine pages of charges covering every conceivable aspect of malfeasance, supported by eight pages of sworn testimony.[12] Armour's file also contains the usual statements in his defense—some of them struck quickly at what was considered the crucial issue. At the crux of the uproar, suggested one statement, were lawyers who were unhappy because "the Court refuses to sustain their imperfect pleas and cover up their defects." While it is evident that some of the attacks on Armour were politically motivated, it is equally obvious that his personal conduct left much to be desired, a fact revealed in correspondence between Governor John Evans and the president.[13]

When the administration remained firm in its support of Justice Armour, the legislature attempted to force his resignation by sagebrushing him to a district which consisted of Conejos and Costilla Counties in the southernmost section of the territory.[14] Colorado's judicial vagabond displayed not the slightest intention of acquiescing, and refused "to visit his adobe castles in Spain or resign his office." [15] Armour passed his time enjoying imported cigars, sipping toddies, and drawing a salary until he had outwaited the legislature; it eventually changed the boundaries of the districts more to his liking.[16] Ironically, Justice Armour was the only one of the three original appointees to serve a full term on the Colorado Territorial Supreme Court.

Stephen S. Harding of Indiana, Colorado's second territorial chief justice, took office July 18, 1863.[17] Since he had
been appointed to the Colorado bench immediately following
a turbulent nine-month tenure as governor of Utah Territory,
Harding was immediately suspect. But instead of making
amends for his failures in Utah, the new chief justice aroused
the ire of Coloradans through his general incompetence and
venality, and by an alleged affair with a woman he had supposedly brought with him from Utah. With reference to the
corruption apparent in a particular mining decision, Samuel
Bowles, a contemporary editor-traveler-commentator, observed
that "the judicious grieved, the unskilled laughed, and everybody said there could be no contempt too great for such a
court."[18]

Harding's repugnant official decorum probably inspired
some of the accusations of an illicit affair. In a lengthy letter
(marked "Private") to President Lincoln, the chief justice
vehemently denied having a paramour and explained the
charges as the work of his vengeful and unscrupulous associate,
Armour.[19] According to Harding, Justice Armour perpetrated
the malicious rumors in retaliation for the redistricting which
included a fee system detrimental to him. Harding went into
minute detail about Armour's predicament but conveniently
omitted his own difficulties. Nevertheless, the tone of the
opening paragraph infers the existence of a great clamor
over the "Mormon woman." After the usual references to his
duty and trust, Harding pleaded," I beg of you in return that
you will not cast it [this letter] aside without noting its
contents." Why would Harding expect Lincoln, who had
given him two appointments, to be predisposed not to read
the report? The president's reply, if any, has not been found.
The pressures for Harding's removal were successful, and the
former chief justice returned to his law practice and his family
in Indiana.

In response to Colorado's pleas for the appointment of
local men to the bench, Charles F. Holly was named to the
supreme court, but his tenure was brief and personally tragic.

His own Second District Grand Jury at Central City indicted him at its April 1866 term for "Adultery and Fornication" and petitioned for his replacement.[20] His Honor, it was alleged, had been caught *flagrante delicto* with the young wife of an elderly physician in whose home the judge was boarding. At the July 1866 term of the Second District Court, with Chief Justice Moses Hallett presiding, the judge was acquitted when no witnesses appeared to testify against him.[21] Though Holly had been replaced even before the trial, he persisted for a year in his attempts to remain at his post. The chief justice finally had to intervene since Holly would not recognize the appointment of his successor as valid.[22]

No one territory had a monopoly on judges guilty of malfeasance and exploitation, nor was such conduct by any means confined to the western frontier. Surely the reconstruction governments and many northern and eastern states had their share of such conduct. In this context, the exploitive attitude of Hezekiah Lord Hosmer, first chief justice of Montana Territory, serves as an excellent example. The correspondence of Hosmer's business associate, T. C. Everts, leaves little room for doubt about their motivations. Writing to Hosmer from Bannack City soon after territorial organization, Everts mentions their joint ventures in mining, roads, and ranches before explicitly revealing the objectives of their stay.

> I am much pleased at the prospect ahead for us. Now is the time to strike and I do not mean to leave any effort untried to make our stay in this Territory a success. I think we can make enough to satisfy us in two years, which is long enough to live in this country.[23]

Part of their scheme evidently was to keep Hosmer's district assignment in the area of action, as Everts reassured his cohort that Justice Lorenzo P. Williston should not be considered "a competitor." Conjecturing that Williston would be assigned out of the mining area, Everts wrote a week later, "he has been dead for a long time but don't [*sic*] know it." [24]

Hosmer was not completely averse to sharing the action with his colleagues. Ammi Giddings of Connecticut had been formally commissioned when his wife's infirmities unexpectedly prevented him from actually serving on the bench with Hosmer. Giddings's letter to the chief justice reflects his disappointment at not being able to share in the speculative activities.[25]

The national implications of these activities are indicated by Everts's remarks that one Mr. Ashley "wants to be let into any speculation going on here," and that Ashley would help sell any company of which he was made a part.[26] It is highly likely that James M. Ashley was the party to whom Everts referred. As a member of the House Committee on Territories, Ashley was actively involved in the territories, and in 1869 he was named governor of Montana Territory.[27] Ashley also had interests in Toledo, Ohio, where Hosmer, who had been secretary of Ashley's committee, was at one time editor of the *Toledo Blade*. Everts's letters also leave little doubt about Hosmer's attempts to secure passage of favorable legislation by the first assembly.

While men such as Hosmer were exploitive, coming from the East and moving on after their terms, the level of their ability and achievement is often surprising. Hosmer, for instance, not only founded and edited the *Toledo Blade* but also wrote plays, addressed learned societies, and gave temperance lectures. After his service on the Montana bench, Hosmer spent the balance of his life in San Francisco engaged primarily in literary pursuits.[28]

By playing the spotlight on the Armours, Hardings, Hollys and Hosmers—and the roster is by no means complete—attention has been distracted from men whose contributions were many, or, in some instances, whose goals were noble though their activities were less fruitful. Admitting that Wyoming's early appointees were soon embroiled in controversy, Professor T. A. Larson has nevertheless recognized "the superior competence of the group as a whole," and seventy-five years before Larson, Hubert Howe Bancroft arrived at a similar conclusion about Montana's justices.[29] Adherence to the functional view of territorial development dictates that achievement and contribution are more relevant than the forces which originally steered the justices to the territories.

Certainly, the majority of territorial pioneers in Colorado, Montana, and Wyoming had opportunistic tendencies, a fact which they at times conveniently overlooked. It was ludicrous, in some respects, for settlers to speak of themselves as Coloradans when they had only been in the region for two or three years. Nevertheless, the "Pike's Peakers" considered themselves the local citizenry. For the purposes of this study, the opportunist is distinguished from the carpetbagger by his constructiveness, permanency, and interest in the development of the region. Into this category many supreme court justices should be placed, thereby putting the emphasis on their contributions to territorial society.

One of Montana's opportunists was Justice Henry N. Blake who, according to historian Merrill G. Burlingame, "probably held more public offices over a longer period of time than any other man in the Territory." [30] Burlingame was not measuring Blake's contributions solely on a quantitative basis. A native of Boston, Blake fought in the Civil War first as an enlisted man and later as an officer. Before the war he had received a law degree from Harvard and had been, briefly, in private practice.[31] Like innumerable veterans following any war, Captain Blake sought a new start. He arrived in Montana Territory in 1866 and "took roots." Before his career ended, Blake played many important roles—attorney, newspaper editor, Indian fighter, district attorney, legislator, court reporter, associate justice, and chief justice of the Montana State Supreme Court.

Henry N. Blake attributed his involvement in the newspaper business to his formal education and his New England background.[32] For brief periods he was editor of the *Montana Post* and *The Montanian,* and there is no doubt that his literary abilities were considerable. In addition, Blake's knowledge of the nation's growth would be a credit to any historian. His address to the bar association in 1887, "The Rise of the Territories of the United States," remains a creditable piece of historical writing.[33] Blake's intellectual capacities are evident in his other works as well, reason enough for his choice as supreme court reporter in 1872.[34] Though his record of a succession of both elective and appointive offices points toward integrity and public acceptance, Blake was not without his critics. However, as was usual in the territories, the complaints tended to be political and vindictive in nature. In this case, the charges came primarily from Alexander Woolfolk whose favorite targets appear to have been judges.[35] Unlike many of his more popular colleagues, Blake was proud of his abstinence from tobacco and alcohol. In its editorial on the newly appointed justice, *The Montanian* made a point of this fact, noting that its former editor had "retained the temperate habits he acquired in his eastern home, and does not use either tobacco or liquors." [36]

The other territorial benches also included men who rendered valuable service, although their original goals had been the seeking of increased fortune on the frontier. While Colorado's Moses Hallett serves as a prime example, others should not be neglected; one of the most colorful was Allen A. Bradford. Though Maine was his home state, Bradford had wandered over America's frontier several times—once as far west as California. He arrived at the Gregory Diggings in 1860, only six months prior to the creation of the Territory of Colorado.[37] In June 1862, Bradford was appointed to fill the vacancy on the territorial supreme court created by the resignation of S. Newton Pettis, an original appointee. Though he had lived in the territory for less than two years, he was considered a local man and was thus saved from the disgrace of the carpetbagger label. While it was surely the challenge and opportunity of the gold fields that had attracted Bradford, he had experience at the bar in Missouri, Iowa, and Nebraska

Territory and had also served as a judge of a lower court in Iowa.

Though Bradford discharged his responsibility with unchallenged competence and humanity, his total disregard for traditional decorum soon became legendary. Unconcerned with sartorial standards, he preferred either a Mexican sarape or a tobacco-stained linen duster to the usual formal business attire worn by his colleagues.[38] His prejudices caused few repercussions, for they were basically apolitical—one against mule thieves, for he was once their victim; another against poker players who had won from him.

Neither his fellow citizens nor his colleagues allowed Bradford's eccentricities and unseemly appearance to distract them from recognizing his ability, benevolence, and high aspirations for Colorado's growth. Perhaps his unpolished manner was wisdom in disguise, for while letters of recommendation mentioned his "unflinching courage," they stressed that he was "well adapted" to the new territory and that he knew "its wants and how to meet them." [39] Bradford stepped down from the bench in 1865 to represent the territory as delegate, a position he held for two terms, 1865–67 and 1869–71. Since the delegate was the only elected official representing the entire territory, Bradford's selection for the post verified that he did indeed understand the desires of his fellow settlers. After he had finished his service in Washington, Bradford returned to Pueblo, Colorado, where he devoted his energies to his practice and to the development of the community during the balance of his years.

After the members of the "wartime" court had either served their terms or been removed, the Colorado Territorial Supreme Court, under the aegis of Chief Justice Moses Hallett, was dominated by men whose personal gains were equaled or outweighed by the benefits their services brought to the territory. Men of great stature also served Wyoming's bench in its maturity—men whose careers would fall into a similar category. Plentiful recognition has been given to Joseph Maull

Carey, who served a full term from 1872 to 1876, and to Willis Van Devanter, who sat as chief justice for a brief period immediately before Wyoming became a state.[40]

It is presumptuous to assign pure motives to anyone. Nevertheless, some men are unquestionably governed by higher ideals than others, and the number of supreme court justices who sought their posts primarily because they wanted to serve has been underestimated at least by intimation.[41] Some jurists have been defamed intentionally by their contemporaries and inadvertently by reporters who have played up the sensational aspects of their careers. Because he clashed with Acting Governor Thomas F. Meagher and was sagebrushed by the Montana legislature, Justice Lyman E. Munson was relegated by insinuation to the role of carpetbagger or *pilgrim,* a term disparagingly applied to officials sent from the outside.

A descendent of New England Puritans and a graduate of Yale Law School, Munson left one of the most highly regarded firms in New Haven to take the place of Ammi Giddings on the Montana Territorial Supreme Court. Munson's first partnership in New Haven had been with an eminent professor on the Yale faculty, Henry Dutton. Later he formed the firm of Munson and Sheldon with Joseph Sheldon, and their practice was reputed to be extensive. When Giddings informed Chief Justice Hezekiah L. Hosmer that he would not be able to serve, he was high in his praise of Munson.[42]

In addition to the news he made by his feud with the legislature and his altercation with Meagher over the supremacy of the courts, Judge Munson was in the headlines because of public charges of corruption pressed by Alexander M. Woolfolk, lawyer and publisher. Though this controversy had factional overtones, Woolfolk's tirade was triggered by the fact that Munson had fined him $100 for his role in a cane-breaking, knife-wielding ruckus before the court. Justice Munson denied the allegations point for point, offering reasonable explanation of his conduct.[43] Woolfolk, who was considered by some citizens to be an "incorrigible idiot," con-

stantly attacked the judiciary; he did not even spare four-term
Justice Decius S. Wade. Thus his charges can hardly be
accepted as evidence of Munson's venality.[44]

Munson frequently held court for his absent associates and
was unusually conscientious; he did not leave the territory for
a year and a half after his arrival. When he did leave to get
his family, the judge was given a "$300 gold watch" as a token
of respect for him "as a man, judge, and citizen." [45]

After his sagebrushing, Munson remained out of the territory, and he eventually resigned because of illness in his
family.[46] He returned to his practice in New Haven where
he lived to be the oldest member of the Connecticut bar.
When he died in 1908, the New Haven papers, as might be
expected, were extremely laudatory in their obituary columns.[47]
The *Helena Independent,* however, did not have to express
such admiration for a former sagebrush victim. While it is
customary to make statesmen of dead politicians, it is still
surprising to find that the *Independent,* once edited by
Woolfolk, praised Munson as "a vital force" in Montana's
"social, religious, commercial, and, above all, its judicial
history." [48] The highest compliments are found in the 1913
history of Montana by Helen Fitzgerald Sanders (still a valuable work) in which she suggests that Munson's courage in
opposing Meagher "was worthy of John Marshall." [49]

My intent here is not to assiduously categorize the justices
but to dispel the carpetbagger myth in which the judiciary,
as a whole, has been too long enshrouded. It is impossible
to determine what the motivations of each judge were, and
Justices Hiram Knowles and Decius S. Wade are presented
here merely to illustrate the quality and achievements of
territorial jurists who were builders of the territory just as
much as any other type of official or resident.

Born in Maine in 1834, Hiram Knowles covered an astound-
ing amount of ground before he arrived in Montana in 1866
to take his place on the territorial supreme court.[50] Educated
at Antioch College in Ohio and Harvard Law School, Knowles

had firsthand knowledge of much of the West before he began his nearly eleven years of service as a territorial justice. His western odyssey began in 1862 when he visited California and then took up a law practice in Nevada. After approximately three years, he moved to Idaho, but he remained at the bar there for only a year. In 1866 he finally arrived in Montana where he remained until his death in 1911. Knowles's close to half a century of residence in Montana and his rigid early training indicate that his brief but wide wanderings were merely an expression of youthful independence. Correspondence from his father, a sea captain and physician, reveals that his eminence on the bench was due at least in part to his heritage. As a student, Knowles was admonished to avoid "the quibbles and technicalities incident to every intellectual pursuit" and to seek the "naked heart of every question, stripping the shams and disguises that tend to cover and obscure it." [51] The elder Knowles continued by exhorting his son to seek "truth and only truth" and to "stow" in his mind great principles that would never desert him in times of temptation. In closing, the captain expressed confidence that his son would not become an imitator, for such a course would be "too poor and ignoble." It is a commentary on the character of Hiram Knowles that he preserved this letter through all of his travels. The justice also saved an essay of which he was evidently proud, written April 26, 1856, and entitled "Life and Death of Brasidas." [52] It is comfort of a sort to see his professor's warning penned in red, "attend to Spelling!"

In 1879, after two and a half terms, Knowles resigned from the court probably for financial reasons.[53] Besides contributing notably to the advancement of his profession as a founder of the bar association in 1885, Knowles played an important role at the Montana Constitutional Convention. In 1890, after statehood had been granted, he was appointed to the United States district court in Montana, a position he held with distinction until 1904. The petitions by the bar for his selection as a federal judge reflect the genuine regard and respect with which Knowles was held.[54] While it would have been poor politics not to sign such a petition, it was not a requirement of etiquette for so many of the signatories to include personal endorsements, notes which seem sincere and not merely perfunctory. Considering both territorial and federal service, Knowles devoted a quarter of a century to the judiciary in Montana. However, his warm human qualities also contributed to his popularity. Among his papers is a letter written in 1909 by a former reporter for the *Rocky Mountain Gazette* (Helena), filled with reminiscences of boisterous frontier escapades—"sampling the old Frenchman's best Valley Tan," for instance—which add to, rather than detract from, his image as a man.[55] And if there is anything that Knowles was not, it was a carpetbagger. In 1911 he went to Los Angeles for treatment of Bright's Disease. Realizing the end was near, Knowles boarded a train so that he might die in Montana. But death thwarted his hopes, and he died aboard the train near Idaho Falls.[56]

The only territorial justice in Colorado, Montana, or Wyoming to complete four terms was Decius S. Wade.[57] His judicial career in the West may have begun in a manner similar to that associated with carpetbaggers, but before his service was concluded he would be known as the father of Montana jurisprudence. A native of Ohio, Decius S. Wade was the nephew of two prominent Ohio politicians, Senator Benjamin F. Wade and his brother, Congressman Edward Wade. It was in their office that Wade read law for his admission to the bar in 1857. Prior to this, he had taught school for six winters and studied at Kingsville Academy in the summers. His law practice was interrupted by the Civil War, in which he fought as an officer. After his military service, he gained experience as a probate judge, and when President Grant appointed him chief justice, he was serving his second term as a state senator.

Commissioned in 1871 at the age of thirty-six, Wade was

diligent from the beginning, working steadily at the bench for an entire month during the first term. To his more experienced associate, Wade confessed that he had "done more labor than doubtless was really necessary," but he added that he was aware of the importance of his first term and that he wanted to be "sure of the law and the right." [58] The new chief justice also admitted that circumstances in Montana were "peculiar and different." Wade had genuine literary talent, and he was not averse to work. Not only do his opinions occupy approximately half of the first six volumes of the *Montana Reports,* but he accrued an enviable record of being sustained by the United States Supreme Court. His decisions were reversed in only two of seventeen cases appealed to that body.[59] Wade wrote an article on self-government in the territories, which still bears reading, and a novel, *Clare Lincoln,* which evidently was well received. He also wrote pamphlets of local interest, particularly dealing with the need for the codification of laws.[60]

Despite his distinguished and record-setting tenure on the territorial supreme court, Wade is most noted for his leadership in a successful struggle to properly codify Montana's laws. In 1890 Wade was appointed to the commission authorized for this purpose, and it is generally acknowledged that his was the dominant role in that effort which included arrangement for publication as well as the actual codification, a task several years in its completion. Though other lofty figures in Montana's legal history, namely Hiram Knowles and Henry N. Blake, were his contemporaries, Wade's achievements in codification have earned him the title "founder of Montana jurisprudence." Since a number of the cases decided by these men are analyzed in chapter 9, it is sufficient to merely state here that their intelligence, training, and experience are amply reflected in the opinions they authored. A careful reader of the *Montana Reports* is impressed with the depth of their research and their individualism, not to mention their literary accomplishments. Wade and Knowles, in particular, were not reluctant about expressing disagreement—both men frequently wrote elaborate dissenting opinions. The court on which these men sat cannot be characterized as a "rubber stamp" operation.

Of the fifty men commissioned as territorial supreme court justices in Colorado, Montana, and Wyoming, none has files that can compare in magnitude with those in the Justice Department for Associate Justice Everton J. Conger. The story disclosed in these bulging folders illustrates that some judicial failures are as difficult to categorize as some successes, and that perhaps some cases deserve as much pity as derision.

Conger's recommendations, though they stressed his war record, wounds, and Republican loyalty, were average to better-than-average for the period. Letters came from the whole spectrum of Illinois society—from bankers, local attorneys, and the usual battery of public officials.[61] Like most new justices, this former war hero found himself at the center of raging controversy not long after his appointment in 1883. Conger's district encompassed approximately half of Montana Territory, and the strain of serving so vast an area led him to rely more heavily than was prudent on morphine and alcohol to relieve the constant pain of his war wounds. In response to the barrage of conflicting reports sent to Washington—half of his district understood his conduct, the other half found it intolerable—the Justice Department decided on the unusual course of sending a special examiner to investigate Conger's conduct. On June 6, 1883, the hearing got under way in Bozeman, with former Chief Justice Peter C. Shannon of Dakota Territory acting as a special examiner.[62] The hearing lasted the entire month, during which 62 witnesses offered 880 pages of testimony varying from the most damaging and vitriolic criticism to the staunchest support of his integrity. It appeared that there was more to the matter than Conger's behavior, for his opposition and his support were concentrated in different communities. It hardly seems likely that His Honor would behave one way at Virginia City and another at Bozeman and Miles City.

In his formal report, Shannon admitted that Conger's effectiveness was impaired in portions of his district, but he concluded that mercy should be exercised in view of the judge's war record and his crippled condition.[63] Two months prior to the hearing, Conger had been suspended by President Chester A. Arthur, but the suspension was revoked in January 1884. Conger was restored to his position because the president sympathized with his "suffering as a soldier" and because of the "extenuating circumstances connected with the charges."[64] It is not clear from the message whether or not the "extenuating circumstances" referred to his infirmities or to other factors. Concluding the letter was an affirmation of Arthur's confidence in Conger's personal and official integrity. Conger was permitted to complete his term, though his request for reappointment was ignored.[65] Regardless of the merit or lack of merit in Judge Conger's predicament, his prolonged suspension was a source of untold hardship for Montana's other two justices and its litigants as well.

A denial of the malfeasance of certain jurists has no place in a reevaluation of the constructive role of the territorial supreme court justices. Recognizing the venality of some of the judges is necessary so that the extent of wrongdoing can be kept in proper perspective. While corruption was never totally absent from the territorial benches of Colorado, Montana, and Wyoming, the incidence of dishonesty dropped as the territories matured, a natural phenomenon perhaps, or a reflection of the national political atmosphere—possibly a combination of these factors.

The noted traveler Samuel Bowles provided a somewhat exaggerated but classic account of the corruption which was undeniably at a high level during and following the war.

The men sent out to these new Territories as judges are not apt to be of a very high order either of morals or intellect. They are often hungry adventurers, and their salaries bearing generally no comparison to the cost of living in these remote regions, and large pecuniary interests often

being involved in the questions brought before them,—as
is especially the case in the mining Territories,—they are
too apt to yield to the temptations offered them, and to
sell their judgements for a price.[66]

In Senate debate Henry M. Teller orated with great rancor
over the improbity of some justices in Colorado's early territorial period. Without mentioning names, Teller actually did
speak of one justice who "sold his judgements" and was on
the payroll of a New York firm, the records of which the
Senator professed he had seen.[67] But Bowles's reflections on
the voting habits of the electorate paint a similar picture of
dishonesty. Territorial residents, he observed, were prone to
"vote early, vote often, and see that their neighbors vote";
they sometimes accumulated a total ballot greater than the
population.[68]

Cupidity was common to all of the territories, though temptations in mining districts were undoubtedly greater. The
diaries of Governor John A. Campbell of Wyoming contain
entries which suggest the problem of bribes. The word *suggest*
applies here because the use of harsher terms would mean
that one's mind was closed to other possibilities. For example,
one entry reads, "Received a present of $1000." [69] Other
references, some mentioning judges, leave little doubt about
attempted bribery.[70] Since railroad and stage passes were
commonly accepted by officials, they are not discussed here
in terms of dishonest practices, but gifts of land from railroads are another matter.[71]

Montana had its share of questionable practices too; hardly
a single judge was not accused of some breach of integrity.
Even Decius Wade was charged with accepting a $1,000 pay-
off, but he was cleared, as were many of his colleagues.[72] The
so-called Indian Rings provided another area of shady deal-
ings, and judges were also associated with them. In the 1870s,
exposures of Indian frauds in Montana led one man to ob-
serve that "they have already unearthed more rascality than

the poor Republican party of the territory can pack." [73]
Considering the tenor of nationally accepted conduct, malfeasance was probably less prevalent among members of the
judiciary than among other officials—especially after the initial territorial periods. Not only were the new justices men of
high quality, but they were subjected to constant scrutiny, a
legacy of their more corrupt predecessors.

There is little doubt that men with even a few years'
previous experience in the Rocky Mountains performed with
greater distinction on the supreme courts and made their
presence felt in more lasting fashion than men appointed
directly from the East. Hallett, Knowles, Blake, Bradford,
Carey, and others had an opportunity to adapt before being
elevated to the bench. Wade was a notable exception, but he
immediately recognized the "peculiar and different" environment into which he had moved.[74] In addition, he had come
from the more western state of Ohio—whose frontier was
still within memory—where he had had the tutelage of two
worldly uncles. The performance of the bench improved as
the territories matured, and a growing tendency to appoint
local men contributed to this improvement. Shortly before
statehood was granted to Colorado, Henry M. Teller observed, "In the early history of this Territory we were cursed
with incompetent Judges, and for the last eight years we
have had an able and I believe honest judiciary." [75]

Apparently youthfulness was another factor, which, while
difficult to measure accurately, worked in behalf of some
justices. The flexibility of youth seems to have been a catalytic
agent in the innovating process. A number of outstanding
jurists were not young when appointed to the bench but had
possessed the resilience of youth when they arrived in the
territories.

The law has always been a learned profession, demanding
an inordinate amount of "book learning." However, most
nineteenth-century lawyers received their training by reading
the law, rather than in a formal law school. In addition, eager

young attorneys mastered their profession by emulating their
respected elders, men whose words, tactics, and mannerisms
were scrutinized in the hope that their skills could be ab-
sorbed. In terms of their formal education, the territorial
supreme court justices of Colorado, Montana, and Wyoming
were an impressive lot. Approximately half had A.B.'s, nearly
a quarter had LL.B.'s, and a few had M.A.'s. More impressive was the frequency with which former justices settled in
the territories and contributed substantially to their growth,
a process which continued after the territories became states.
Did these territorial judges, as a group, operate any differently
in terms of integrity and performance than other political
groups across the nation during the postwar era? A few judges
were certainly not moral or intellectual pacesetters; the
majority performed at least up to par; a surprising number
were truly builders and innovators. Political derelicts all?
Hardly, although the bench undeniably had its share.

7
William
Ware
Peck

In its waning hours, the Fifth Legislative Assembly of the Territory of Wyoming redefined and reassigned territorial judicial districts for the specific purpose of sagebrushing Justice William Ware Peck.[1] The resulting controversy raged with such intensity that Peck became a household word in Wyoming, and his predicament was followed in newspapers throughout the entire nation, thus making Peck perhaps the most celebrated of all sagebrushing victims.

Ostensibly, the source of this cause célèbre was the exorbitant expenses incurred by the terms of district court held by Judge Peck in Uinta and Sweetwater Counties on his arrival from New York in the summer of 1877. Though the figures cited by his friends and his foes vary, in Uinta County the costs of conducting his July term of district court in 1877 ($11,000) were more than three times the costs for the preceding July ($3,000).[2] It appeared that the people of the remote and sparsely settled counties of Uinta and Sweetwater simply could not afford Peck's "eastern" brand of justice, and this aspect of the conflict generally received prominent treatment.[3] However, the actual cause of Peck's problems was a conflict of personalities and heritages—a conflict which led to a compounding of irritations. During this collision of cultures, local officials lined their pockets by taking advantage of the judge's lack of familiarity with Wyoming's court finances. Through his deliberate conduct of the court, Peck did unwittingly let court expenses get out of hand.[4] But once he caught on to the capers of the court officials, he put an end to their lucrative practices and demanded to approve all bills rendered by the county. Peck not only curtailed these activities, but he also passed around court appointments which had been reserved by his predecessor for a select few— he had challenged the ring.[5] The newly appointed jurist fined a lawyer, who was a delegate to the state legislature, ten dollars for contempt, and the embittered attorney publicly announced his plans for retaliation.[6]

Though the usual vague charges of incompetence were heard, it was clearly Peck's eastern notions and prim manner rather than a lack of ability that was the source of the opposition to him.[7] Several members of the Senate Judiciary Committee defended his professional qualifications but admitted that he would be more acceptable in a "settled community" and that "he was not constructed for the kind of people who seem to hold sway" in Wyoming. The people of Wyoming, moreover, did not go uncriticized. In speaking of Peck's appropriateness for communities with settled habits which restrain the behavior of men, Senator Isaac P. Christiancy of Michigan referred to a "certain portion of the people" of Wyoming who were "somewhat addicted to drinking and gambling." [8]

Considering the attitudes and mannerisms of William Ware Peck, the causes of his predicament are not difficult to fathom. Even the hustle of his entrance—he arrived in Evanston at two in the afternoon and held court at three—must have ruffled a few feathers.[9] While perhaps the epithet "experimental moral philosopher" was too derisive, it does accurately convey the reaction of many frontier men to a judge who tended to flavor his justice with ample doses of morality.[10] A staunch Episcopalian, Peck taught Sunday School and often opened his court with a prayer, activities which provoked Senator Algernon S. Paddock of Nebraska to describe the justice as a self-acclaimed "apostle to the border country, sent there for missionary work to reform a depraved people." [11] Some years later, an observer referred to Peck's courtroom prayers on the western fringes of Wyoming and suggested humorously that the community "would have been less astonished had one of their number opened a jackpot in the same manner." [12]

Peck's own letters reveal his missionary zeal and suggest he may well have envisioned himself as a great conveyor of law and order. To President Rutherford B. Hayes, Peck depicted his work as a "sharp contest, a *close throat-grapple* between law and crime," and he seemed to be preoccupied with the "lawless element." Years after leaving the bench, Peck described a successor to the court as "without talent, poorly read, ill trained and unbalanced—in professional development below his years (and they are but 28), a judicial crudity—is profane, given to low intimacy and a frequenter of saloons." [13]

Peck's religious bent was not his only annoying characteristic. He was so deliberate and fastidious that, in the jargon of twentieth-century psychology, he could be properly labeled compulsive. His files in the National Archives reveal, for example, that only the pages of messages from His Honor are carefully glued together, and his clerk surely swallowed exasperation as Peck inserted extra punctuation marks before signing a letter.[14] The judge, by his own admission, was thorough in the conduct of his court; his notations must have irritated those of his neighbors who were accustomed to speedy frontier justice.[15] And it is easy to imagine the astonishment of his colleagues when he suggested that the supreme court don robes. Mannerisms such as these were behind one allusion to William Ware Peck as "one of those gentlemen to whom it is a pleasure to part their names in the middle," and another to the "lordly air" with which he mounted the bench.[16]

Whether viewed as humorous or pathetic, these idiosyncrasies were neither the sole nor the sufficient cause of the sagebrushing of Justice Peck. Local politicians, including Peck's predecessor, E. A. Thomas, were more disturbed by a fear of losing control than by the judge's religious zeal.[17] Another ingredient in Peck's explosive situation was a legislative custom in Wyoming which was the epitome of logrolling —by agreement and precedent, memorials and resolutions on purely local issues automatically received nearly unanimous support from other delegates.[18] This tradition provided just the fuse needed to explode the grievances of Peck's rivals into an incident of national proportions. That the Peck affair basically began as a localized quarrel is indicated by the absence of comment in the *Cheyenne Daily Leader,* which covered the territorial news closely prior to the legislative action.

Peck was sent to Wyoming to replace Justice E. A. Thomas on an interim appointment which required Senate confirmation at the next session of Congress. Since he had already alienated some of his constituents before this session convened in Washington, his opponents hoped to block his confirmation. It was at this juncture that the logrolling practices assumed importance, for the offended delegate to Wyoming's 1877 assembly had no difficulty in passing a memorial requesting the president to withdraw the nomination.[19] The same resolution instructed Delegate W. W. Corlett to work toward this end. Despite the claims of Wyoming's legislature about Peck's "incompetency and gross extravagance," the president's choice was confirmed on December 14, 1877.

At the time of Peck's arrival in the territory, Wyoming had five counties, all of which extended from Colorado to Montana—from east to west, they were Laramie, Albany, Carbon, Sweetwater, and Uinta. Chief Justice Joseph W. Fisher was assigned to the First District which covered only Laramie County. The Second District, Albany and Carbon Counties, was assigned to Justice Jacob Beeson Blair, and the Third

District, composed of Sweetwater and Uinta, was to be that of Justice Peck.[20]

In retaliation for the confirmation of Peck against its wishes, Wyoming's legislative assembly passed a redistricting bill which altered the existing districts and relegated Peck to the unorganized counties of Pease and Crook in the extreme northeastern corner of the territory. The legislation was entitled "An Act to provide for the Organization of Crook and Pease Counties, and to provide for Holding Courts therein," and its provisions were simple but of vast implication.[21] Basically, the act ordered the governor to organize Crook and Pease Counties, designated them the Third Judicial District, assigned Peck to it, and attached the counties of Sweetwater and Uinta (the old Third District) to Blair's Second District. The assembly's desire to circumvent the intentions of the Organic Act was clear, for the act also authorized the governor, in the event of a vacancy in the Third District, to redistrict the entire territory and to reassign the judges. The redistricting bill, according to some reports, was actually passed after the expiration of the last (fortieth) day of the session, but it is recorded on the books as having been enacted December 15, 1877, the day following the Senate confirmation. On the same day, the Wyoming legislature provided extra compensation of $800 per year for Judge Fisher and $1000 per year for Judge Blair upon whom the lion's share of the work would fall.[22]

Though the intended victim of the sagebrushing did not yield, Governor John M. Thayer, who approved the bill, was soon replaced. Thayer defended his approval on the grounds that he had previously vetoed a similar measure and by the fact that the assembly was now determined to override his objection. In addition, delay would be an imposition on the growing population of Crook County.[23] The first bill called for organization of the new counties only after petition by five hundred voters; in its enacted version, immediate organization was stipulated. Additional ulterior motives, connecting his approval with political advantages, have been attributed to Thayer's actions.[24] Regardless of his motivation, the governor's assent to the sagebrushing was interpreted by both the president and the Senate as a rebuff, and the signature cost Thayer his job.

The legality of the sagebrush was never recognized by Peck, and for a brief while, he attempted to maintain possession of his Third District Court. The judge soon recognized, however, that discretion might be the better part of valor, and he moved to Cheyenne where he remained during the balance of his term. Perhaps his move was wise. Affidavits submitted to the Senate Judiciary Committe indicate that the sheriff, appropriately named George Pepper, refused to serve Peck's court orders and threatened to "club him and his whole damned gang out of there" if the judge tried to hold court. Peck reported to the attorney general that Sheriff Pepper locked him out of the building, threatened to shoot him, and escorted Justice Blair into the courtroom to act in his stead.[25]

Though Peck retreated from Evanston, he had by no means deserted the struggle. Actually, he had only begun to fight, choosing to do battle in Washington where his strategy was to secure congressional annulment of the redistricting bill. Peck's efforts bore fruit in the Senate, and on February 13, 1878, Senate Bill S 732 was favorably reported from the Committee on the Judiciary. After a vigorous debate, which revealed sectional attitudes toward the territories, the Senate passed the annulling legislation on February 20, 1878, despite Delegate Corlett's rigorous attempts to block its passage. The next day, the bill was sent to the House Committee on the Judiciary where it died as a result of Corlett's diligent and skillful opposition.[26]

The Senate interpreted the action of Wyoming's legislature as an expression of defiance, not just the punishment of an unfortunate judge, and the debate boiled down to two basic issues: first, the supremacy of Congress, and second, the unanimity of the resistance to Peck.[27] Though they understood the situation, eastern senators stressed their demands for the conformity of the territories and insinuated that a New Yorker was being persecuted for his eastern notions.

Solons from the newer states west of the Mississippi adamantly defended the Wyoming legislature; the most vociferous was Colorado's Senator Henry M. Teller. Teller chided his eastern colleagues, particularly directing his remarks at Vermont's Senator George F. Edmunds, with the observation that there was "not such a wonderful difference" between the practice of law in Wyoming and in Vermont.[28] The Colorado Senator challenged the suggestion that Justice Peck had "introduced any new system of practice" into the territories.

The senators, however, particularly the Committee on the Judiciary, refused to accept Corlett's estimate of the scope of Peck's opposition. Indeed, the committee had too much evidence to the contrary, and it is likely that the administration also had the advantage of firsthand observations made by Washington officials who traveled through the territory.[29] Much has been made of the friendship between Peck and President Hayes, and this relationship has been offered as the explanation for the Senate's action as well as for the administration's failure to remove him from the bench. The justice and the chief executive had been classmates at Harvard Law School, and evidently the friendship had been maintained.[30] However, the evidence heard by the Justice Department and the Senate indicates that Peck's tenure cannot be explained simply in terms of either his relationship with the president or the eastern bias of the Senate.

The voluminous files of charges and countercharges which accumulated during the Peck affair are worth analyzing, not because of their color and humor but because they reveal the true complexity of the environment in which territorial supreme court justices performed. Typically, this episode in

Wyoming territorial history has been depicted as just another amusing carpetbagger anecdote. However, in the mass of correspondence can be found illustrations of the diverse pressure which affected the judiciary. In addition, the files make it clear that the justices were men as well as officials, men who often left their marks in uncommon ways, some in success, others in failure.

Deep emotions were revealed in most of the communications—both pro and con—about Judge Peck, and in view of his personality and religious fervor, it would be surprising if this were not the case. Therefore, the intensity and volume of the correspondence should be given less consideration than the sources of the remarks and the plausibility of the claims. As was so often the case in disputes on the frontier, both factions indulged in excessive assertions. Peck's adversaries, however, appeared to be completely unreasonable in some of their statements. While the governor, using official county statistics, reported that court expenses in Uinta County had tripled, one petition to the House of Representatives charged that the costs of the court term had increased eight to ten times.[31] The same petition estimated that ninety percent of the residents were against the judge, and his supporters were castigated so severely that questions were raised about their reliability. Since the "spoils system" was also in operation at the county level, it was to be expected that Peck's supporters were in line for court patronage, and the protégés of his predecessor surely understood that reality. Nevertheless, the sheriff, the former supreme court justice for that district, and their followers found only evil, venality, and nepotism behind the Peck supporters, and they coined a new but highly descriptive phrase when one attorney, Henry Garbanate, was dubbed a "briefless lawyer."[32]

Delegate Corlett expressed the feelings of at least part of his constituency when he wrote of the "idiosyncrasies of character" which had "rendered him [Peck] so odious to the people of Wyoming."[33] But the propriety of other remarks is questionable. In this category falls a resolution which was railroaded through a territorial convention—it declared that the jurist suffered from "certain infirmities of mind." [34] At the time the "resolution of insanity" was passed by a controvertible voice vote, Peck's archenemy and predecessor, E. A. Thomas, was wielding the gavel, and even the Republican candidate for delegate repudiated the resolution.[35]

While the pleas in defense of Judge Peck were as zealous as the attacks of his critics, their sources were often more credible, and their assertions more reasonable. Peck was fervently endorsed by the clergy, and considerable clarity can perhaps be gained by discussing this group's significance separately. The little that has been written about Judge Peck tends to stress his religious affiliations and neglects evidence of much wider support.[36] It was strong clerical sympathy, no doubt, which further intensified the opposition to Peck in some circles. In the heat of the controversy over Peck's confirmation by the Senate, the Reverend F. L. Arnold, pastor of the Evanston Presbyterian Church, praised the "good and noble Judge Peck" in the most glowing terms, blaming the "Saloon, Gambling and *Impure* houses" for his tribulation.[37] This Presbyterian pastor added a postscript, apparently feeling that it stood as testimony to his lack of bias: "Judge Peck is an *Episcopalian!*" On January 1, 1881, toward the end of his tenure, Peck was sent a letter signed by thirteen pastors in which they conveyed the "compliments of the season" and commended him for his work.[38] At the bottom of the message was penned, "Signed by all the clergymen except possibly one."

Had Peck's support been derived solely from the clergy, it is possible that ninety percent of the population was, indeed, hopeful of his removal. However, such was not the case. The source of his support was surprisingly broad and generally of apparent credibility. Particularly impressive is the appraisal of Judge Peck, a Republican, by the Democrat William R. Steele who served two terms as delegate. After knowing Peck for over a year, Steele depicted him as "an honorable, conscientious gentleman, a good lawyer, and an able Judge." Earlier, during the first efforts to remove him, Steele had also defended Peck, though he admitted that the judge was "slow in trial" because of his lack of familiarity with the codes.[39]

The experience of a full term on the first Wyoming Territorial Supreme Court had given John W. Kingman ample knowledge of Peck's predicament, and the former justice staunchly defended Peck as having been "outraged by an insignificant cabal." While many newspapers blasted Peck, especially William E. Wheeler's *Evanston Age,* a number of them, including some of considerable influence, were sympathetic to the judge. Though the most prominent of the latter was the *Laramie Sentinel,* the *Cheyenne Leader* eventually wound up in the Peck camp too.[40] The *Sentinel* argued that no respectable man could afford to join in the cry against Peck since the simple truth was that Peck had been rejected in Evanston because of his morality and integrity. Furthermore, the editorial continued, Peck's persecution might "create the impression that the people of Wyoming are a set of heathens and savages." A reader from Evanston shared the *Sentinel's* attitude, writing the editor that "John Marshall himself" could not have escaped the wrath of Peck's enemies in the Third District.[41]

Just as there were petitions seeking Peck's removal, there were petitions loud in their praise for him. Though there is always a question about how many of the signatures were valid, enough petitions were offered in his behalf to gainsay Delegate Corlett's estimate before Congress that nine-tenths of Wyoming's citizens were not in favor of Peck.[42] Assuming an equal proportion of fraudulent names on the lists of both factions, Corlett's assertion would still have been far out of line. Some of the memorials supporting Peck could have readily been checked, such as the one signed by "eight of the nine resident and practicing attorneys" in the Third

Judicial District. Though it is impossible to detect fraudu-
lently prepared lists with the available records, Peck's friends
offered a petition arranged by precinct in Evanston which
at least precluded the possibility of more signatures than
voters. Of course this petition showed a substantial majority
behind the judge. An attorney, Charles M. White, swore in
an affidavit that he had made a similar poll of Uinta County,
using a list of voters obtained from the county clerk, and
that his poll also indicated a strong backing for the judge.[43]

In addition to battling for the longest list of signatures,
both sides engaged in a war over the quality of their ad-
herents. During the confirmation struggle, Peck's side produced a truly formidable petition which stressed the fact that
the signatures had been volunteered by responsible taxpayers
rather than by "promiscuous crowds." Attached to the document were letterheads from ten obviously substantial business
firms, and beside each signature the occupation of the signer
had been noted. Also appended was a list of all county tax
assessments, and it was pointed out that one William Hinton,
a "prime mover" of the campaign against Peck had not been
listed for "one Quarter of a Dollar of Assessment." [44] Each
of these items was carefully notarized.

Some of the charges and countercharges were as humorous
as they were indicative of political chicanery. It is easy to
imagine the guffaws in the committee room when the affidavit
of Samuel H. Stevenson was presented, complete with the
tiny scraps of what had supposedly been a list of fictitious
names that he had applied to a petition for Peck for a fee of
eighteen dollars.[45] The statement had been sworn to before
none other than Sheriff George W. Pepper who had noted
that the "bits of paper were appended by me."

Finally, the outcome of the 1878 race for delegate confirms
that Peck's unpopularity had been recklessly exaggerated.
Stephen W. Downey of Laramie was nominated by the same
Republican convention which declared Peck non compos
mentis, even though Downey repudiated the resolution.[46]

E. L. Pease, the Democratic nominee from western Wyoming, had been instrumental in the passage of the redistricting bill. By his own admission, and in the judgment of the *Sentinel,* Pease was defeated because he lost his own western counties where his persecution of the judge was resented.[47] Evidently, residents of the area appreciated Peck's contributions. Besides interesting himself in religious activities, Judge Peck established libraries—a total of fourteen hundred volumes plus subscriptions to twenty monthly and twenty weekly periodicals—in Evanston and Green River.[48]

The legislature did the citizens of Wyoming a grave disservice through its redistricting act. It was not only a failure in its primary objective, the removal of Peck, but it backfired completely, badly crippling an already handicapped judicial system. For some time after redistricting, the considerable confusion over jurisdiction worked to the advantage of the lawless element, particularly debtors who were able to abscond with sizable quantities of property. As the former justice J. W. Kingman had warned, the redefined Second District could not possibly be served properly by one judge.[49] The resulting confusion was not limited to district court matters; it was also in evidence when the supreme court sat in its appellate jurisdiction. Since Justice Peck was in Washington, D.C., aiding in his defense during much of 1878, the supreme court was delayed in hearing appeals which required the full bench. Thus the load on an already crowded docket was increased. It was not long after the sagebrushing that all of these "serious complications" were recognized by the territorial leadership, and the folly of redistricting became clear.[50] Perhaps these hardships explain the infrequency with which sagebrushing was practiced, though the power of redistricting remained an effective, but somewhat less potent, legislative weapon.

Regardless of the price that the territory paid for its action, enmity toward Judge Peck remained at a high level in the territorial legislature. Consequently, nearly two years after the redistricting, the governor suggested to the president that Peck's effectiveness had been lost even though the judge had overcome much hostility among the populace which now recognized his ability.[51] The governor's recommendation of a transfer was ignored, and Peck served his full term. By the end of his tenure, Peck's talents were recognized by his colleagues as well as the press. On occasion he sat on both the First and Second District Courts in the absence of the other judges, receiving praise for the manner in which he conducted the court.[52]

It was in the capacity of an appellate judge that Peck made himself felt most effectively during his tenure in Cheyenne, where he had remained since his own district was nonexistent.[53] His colleagues were not reluctant to have Peck use his considerable time—since he did not have district duties—to write their supreme court opinions. During 1878–79 he authored 21 of the 25 opinions handed down by the court. And the opinions he wrote during his four years on the bench fill 269 pages of the *Wyoming Reports* compared to a total of 85 for his associates.[54] A senior law student at the University of Wyoming in 1956 affirmed the competency of Peck's appellate work, noting that Peck cited authorities in substantiation of his views perhaps more frequently than any of the other justices.[55] The strongest affirmation of Peck's ability, found thus far, has been made by Professor John W. Smurr who placed Peck in the same category with Montana's Justice Hiram Knowles in terms of intellectual competence. Smurr was particularly impressed with the brilliance of Peck's analysis of the nature of territorial courts.[56] Another feather in the judicial cap of this sagebrush victim was his dissenting opinion in a railroad case in which the majority decision was eventually reversed by the United States Supreme Court.[57]

There is incongruity in a "Sunday School" image on the raw frontier, and Peck would never escape this stigma. Nevertheless, in his own way, the justice was not short of spunk, or guts, as his critics would have preferred. At the very moment in which Peck was reminding Hayes of the necessity to renew his commission at the next session of Congress, he was also requesting promotion to chief justice when the vacancy occurred.[58] News of an impending opening for that post sparked similar requests two years after the Wyoming legislature had attacked him, indicating the judge's disdain for that body as well as his ample supply of intestinal fortitude. In 1880 the Justice Department attempted to transfer Peck to New Mexico Territory, but Peck refused to resign his Wyoming office until he was confirmed for the new position, an event which never materialized.[59] On news that Wyoming's controversial jurist was to remain, the *Cheyenne Daily Leader* praised him as "one of the best jurists that ever graced the Wyoming bench." [60] In January 1882, Samuel Chipman Parks replaced Peck who practiced law in Cheyenne for the next decade. Though the former justice remained in good stead with Republican officials in Washington, he never received the appointments which he solicited from time to time.[61] Before returning to New York where he died in 1899, Peck proved that even "Sunday School" men could be vengeful. Shortly before Wyoming became a state, Peck successfully blocked Corlett's appointment to the territorial bench by supplying the president with irrefutable evidence of Corlett's temporary defection in 1884 to support Cleveland. The judge also went to great lengths to injure Francis E. Warren, but Warren's power was sufficient to repel the attacks.[62]

While the national implications of the Peck incident were many, some have been exaggerated. During the fight over senate confirmation, Peck's backers tried to connect his Wyoming enemies with the forces of Senator Roscoe Conkling of New York who were at odds with Hayes. Alfred G. Lee of Evanston wrote the president's secretary that "one E. A. Thomas, formerly Associate Justice of this Territory is working with Conkling in this movement." While Conkling's followers did attack many of the Hayes appointments, debate in the Senate does not substantiate this claim, for Conkling vigorously defended Peck, a New Yorker, against attack by western senators.[63]

However, national interest in the case is undeniable, and newspaper accounts show that the incident did little to improve the image of territorial residents. Americans to the east indulged in great satire, depicting Wyoming courts as havens of profanity and tippling, where the jug was passed around the jury after the advocates had their swigs.[64] The sarcasm of a Washington, D.C., paper bears repeating, as does its misconception of Wyoming Indians. "The salary is $3000 per annum, and if the judge be not shut up in a stockade, and his judicial jurisdiction be not confined to counties where the Red men of the forest hold unlimited sway, the position is a very pleasant one." Judicial diets of "sagebrush and alkali" were the topic of banter in other versions.[65]

The temptation to treat the Peck narrative as just another local story about a "funny easterner" is strong. But as historians try to place the territories in their proper perspective, this humorous case of sagebrushing becomes much more. It reveals the interaction of the varied and complex forces involved in territorial development, a process in which the judiciary actively participated. In the plight of Judge Peck, political realities are graphically illustrated, as is the perpetual struggle for the independence of the territorial bench. It is also clear that the Peck affair, with its beginnings in the most remote areas of Wyoming, grew into a full-fledged battle over congressional authority and local control. Despite the understanding and sympathy of many senators, as a group they were unyielding on the principle of territorial subordination. The importance of property was also revealed in the debate, as both sides used this qualification as a measure of the credibility of their partisans. In the end, the national force dominated—Peck, as the administration and national politicians desired, remained. Nevertheless, and despite his contributions as an appellate judge, Peck was a failure. With all of his attributes, William Ware Peck was not able to adapt, an often fatal deficiency on the frontier.

8

Moses
Hallett

On February 8, 1866, the Fifth Session of the Colorado Territorial Assembly adopted a joint memorial imploring the president of the United States to appoint a local resident as chief justice of the territorial supreme court.[1] Displaying little timidity, the legislators carefully explained the legal problems peculiar to mining and irrigation, problems unfamiliar to and thus not understood by easterners. The boldness of these pioneer Coloradans increased with the length of their memorial; they even announced to the president their choice for the position, Moses Hallett!

In Moses Hallett the territorial assembly selected a man who had, in six years on the frontier, proved his understanding of local needs and whose performance on the bench would in time serve as a model of adaptability. Indeed, Moses Hallett had all of the characteristics lacking in his colleague to the north, William Ware Peck, a fact of which the legislators were acutely aware. Their memorial was only the formalization of a long-standing desire, for many "Pike's Peakers" understood the need for government officials appointed from within their ranks. In the case of the judiciary, Moses Hallett was their man. Samuel Bowles noted, "One especial motive with the Coloradans . . . is to get a judiciary of their own that shall be both more intelligent and independent than that furnished by Washington authorities." [2]

The bar in Colorado began its fight for the appointment of a judiciary from among its ranks even before the original panel of jurists had served its term. Hallett was among the signatories of a petition in July 1863 calling for the ouster of Justices Benjamin F. Hall and Charles Lee Armour. Minutes of the Colorado Territorial Bar Association indicate that the young attorney had also served on the committee which had drafted the document.[3] Some three months later, sensing victory in their drive to expel the foreign justices, the territorial bar recommended Hallett and William R. Gorseline as local attorneys who knowledge of Colorado's problems qualified them for elevation to the territorial supreme court. Governor John Evans added his recommendation, stating to President Lincoln that Hallett was preeminently qualified, an opinion which was repeated at every opportunity.[4] The nomination of Moses Hallett was also actively pushed by Delegate Allen A. Bradford, former associate justice in Colorado, who stressed Hallett's success as a practicing attorney in the territory.[5] After the failure in the same district of two judges from "the states" within two years, the pleas of the Coloradans were heeded, and in March 1866 their brilliant and youthful candidate was nominated for chief justice of the Colorado Territorial Supreme Court.

When his nomination by President Andrew Johnson was confirmed by the United States Senate on April 10, 1866, Moses Hallett was only thirty-two years of age. The lure of a quick fortune had brought him to the mining districts of Clear Creek and Gilpin Counties in the spring of 1860. Son of a successful though not wealthy Illinois pioneer, Hallett was born in Galena and was educated at Rock River Seminary and Beloit College. After reading law in the office of an attorney in Chicago, he was admitted to the bar in 1858. He practiced in Chicago until overcome by gold fever on hearing and reading about the success of the "fifty-niners." [6]

The two hundred dollars Hallett brought from Illinois was soon depleted, and the future magistrate found working a rocker on Clear Creek far less financially rewarding than he had anticipated.[7] By the fall of 1860 Hallett was in

Denver. The luck that had avoided him in the gold fields came to him there, for he soon became a partner of Hiram P. Bennet, one of the most prominent attorneys in the area. One account credits the formation of this partnership to the recommendation of a local businessman, Steve Hempstead, who promised to reimburse Bennet for Hallett's wages. It was years before Hallett discovered the true source of his first five-dollar fee for preparing a mechanic's lien.[8] Catching Steve Hempstead's eye was only the beginning of Hallett's good fortune. Bennet, who had arrived in Denver with the first wave of lawyers in 1859, was a man of influence and the proud possessor of the most extensive library available—a total of some fourteen volumes.[9] A paucity of law books is hard to visualize today. But in Gilpin County, for example, there was only one set of Illinois Statutes, and many of Colorado's new territorial statutes were adopted from those of Illinois.[10] Again Hallett was in luck, for he enjoyed the advantage of having been trained in those codes.

Hallett was among the first twenty-seven attorneys formally admitted to practice before the newly organized territorial courts on July 11, 1861.[11] The following September, Bennet was elected delegate to the United States Congress; thus the Hallett-Bennet partnership dissolved shortly thereafter. By then, however, the younger partner was on the way to prominence of his own, as well as considerable financial success. His name often appeared in reports of court cases in the columns of the *Rocky Mountain News*. Files of the civil cases of the First District Court as well as the first several volumes of the *Supreme Court Opinions of the Territory of Colorado* indicate that Hallett enjoyed an active practice prior to his appointment as chief justice.[12]

Correspondence with the Central City law firm of Teller and Johnson is also a barometer of Hallett's activity during the early part of the decade. These letters suggest that Hallett was dissatisfied with the early territorial bench. He described Benjamin F. Hall, Colorado's first chief justice, as an officious, overbearing judge. These two unusually strong personalities clashed. Hallett's feelings about the supreme court as a whole were so strong that he felt justified in planning diversionary tactics to keep it from meeting as an appellate body.[13] "Keep him [Judge Allen A. Bradford] away and it is all right," Hallett wrote, urging his friend to detain the judge in Central City so the supreme court could not be held that week.

For an undetermined time in 1865–66, Hallett and Alfred Sayre were partners. Judge Wilbur F. Stone, himself on the supreme court after Colorado achieved statehood, described Sayre as "the leading lawyer in practice in Denver." [14] This mutually profitable relationship was apparently terminated with Hallett's elevation to the bench. While other indications of his diligence as an aspiring young lawyer appear in the newspapers, perhaps his tenure as the Denver city attorney at an annual salary of $1,000 is the most worthy of mention here.[15] His resignation, tendered March 31, 1866, was accepted with great praise for his promptness and devotion to duty. Reports of the council meetings reflect his leadership.

From the earliest stages of his career in Denver, Hallett displayed traits of personality which explain his later judicial, financial, and social preeminence. Correspondence with other attorneys points to his diligence in preparation and his desire to win. An 1863 letter to Teller and Johnson requests a particular code book "needed badly lest he may be defeated." [16] Hallett accented his concern with an offer to pay the freight charges if no acquaintance was about to depart for Denver who might deliver the book.

Not only did his professional associations place him in good stead, but Hallett appeared to make the best of all contacts, even those at his boardinghouse. Listed as a fellow boarder in his first months in Denver is George Clark of Clark and Gruber minting and banking fame.[17] Throughout his career, names prominent in Colorado history appear among those with whom he associated professionally and

otherwise, offering obvious clues to his ability to enter the
right circles and his alertness to opportunity. The young
lawyer's frequent trips between Central City and Denver,
recorded in the notices of arrivals and departures, are indicative of his interest in and closeness to mining operations.[18]
His later eminence as a progenitor of mining law may well
be traced to these firsthand experiences in mining technology
and finance.

Hallett served as chief justice for the ten consecutive years
which preceded Colorado's admission to the Union. His
accomplishments and performance during his three appointments more than justified the confidence expressed by the
assembly in its 1866 resolution. At the conclusion of Hallett's
first term, Henry M. Teller urged his reappointment, praising
the happiness of lawyers and litigants alike with the conduct
of his court.[19] Teller felt that Hallett's popularity was unanimous among Colorado's attorneys. His contemporaries across
the nation acknowledged him as a jurist of exceptional
ability, and during its final ten years, Colorado's territorial
supreme court was unquestionably a Hallett court. He attended ten terms and averaged ten opinions per term, nearly
double the number of the most productive of his associates.[20]
Of the cases appealed to the United States Supreme Court
during Hallett's tenure, ten were affirmed while only four
were reversed (see table 3).

At his own expense, the chief justice compiled and published the first and second volumes of *Colorado Reports*. An
examination of the original journals containing the *Supreme
Court Opinions of the Territory of Colorado* indicates that
a few discrepancies may have occurred in reports of the
earliest cases before the court.[21] Considering the confusion
which characterized some of Colorado Territory's first
benches, omissions and other inaccuracies are understandable;
and they would in no way detract from the plaudits due
Hallett for his undertaking. The volumes he edited are out-

standing in terms of organization, form, and indexing—qualities not merely academic to the legal researcher. Also indicative of his energy and drive was his willingness to sit for his associates in their district courts, when this was necessary to clear the dockets. At his retirement ceremonies in 1906, a former colleague on the territorial bench, Judge Ebenezer T. Wells, may have embellished Hallett's service a bit. "Almost all the terms of the District Court of Gilpin and some of the terms in other counties, while Judge Gorsline remained on the Bench, were held by Judge Hallett." [22]

Table 3

Appeals to the United States Supreme Court

	Affirmed	*Reversed*	*Dismissed*
Colorado	10	4	—
Montana	26	11	22
Wyoming	4	5	7
Total:	40	20	29

Note: These statistics were abstracted from *Shepard's Citations* (Colorado Springs, Colorado: Shepard's Citations, Inc.). A widely used research tool, the Shepard's series is a compilation of the citation history of every case reported in the various state, federal, and regional reports. Since it is based only on published reports, a few cases heard by the earliest territorial courts may have been omitted. It is not likely, however, that so many cases were omitted that the results would be altered significantly. Since a lack of jurisdiction was the reason given most often by the Supreme Court for a dismissal, authorities are reluctant to consider dismissals in their evaluation of the lower courts. Some attorneys interpret a dismissal as an affirmation because it effectively upholds the work of the lower court.

It is by achievement, not energy, that the performance of officials is ultimately judged. Hallett, through his opinions, sustained previous decisions upholding Kansas law during the transitional stages of the territorial period.[23] Continuity of rule of law was assured; anarchy was avoided. As acknowledged in chapter 9, it was in the formulation or (in the jargon of lawyers) the "making" of mining and water law that Hallett would excel to the point of becoming internationally known at the peak of his career.

In addition to deep involvement in mining and water law, Hallett soon found himself in the midst of another gigantic struggle, the railroad wars. Though exhaustive research on Hallett and the railroads has not been attempted here, random findings indicate that the judge had a propensity to decide in favor of the railroads.[24] After he became a federal district judge, Hallett was at times immersed in railroad litigation, especially that of the Denver and Rio Grande.[25] Aspersions cast on Hallett by litigants in railroad cases constitute the only insinuations of his venality.

The leadership of the young chief justice was felt not only in the courtroom, but through the entire territorial community. Few aspects of Colorado life escaped his influence. He served on a specal committee to advise the federal authorities on Indian policy, and he showed no reluctance to join other signatories in sending a telegram to President Johnson in 1867 to bolster federal protection from the Indians.[26] A director of the Denver YMCA, a trustee of the First Presbyterian Church, and a charter member and director of the director of the Denver Club, Hallett was involved in a wide range of community services.[27] That he was held in high esteem is clearly indicated by correspondence from James B. Thompson, the governor's private secretary, to the War Department which was seeking citizens of some judgment as a source of what would today be called "intelligence." Thompson suggested that the War Department consider Hallett as representative of the top citizenry of the territory.[28]

Though he was chief justice, Hallett's "home" court was that of the Third Judicial District in Pueblo. Like his associate justices, Hallett rode the circuit to hold court in various county seats, and dozens of anecdotes about him have been passed down through generations of Colorado attorneys.[29] In his improvised court in the San Juan region, for example, the celebrated "leather seat" incident took place. When His Honor asked why the same faces always appeared on the jury, the sheriff replied that due to the dangers of splinters from the roughly hewn log benches, only those men who owned britches with leather seats were placed on the venire.[30] The law was serious business to Hallett who, while affable enough off the bench, had little patience with horseplay inside the court. He once became quite offended at the prank of a lawyer in a remote county seat who persuaded the somewhat mentally deficient county judge that he was entitled to share the bench with the chief justice as he held district court.[31] Hallett's sternness, particularly since it contrasted so sharply with the laxity of his predecessor, Allen A. Bradford, rated him the reputation among the Hispanos as *"el juez severo."* [32] The jurors he cited for contempt because they failed to appear in his court as ordered would have agreed that the young judge deserved such a sobriquet. Nor was Hallett a pushover in criminal matters—bails ranged from $1,000 to $5,000 for grand larceny.[33]

When George Q. Richmond, a prominent member of the Colorado bar in the late nineteenth century, immigrated to the Rockies from the East in 1870, he expected to find a "rough and tumble" judicial system in which the participants would be better "versed in Colt on Revolvers than Coke on Common Law." [34] Yet Richmond described the atmosphere of Hallett's adobe-walled, dirt-floored court in these terms, "A more orderly crowd, a more dignified judge, a more respectable appearing lot of attorneys I have never seen than was there collected." Of those present that day, two—Calvin J. Thatcher and Wilbur F. Stone—were destined to serve on the Colorado State Supreme Court.

Despite his severity, Hallett sought fairness as well as consistency, and today's law student might be surprised at his protection of due process. In a case cited well into the present century, Hallett insisted on the proper service of process. "The right of every defendant to his day in court is inviolable," commented Hallett, "and in every case it ought clearly to appear that he has enjoyed it." [35] His opinions were marked by brevity, clarity, and an absence of equivocation. In *Sullivan v. Hense,* the last sentence before his concluding statement of reversal illustrates these qualities. "Enough has been said to determine the substantial questions presented in this record and counsel should not ask for more." [36]

Moses Hallett shared with his associate justices numerous responsibilities which are not apparent from a casual examination of territorial organization. While district attorneys and marshals were available to represent the interests of the United States government, members of the supreme court performed duties associated today with the responsibilities of state attorneys general.[37] For example, they were requested to offer opinions on bills pending before the assembly and on those already enacted.

Before exercising their prerogatives of pardon and commutation, the governors often consulted the judges before whom convicted felons had been tried. Although this was a wise practice, it was another job for the territorial judges in lieu of other state agencies, and frequent communications on such matters indicate that it was not a rare occurence.[38] Another demand on the judges' time was service on various commissions and boards. Evidently the justices rotated their service on the board which examined and certified the accounts of the territorial auditor and treasurer at the conclusion of each fiscal year.[39] The judges were also subject to assignment by the governor, and they occasionally found themselves unexpectedly ordered to occupy the bench of a colleague. While absence from the territory was the most frequent cause of this juggling of court terms, the jurists sometimes disqualified themselves because of "personal interests." Hallett was asked to serve in more than a few instances in this manner.[40] The plea of conflict of interest, especially in Central City, could reveal significant mining speculation on the part of members of the bench.

While each judge had a clerk of the court to take care of details in his district, it was the judge himself who was ultimately responsible for the orderliness of the business of his court. A nine-page booklet containing samples of some twenty-four forms of oaths suggests that by 1875 the operation of the territorial courts had assumed at least a semblance of efficiency.[41] Thus the responsibilities of the court varied from the august to the mundane, and Moses Hallett shared in both.

One Colorado political pundit, a contemporary of Hallett, erroneously concluded that the young attorney from Illinois was incapable of political infighting and had no stomach for politics.[42] This conclusion was primarily predicated on Hallett's decision not to challenge Henry M. Teller for one of the seats in the United States Senate when Colorado was granted statehood. While it is true that Hallett rejected pleas for an active candidacy at this juncture, his entire adult career discredits any idea that he lacked political adroitness.

From his father, Moses Hallett, Sr., young Hallett had a political legacy of sorts, for the senior Hallett had served four terms as sheriff of JoDavies County, Illinois, and had been justice of the peace twice.[43] The younger Hallett's first law partner, Bennet, was successful in his bid to become the territory's first congressional delegate, and Hallett's diligent campaigning contributed substantially to the victory.[44] Hallett served in the Council of the Territorial Legislative Assembly during its third and fourth sessions in 1864 and 1865. The legislation for which he is best remembered was Council Bill No. 22, introduced February 19, 1864, which provided for the incorporation of Colorado Seminary.[45] The seminary, which later became the first building of Denver University, opened the following fall; by December it had fifty students.

On both county and territorial levels, Hallett actively

participated in affairs of the Union Party, backers of the Washington administration. The *Rocky Mountain News* in September and October of 1865 referred to his prudent and honest political maneuvering and reported on his activities.[46] The efforts of this enterprising young attorney were by no means fruitless. Early in 1865, almost a year before the memorial called for his nomination to the court, Hallett had been enthusiastically recommended for that honor by Governor John Evans in a note to President Abraham Lincoln.[47] Prominently mentioned in the correspondence was Hallett's support for the "regular Union ticket." During his first term as chief justice, Hallett was also politically active, journeying to Washington to urge passage of the bill for admission which was under consideration in 1866–67.[48] Only three votes kept Colorado out of the Union when Congress attempted to override President Johnson's veto in January 1867.

The years 1874 and 1875 were precarious times for federal appointees in Colorado Territory; this was the era of the "Grant Purge." Though Hallett was the only territorial official to survive, rumors circulated on the streets of Denver that a clique of his former friends had tried to unseat him.[49] The most interesting of the many explanations of Hallett's durability attributes his longevity in office to the influence of a college classmate, General John A. Rawlins. For years Rawlins had been the most trusted adviser of General, later President, Ulysses S. Grant; he eventually became chief of staff and secretary of war. The association of Hallett, Grant, and Rawlins with Galena, Illinois, undoubtedly worked to Hallett's advantage.[50]

The precise explanation of Hallett's survival of the "Grant Purge" is still a matter of conjecture, but his performance indicates that he was not politically inept. In the years following Colorado's admission to the Union, Hallett was a constant correspondent of Senator Teller, writing about all manner of things political.[51] And the Denver newspapers offered frequent accounts of his activities, indicating a great awareness of the importance of a public image.

With the birth of the Centennial State on August 1, 1876, Hallett's service as territorial judge terminated, but his distinguished career had not yet reached its peak. President Grant appointed him the first United States district judge for the District of Colorado where he remained until his retirement May 1, 1906. Three decades of extraordinary service to community, state, and nation can hardly be ignored if the true measure of a man is to be taken, especially when his expertise has been based on a decade of experience as a territorial justice.

While his most notable decisions from the district bench were in mining, water, and railroad litigation, Hallett also displayed a keen interest in the federal court system. Consequently, he was soon engaged in steady correspondence with Senator Teller about the structure of the courts.[52] New York's Senator Roscoe Conkling was intent on increasing the number of districts, but Hallett advised Teller that a more feasible approach would be the establishment of more court facilities throughout the state, making it possible for one judge to more effectively serve a greater number of citizens. While Hallett admitted that New York might require more judges, he argued that Colorado could be served by one justice who had the proper facilities. On one occasion the Colorado judge wrote four pages of details about the organization of his court.[53] Cynics may interpret Hallett's attitude as a self-interested one, but admirers praise his energy and sense of duty.

Considerable prestige was gained by the newly founded University of Colorado Law School in 1892, when Hallett was named its first dean and professor of American constitutional law and federal jurisprudence, posts which he held until 1902. By 1898, the school boasted a faculty of twenty-seven, most of whom were evidently on a part-time basis.[54] Hallett's

interest in charitable causes was widespread, and he supported
many of them with considerable donations. In memory of his
wife, the Katherine Hallett Home for Nurses at Saint Luke's
Hospital was built. As the trustee of the George W. Clayton
estate, the judge was instrumental in establishing and developing Clayton College for Boys, still a thriving institution in
Denver. While Hallett's generosity was often mentioned in
the source materials I investigated, it seemed ironic to find
stamped in a volume used in research for this work "Gift
From the Judge Moses Hallett Library." [55]

A most fascinating aspect of Hallett's life lies in the fact
that he had accumulated the better part of a million dollars
by the time of his death, April 25, 1913. With scarcely a hint
of corruption during his forty-year tenure in office, his
highly acclaimed perception of the law must have been
matched only by business acumen. In 1866 at the time of his
appointment, a territorial judge's salary was $1,800 per year.
The following year this figure was increased to $2,500, and
in 1870 to $3,000.[56] With the high cost of living, most of his
colleagues had little money left at the end of each year. Since
his father was only a moderately successful Illinois farmer, it
is not likely that Hallett received significant financial contributions from home.[57] In 1882 Hallett did marry the daughter
of a merchant in Galena, Illinois, but by then the judge was
already reputed to be quite wealthy.

The answer to this puzzle seems to be Hallett's ability as a
"promoter." His efforts in this direction evidently date from
his association with Hempstead, who, in turn, arranged for
Hallett's job with Bennet. The first solid evidence of this
sideline was the incorporation on January 9, 1863, of the
Julesburgh [sic] and Fort Lupton Wagon Road Company.[58]
The terms of incorporation gave the company a ten year fran-
chise to build and operate a toll road between Julesburg and
Fort Lupton. Capital stock was $12,000, and there were two
other incorporators, Andrew J. Williams and M. C. Keith.

The nature of Hallett's law practice prior to his appointment is evidence of his connection from the beginning with the moneyed interests in the territory. Frequent notices of Hallett's real estate transactions in the *Rocky Mountain News* attest to his involvement in land deals—some of the sales prices mentioned amounted to one-third of his yearly salary.[59] While no specific record of the judge's mining ventures has been uncovered, the close association of his law practice with the mining industry is ample ground for conjecture that he had financial interests of his own in the territory's most important economic sector during the early 1860s. The exact nature of his connections has not been discovered, but requests for leaves of absence in the Justice Department correspondence files clearly indicate the judge's association with business interests in Illinois, New York, and Massachusetts.[60] It must be recognized that Hallett did not live in an era when conflict of interest was a sensitive matter, and it is quite likely that he was a broker of eastern capital. Since arduous efforts to uncover a significant amount of his personal correspondence have thus far been unfruitful, researchers have to be content, at least for the time being, with merely speculating about this aspect of Hallett's career. The inquiries I made to his descendants did not uncover further details of Hallett's affiliations in the world of finance, though it seems probable that his wife's family was involved.

The history of economic growth in Colorado after the territorial period clearly suggests Hallett was closely allied with several of the state's most powerful financiers. Records of incorporation reveal that Hallett was in frequent company with David H. Moffat, Walter S. Cheesman, and George W. Clayton. In 1886, this group chartered the First National Bank of Aspen with capital stock which grew to $100,000 within two years. With the same men and others, Hallett was an incorporator of the National Trust Company in Denver in 1891; the company soon evolved into one of the city's most important financial institutions, the International Trust Company. In 1895, Cheesman, Moffat, Clayton, and Hallett were

deeply involved as incorporators and directors of the Denver
Union Water Company, which had capital stock of $7,500,000
and was created to consolidate nine water companies in the
Denver area.[61] Hallett's close personal association with Clayton
and with other leaders of Denver's financial community is
also confirmed by entries in the Clayton diaries.[62]

Probate records list the total cash value of the estate of
Moses Hallett at $851,806.19.[63] The real property, valued at
$274,760 consisted of fifty-three parcels of land, primarily lots
in Denver and Pueblo. There was also some acreage in
Jefferson and El Paso Counties, as well as a few mining
properties. The bulk of the personal property, valued at
$576,046.19, was in the form of some 140 notes, mainly to
individuals, a majority of which were bearing seven percent
interest. Only insignificant amounts of stock were listed. In
the first year after his death, Hallett's estate earned $39,813.08;
of this amount, $35,947.58 was interest, with rents comprising
the balance. It is clear that Hallett had divested himself of
all meaningful holdings of stock, and, whether or not it was
his intent, he deprived researchers of an obvious clue to even
his more recent major corporate investments.

Except for a confrontation with the state tax collector over
unpaid taxes in 1909,[64] the only hint of irregularities in his
financial affairs is based on criticism of his railroad decisions,
and only insinuations are offered in that area. Perhaps inten-
sive investigation of the tax litigation would produce a lead.
It does seem that something unusual was involved in the dispute since no one would bid on Hallett's properties at the
auction. Throughout his career only superlatives were offered,
at least publicly, in praise of his integrity, conduct, and
judicial ability—qualities which obviously did not inhibit his
business activities.

Moses Hallett's career completely vindicates the Colorado
legislature's memorial for his appointment. The assembly in
1866 had wisely assessed territorial needs. Mining operations
and titles, together with irrigation, posed "novel and pecu-

liar" problems which could best be solved by a man who understood them and who could identify with the people for whom these problems were of primary concern. Hallett filled both of these qualifications because, unlike William Ware Peck, he was able to adapt to the conditions of the frontier. The two men were similar in a number of ways. They were both able, well educated, and public spirited; both had strong religious convictions. The major difference was that Peck was inflexible. Whatever the source of Hallett's ability to accommodate, this trait, though not sufficient in itself, was unquestionably prerequisite to his contributions in Colorado and the trans-Mississippi West.

9

Making

Law

Justice Oliver Wendell Holmes once observed that "the life of the law has not been logic; it has been experience," [1] and the wisdom of his words can be demonstrated by events in the Colorado, Montana, and Wyoming territories. What could have been more logical than for the territories to adopt the common law as the basis of their jurisprudence? Thus, one of the first laws passed in Colorado Territory was "An Act Adopting the Common Law of England," and only experience would teach Coloradans that a new foundation was needed to enact laws that would be effective for their "peculiar needs." [2]

The territorial supreme courts dealt with the most important possessions of the settler: mining claims, water, and land. On their judgments fortunes were made or lost; the territorial justices had the power of instant wealth. While much has been written about their alleged failures in these trusts, little credit has been given to the judges for their novel contributions to jurisprudence. Though legal commentators had previously recorded these new laws, it was Walter Prescott Webb who related the evolution of the law to the peculiar conditions of the trans-Mississippi West and dramatized the relationship of experience to law.[3] It should not be surprising to devotees of Webb that the territorial justices displayed unusual adaptability in their opinions on natural resources. Indeed, the laws of most consequence which were made via court decisions were in the areas of mining and water. Not only did the justices' opinions add substantially to the body of mineral and water law, but their decisions assured maximum economic development of the territories through the establishment of order in mining and agriculture, no mean accomplishment. In this light, the judiciary might be the real heroes of the period.

The history of American mining law lends credibility to the concept of a world frontier.[4] The story begins in Europe and can be traced by way of Latin America, California, and the successive mining frontiers of North America.[5] While the Spanish mining heritage was particularly influential in the evolution of early mining codes, mineral law represents an accumulation of experience from around the globe. The expertise, for example, shared by the many Englishmen who began arriving in California in 1849 should not be ignored. Nor should the contributions of other nationalities. The vehicle or medium by which the international ingredients were assimilated into a body of law was the miners' meeting or miners' court, which will be described later in this chapter.

Since there was no significant body of American mineral law in 1848, it is understandable that the early statutes have been characterized as loose and lacking in definition. Rodman W. Paul, one of America's most eminent mining scholars, suggests that as lawmakers "the miners were frequently neither sufficiently careful nor up-to-date," and that as real estate operators "they were generally lax." [6] It was for the state courts in California and the territorial courts of later periods to correct the defects of the mining laws. Not only did rapid development leave room for improvement, but the more complex geological conditions which characterized the later strikes also presented ample opportunity for the territorial courts of the Rocky Mountains to update and refine the codes. Hence, it was in the definition and refining of the law, rather than in the initiation of it, that the territorial bench distinguished itself. Specifically, this was true in the lode or vein operations so prevalent in the Rockies. Thus California's contributions were soon overshadowed.

While the regulations of the various mining districts were eventually incorporated into our state and federal mineral law, the American courts were at first reluctant to abandon the common law. Recent legal scholarship reveals that in the conveyance of mining claims, the organized courts of California were initially hesitant about relying on mining camp rules. The persistence of the common law heritage is clear in the following observation of law professor Robert W. Swenson:

> A review of nearly two-hundred California cases between 1848 and 1866 does not reveal that the customs of the miners played a very significant role in the judicial law-making process. Many cases involving conflicting mining claims were decided on the basis of standard property law such as the rule that as between claimants who have no proprietary interest in the land, prior possession alone is a better right.[7]

As I will demonstrate later, mining camp rules were eventually recognized by territorial courts as well as by federal statute. Nevertheless, congressional legislation and the decisions of both territorial and federal courts ultimately replaced local mining district regulations. The standardization of the system by the territorial legal process was a vital link in this chain of events. Territorial courts and legislatures provided Congress and the Supreme Court with valuable guidelines.

The Federal Mining Law of 1866, Congress's initial effort to establish federal control over mining, might well be called the Magna Charta of the miners.[8] It legalized what had technically been considered trespassing. The mineral lands, according to the statute, were declared to be "free and open to exploration and occupation." However, the 1866 law subjected mining in the public domain to such "regulations as may be prescribed by law" as well as to "local custom or rules of miners in the several mining districts, so far as the same may not be in conflict with the laws of the United States." While this act provided an important and much needed statement of policy, it was inadequate as a codification of mining law.[9]

Congressional attention to mining may be a measure of the impact of that industry on the nation's economy and people. In 1872, the acts of 1866 and 1870 were expanded and republished as a single statute. For the most part, the "Mineral Location Law of 1872" still governs a large percentage of the acquisition of mining rights in federally owned lands.[10]

There are few industries that involve as much litigation as mining, and in few businesses is speed so important in settling the issues. These facts, in addition to the inordinate value of the disputed property, explain the vociferous demands from Colorado and Montana for the speedy replacement of less-gifted jurists and for the appointment of men who could deal with the unusual problems of mining law.[11] While Colorado was fortunate in the leadership of Moses Hallett after 1866, Montana Territory was similarly favored with the appointment of men who were capable of handling mining problems.[12] Hiram Knowles, who had spent time in the gold fields, was appointed in 1868, and for nearly eleven years Montana had the benefit of his particular qualifications. Most of that time he shared the bench with Decius S. Wade; thus the territory had a most able bench. Because of his competence in mineral law, Knowles was vigorously defended by the *Helena Weekly Herald* during one of the recurrent drives for judicial rotation. The editor warned, "Should a new Judge be appointed who is not familiar with mining law and usages, it would be prejudicial to the interests of the entire Territory." Knowles's decisions were often included in the columns of local papers.[13] When he resigned, the man who replaced him was also well versed in the territory's particular needs. Appointed in 1879, William J. Galbraith served two terms, and Justice Department files indicate that mining interests were pleased with his performance.[14] Though he was

a Republican appointee, Montana Democrats were also happy
with his abilities and urged his reappointment.[15]

The geology of the Rocky Mountains gave the territorial
justices of Colorado and Montana a rare opportunity to use
their talents fully, for the lode mining in their districts
jammed the courts with problems of incredible complexity.[16]
Veins of valuable minerals, created during the formation
of the earth's crust, display a complete lack of uniformity.
Herein lay the problem. Placer locations could be defined as
readily as any other surface land claim, but quartz or lode
claims involved subsurface rights to veins which often pursued
unpredictable courses.[17] Making the statutes conform with
the realities of geology was an inhuman task. The territorial
supreme courts of Colorado and Montana were constantly
called upon to clarify or define statutory terms. United States
Justice David J. Brewer commented on this fact:

> If the surface of the ground was everywhere level and
> veins constantly pursued a straight line, there would be
> little difficulty in legislation to provide for all contingencies,
> but mineral is apt to be found in mountainous regions
> where great irregularity of surface exists and the course or
> strike of the veins is as irregular as the surface, so that
> many cases may arise in which statutory provisions will fail
> to secure to a discoverer of a vein such amount thereof as
> equitably it would seem he ought to receive.[18]

The complexity of lode mining with its battery of puzzling
terms is overwhelming for the layman: end lines, side lines,
side-end lines, parallelism of end lines, apex rule, intralimital
rights, extralateral rights, etc. And the intricate diagrams
which often accompanied court opinions look as if they just
tumbled out of a kaleidoscope. Though entanglements involving mineral rights were often finally resolved at the bar of
the United States Supreme Court, this body tended to follow
the doctrines developed in the Rocky Mountains.

The territorial courts of the Rockies, in turn, relied heavily on the experiences of the miners in an effort to establish order in their most important industry. At the time of Colorado Territory's organization, the gold fields were governed by mining districts and miners' courts—extra legal, but pragmatic and surprisingly effective. R. S. Morrison traced the origins of this system from the Spanish in Mexico and from the Californians, and Charles Howard Shinn described the operation of mining camp law in minute detail.[19] While both men stressed the lack of uniformity and the need for the development of a uniform code, Shinn commented that "from an institutional stand-point, this irregular and spontaneous element is their [the mining courts'] strongest claim to a place in Western history." [20]

In one of its most significant bills, Colorado's territorial assembly validated claims made under the various mining district rules. When the law was tested in the case of *Sullivan v. Hense,* the Colorado Territorial Supreme Court upheld the act.[21] The opinion of the court, written by Chief Justice Moses Hallett, made the rules and regulations of the mining districts legitimate, particularly those concerning the vital question of the validity of claims. Hallett's recognition of the validity of mining district rules was one of the earliest and most important by a state or territorial court. Since the Colorado miners entered the public domain with no legal authority, the validation of mining district rules was actually a departure from the English common law.[22] Under the common law, some type of permission from the central government would have been prerequisite to valid claims. In effect, the Colorado Territorial Supreme Court was endorsing the more individualistic and exploitive conduct of the Pike's Peakers.

In an 1870 opinion, Montana's Hiram Knowles incorporated into his territory's jurisprudence the basic mining customs which pertained to location, relocation, and forfeiture. He also recognized the validity of mining district rules in general.[23] Mining customs, wrote Knowles, "have the force and effect of laws, or, in other words are laws"; he recognized an "American common law on mining." While the Montana court relied on past experience, it was not reluctant to strike down specific rules if they were judged to have an adverse effect on the orderly development of natural resources. The justices felt that customs "must not be inconsistent with the full and rapid development of all the mining resources of the country." [24]

The flood of litigation over rights and definition seemed endless. Until 1969 the most comprehensive treatise on mining had been compiled by Curtis H. Lindley of the San Francisco bar. His table of cases includes at least sixty territorial opinions from Colorado, Montana, and Wyoming which are cited in dozens of different sections. The eminent Colorado mining authority, R. S. Morrison, incorporated many of these same law suits into his twenty-two–volume *Mining Reports*. Even the *American Law of Mining*, completed in 1969, cites large numbers of these cases. Several which illustrate the quality of the territorial bench's work will be reviewed here.

The federal mineral laws of 1866 and 1872 did not slow down the pace of litigation. If anything, they were a stimulant. The oft-cited opinion of Chief Justice Decius S. Wade of Montana in *Belk v. Meagher*—affirmed by the United States Supreme Court—is an excellent example of Wade's ability to cope with complicated questions about the validity of claims to public mineral lands.[25] The facts and conclusions are as follows. Litigant A, peacefully and with no use of force, relocated a claim on land that had previously been claimed by B; B was neither working the mine nor in possession of it. Party C again peacefully and with no use of force, subsequently relocated a claim to the same property only two months later than A. B's claim was still valid when A relocated, despite B's absence from the location. B's claim had expired for lack of improvement by the time C relocated. A sued for the ejectment of C. The territorial courts ruled against A, giving C clear title to the claim. This description is simplified because the claims of B were conveyed several times and the validity of those transactions was challenged, as was the admissibility of the record book—a book extracted from early mining district records—in which B's claims had initially been registered.

In addition to deciding whether to accept disputed testimony and evidence (claims and deeds), both the Montana court and the United States Supreme Court had to answer four questions: (1) Did the 1872 law apply—the law regarding the annual labor (representation) required to keep B's claim in force? (2) Was A's relocation, if valid, good against everybody but the original holders? (3) If A's relocation was invalid when made, did it become effectual on the extinction of the original (B's) claim? (4) If A's relocation was invalid, could C, after the expiration of the original claim, make a valid relocation? Chief Justice Morrison R. Waite, writing the affirming opinion for the United States Supreme Court, held that "mining claims are not open to relocation until the rights of a former locator have come to an end." Claimant A, according to Justice Waite, was not entitled to the mine after the expiration of the original claim because his possession was illegal in the first place. A had no valid location, though he could have prevented C's location if he had been in a position to prove that C was trespassing. However, since C's entry was peaceful and without force, his location was upheld.

Even without matters involving subsurface rights, the litigation was extremely complex. Justice William J. Galbraith in *Garfield M. and M. Co. v. Hammer* wrote another of the many Montana opinions, affirmed by the Supreme Court, which demonstrate this point.[26] In this dispute about title under federal laws, Galbraith had to deal with five questions involving procedure as well as claims or locations. (The term *location* was used interchangeably with *claim* to mean a perfected claim.) First, it was decided that location is not made by possession alone; it is made by marking and recording, and then by fulfilling all the requirements of congressional as well as local laws and regulations. Thus the right to possession is derived only from a valid location. Secondly, a plaintiff in an action to quiet title (to clear title) to a mining claim must prove valid location. Thirdly, locators are presumed to be citizens in absence of evidence to the contrary. Fourthly, notice of location describing it by metes and bounds and in reference to a well-known claim is sufficient. And last, cumulative evidence is not sufficient grounds for a new trial. As this case demonstrates, federal legislation invited a retesting of mining customs and assured the judiciary that there would be no relief from crowded dockets.

Under the laws of 1866 and 1872, a number of significant conflicts developed between mining operators and townsite developers, and the territorial courts protected the interests of the miners. In one of the most celebrated townsite lawsuits, *Silver Bow M. and M. Co. v. Clark,* Montana's Chief Justice Wade ruled that the owner of a valid mining claim under federal law cannot be deprived of his rights by later settlement thereon for purposes of commerce and trade.[27] In this instance, the land office had issued a patent for a townsite after a valid mining location had been entered within the limits of the then unpatented townsite. Wade declared that this act by the land office was unauthorized and that it could not defeat the title held by the miner. Furthermore, it was held that the miner was under no obligation to file an adverse claim to the townsite entry. The purpose of Congress, according to Wade, was to sell its mineral lands. The right to purchase is the right to full title which carries with it exclusive rights to both surface-ground and subsurface minerals. This case was one of the longest reported during the territorial period—a measure of its significance. The briefs were lengthy and Wade's opinion reflected an unusual amount of research in state and federal statutes and opinions.

The Silver Bow decision is another example of the territorial court's determination to secure the economic development of the territory; the highest priority was clearly assigned to mining. Town building must have been recognized as an integral part of economic growth, but mining was protected as the basis of territorial wealth in Montana at this time. In 1887 the question was reconsidered in thirty-three suits tried jointly as the *Butte City Smokehouse Lode Cases.*[28] The court agreed to hear these cases because it had been reorganized. It was now composed of a total of four justices, two of whom had been recently appointed. However, the opinion of the body had not changed; the new appointees concurred with Wade that the principles established in *Silver Bow M. and M. Co. v. Clark* and *Talbott v. King* should be reaffirmed.

Perhaps the jurists' most demanding task was the definition or clarification of territorial and federal legislation regulating lode mining. Firsthand knowledge of the industry was virtually a prerequisite for judicial excellence in this realm, and, indeed, the opinions of the more outstanding territorial justices reveal a practical understanding of the geological problems encountered. In *Foote v. National Mining Co.* the court was asked to clarify a Montana statute which defined a lode claim as existing fifty feet on either side of the lode.[29] Was this distance measured from the center or from the edge of the lode? Wade ruled that since the fifty-foot allowance was intended to provide working space, it was necessary to measure from the outer wall of the lode, for veins or lodes varied in width from less than an inch to a hundred feet or more.

The "apex rule" was the foundation of lode mining laws. This rule evolved from mining customs which permitted the following of the downward course of discovered veins to any depth, and it governed the all-important extralateral rights.[30] Extralateral rights are rights to minerals beneath the surface claim of another party—rights gained by virtue of the downward direction of the vein, provided that the apex or top of the vein is inside of the downward vertical extension of the claim's side lines.[31] The 1866 law granted the "right to follow such vein or lode with its dips, angles, and varia-

tions, although it may enter the land adjoining," and it provided that the sale of the adjoining land was subject to this
condition. The 1872 statute maintained this principle and incorporated the apex rule. The apex of the vein must be
found within the surface boundaries of the claim in order for
extralateral rights to exist.

Considering the irregularities of lodes, the possibilities for
litigation over extralateral rights are limitless. The controversies often centered around the definition of the apex and
of a lode. Justice Thomas C. Bach defined the apex as the
highest point of the lode, whether at the surface of the ground
or at any point below.[32] Though United States Justice David
J. Brewer added in his affirming opinion that the apex "is
not necessarily a point, but often a line," Bach's definition is
still generally accepted. Another prerequisite to extralateral
rights, parallelism of end lines, is often traced to one of the
first decisions rendered by former territorial justice Hiram
Knowles after he was appointed United States district judge in
Montana.[33] Knowles ruled that while side lines could zigzag,
the end lines of a claim must be parallel in order to obtain
extralateral rights. The Montana Territorial Supreme Court
unquestionably distinguished itself in its opinions on mineral
law, a fact recognized by Justice Stephen J. Fields of California, the United States Supreme Court's most knowledge-
able member in this area of the law. Justice Fields described
the opinions emanating from Montana Territory as "very able
and learned." [34]

The territorial court's brilliant interpretation of mining
law had a generative effect, and Colorado's Moses Hallett
achieved national preeminence as a mining law authority
during his thirty-year tenure as a United States district judge.
Fellow members of the bar estimated that during his judicial
career, Hallett heard nine-tenths of the mining suits argued
in Colorado.[35] The *Federal Reports,* a compilation of federal
court opinions, contains many of his mining decisions—a
considerable number of which were affirmed on appeal. Of

his numerous contributions to the clarification of extralateral rights, the one for which he is most often remembered is the definition of a lode. In *Iron Silver Mining Co. v. Cheesman,* Hallett defined a vein or lode as "a body of mineral or mineral bearing rock within defined boundaries in the general mass of the mountain." [36] In its affirming opinion, the highest tribunal noted the lack of a precise definition, praised Hallett's work, and adopted his terminology. While there are dozens of definitions of a lode, Hallett's is still prominently mentioned.[37] And although no authoritative tally exists, it is doubtful if any case has been cited in other opinions as often as *Del Monte M. and M. Co. v. Last Chance M. and M. Co.,* another of Hallett's opinions affirmed by the Supreme Court.[38]

Perhaps the clearest abrogation of common law in the West was the abandonment of the riparian rights doctrine in response first to the demands of mining and then to those of irrigation. Experience was definitely the life of water law in the Rocky Mountain territories. Since water was a vital part of early mining techniques, it is natural that experiences in Colorado would greatly influence the evolution of the systems of water law in Montana and Wyoming, as well as those in many other western states. In the mining process, water was often diverted or appropriated from streams for use at locations at varying distances from the point of diversion. Consequently, the necessities of mining gave rise to a western common law of water—the doctrine of prior appropriation.[39] An abrupt departure from the English common law doctrine of riparian rights, prior appropriation became still more significant as it was extended to meet the demands of irrigation on the high plains.

According to the common law doctrine of riparian rights, the owner of the banks of a river had exclusive rights to the waters therein.[40] He and his downstream neighbors were entitled to the accustomed flow of water, undiminished in quantity and unimpaired in quality. The nonriparian owner had no rights whatsoever to the waters of the riparian owner; nor could a party whose land was away from a stream demand or receive water. Prior appropriation, on the other hand, was based on priority of use rather than on stream bank ownership. *Qui prior est in tempore potior est in jure.* The maxim "first in time, first in right" is the heart of the appropriation system. Basically, this system involves the right to divert the *unappropriated* water of natural streams to beneficial uses, following, of course, the "first in time, first in right" rule. An appropriation is more than the mere diversion of water from a stream; for an appropriation to be upheld, the water must be used for beneficial purposes within a reasonable time after it has been diverted. Priority acquired through the satisfaction of these requirements becomes a right—a real property. Just as a mining claim may become extinct if it is not developed, an appropriation may be lost by abandonment, and once the water has been returned to the stream, it is available to satisfy other downstream priorities. The appropriation system was developed as an adjunct to mining, and, of course, precedents from California were followed in the Rocky Mountains. However, these earlier cases dealt primarily with mining and concerned individual appropriations.

Leadership in developing an actual system of water law is often attributed to Colorado, an assertion usually based on an early irrigation, case, *Yunker v. Nichols.*[41] Yunker, the plaintiff, had constructed an irrigation ditch across Nichols's land. Nichols and an accomplice diverted the water from Yunker's ditch. In the district court the jury found for the defendant, but in a unanimous decision the Colorado Territorial Supreme Court reversed the lower court and ruled in favor of Yunker. A landmark of western water law, this 1872 opinion renounced the doctrine of riparian rights as not being applicable in Colorado and thus boldly departed from centuries of English legal precedent. Though both associates wrote concurring opinions, Hallett spoke for the court. First the chief justice reviewed the history of riparian rights under the common law, specifically referring to the humid climate of England

and the eastern United States. Then, in a few powerful words, he sanctioned a new system.

> The principles of law are undoubtedly of universal application, but some latitude of construction must be allowed to meet the various conditions of life in different countries. The principles of the decalogue may be applied in the conduct of men in every country and clime, but rules respecting the tenure of property must yield to the physical laws of nature, whenever such laws exert a controlling influence.

> In a dry and thirsty land it is necessary to divert the waters of streams from their natural channels, in order to obtain fruits of the soil, and this necessity is so universal and imperious that it claims recognition of the law.[42]

Relying on his judgment rather than authority, Hallett continued with a statement that when the government made land available to individuals, it "intended to convey to the citizens the necessary means to make them fruitful." Private lands are thus held in subordination to the dominant rights of others who must necessarily pass over these lands for purposes of irrigation. In his conclusion, Hallett explicitly declared that this right to pass over the lands of others to obtain a water supply exists "not by grant, but by operation of law." [43]

Hallett's two lesser-known associates, James B. Belford and Ebenezer T. Wells, wrote concurring opinions in the Yunker case. While neither displayed Hallett's command of language or his incisiveness, they shared his view that law is founded upon the necessities of those whom it is to serve. Drawing on opinions from courts across the nation, Belford illustrated the equivocations found in the law with dozens of cases which pointed to public needs. Then he philosophized on the nature of law.

> As has been well said by another, the law is not a system marked by folly, based on bold sentences, without reason;

it is a grand code, founded on the necessities of men, erected by mature judgement, gradually expanding in beneficence and wisdom as time progresses, and regulating with care the interests of society and civilization.[44]

But Belford, in comparison to Hallett, was reluctant in his departure from the "tried and true." Wells, the other associate, was more positive and straightforward. The right which "springs out of the necessity," according to Wells, "existed before the statute was enacted and would still survive though the statute were repealed." [45]

Though Colorado's court has held much of the limelight, the accomplishments of the Montana territorial court were certainly not meager. Apparently, it was in an opinion affirming a Montana case that the United States Supreme Court first expressed itself regarding the appropriation of water.[46] In *Atchison v. Peterson,* Chief Justice Wade had upheld the custom that "the first appropriator of water for mining purposes is entitled to water of a stream as against subsequent appropriators without material interruption in the flow thereof or in quality or quantity." [47] In affirming Wade's opinion, United States Justice Field commented on the acquiescence of the United States government to territorial and state rules governing water, particularly in their departure from riparian rights. In 1867, even before the territorial supreme court ruled on prior appropriation, that doctrine had been upheld in Montana by Lyman E. Munson, sitting as judge in the Third District. The *Helena Weekly Herald* gave prominent and detailed coverage to this decision which revealed Munson's respect for the validity of the priority system.[48]

It is interesting to speculate on the possible impact of Hallett's Yunker opinion on the Montana bench; it reached an almost identical conclusion just six months later in *Thorp v. Freed.*[49] This Knowles opinion is a brilliant treatise justifying abrogation of the common law doctrine of riparian rights in Montana Territory, despite the legislature's adoption of the common law. Knowles felt that riparian rights were at variance with natural equity and therefore fatal to agricultural improvement. Irrigation had been practiced commonly in Montana Territory since its settlement. Citing Coke, Knowles argued that where the same reason exists, the same law prevails; appropriation is necessary for mining and it is likewise necessary for agriculture. The opinion concluded with the declaration that priority of appropriation applied not only for irrigation but for any beneficial use. In affirming another Montana case of a similar nature, *Basey v. Gallagher,* the higher court praised the Thorp opinion and cited it as "controlling." [50] In so doing, the United States Supreme Court endorsed the appropriation doctrine as applicable to mining, agriculture, or manufacturing.

Those who are skeptical about the quality of the Montana Territorial Supreme Court are invited to study *Thorp v. Freed.* Wade's concurring opinion is of particular interest, for he arrived at the same conclusion though he followed an entirely different line of reasoning. Wade's opinion shows how thoroughly ingrained common law was. In short, this justice viewed prior appropriation for irrigation as an extension, rather than an abrogation, of the common law. He admitted that the doctrine of riparian rights had evolved under different climatic circumstances, but he insisted that the reason and principle upon which common law was founded could be a guide in the equitable distribution of water. Wade was adamant that "the principles and the reason of the common law adapts itself [*sic*] to the physical conditions of every country as dictated by the natural wants of the people in whose behalf the law is invoked." [51] Starting with Coke and Kent, and using numerous American precedents, the chief justice diligently documented his line of reasoning.

With his colleagues, Wade recognized the need for an orderly and pragmatic system of water law which would facilitate economic development, but he displayed in the concluding portions of his concurring opinion a greater depth of thought. He closed with a warning about the dangers of unbridled appropriation and clearly outlined the need for some type of administrative system which would protect the rights of future residents and the government. Specifically, Wade was concerned that the lands reserved by Congress for support of public education would become worthless without some protection of future appropriations. The justice's concern was not for financial considerations, but for the loss of educational opportunities. This opinion categorized Wade as both a realist and a visionary, and the administrative systems which were later developed verified his wisdom.

In addition to establishing broad legal principles which assured economic growth, the judges were responsible for sorting out the technical controversies which arose in water law just as they had in mining law. Again, experience and good judgment were the major determinants of the decisions. In a case which was still being cited as late as 1951, the Montana court ruled that an appropriator is limited in his appropriation by the capacity of his ditch at its head, and that in his original appropriation he had to allow for evaporation and seepage before the water reached the place of beneficial use.[52] That an appropriator may change the place as well as purpose of the water's use was determined by Montana's early bench in *Woolman v. Garringer*.[53] Here the court also dealt with three other technicalities: (1) Claimant of water must pursue his appropriation with reasonable diligence. (2) Notices of the site of appropriation are sufficient. (3) Waste water not yet returned to the stream is the exclusive right of the first appropriator. A survey of the *Montana Reports* and *Shepard's Montana Citations* reveals many other water cases of similar importance and leaves the researcher with little doubt about the contributions of Montana's territorial court to the water law of Montana and the Rocky Mountains.

By incorporating the doctrine of prior appropriation into Colorado's state constitution, the convention resoundingly endorsed the work of the territorial courts. Prior appropriation was sanctioned with these words:

The waters of every natural stream, not heretofore appropriated, are hereby declared to be the property of the public,
and the same are dedicated to the use of the people of the
state, subject to appropriation as hereafter provided.[54]

Domestic, irrigational, and industrial uses were authorized, in
that order of preference, in the constitution. This order of
preferential use is not to be confused with priorities. Actually,
the only practical effect of this section was to give cities the
right to secure water by condemning subordinate uses—the
right to secure irrigation water for urban use by eminent domain, for example. After considerably more debate than had
occurred in Colorado, the Wyoming convention also adopted
the appropriation system which had been written into law by
her courts.[55] In Montana, water rights became entangled with
other highly controversial issues, and the convention failed
to incorporate a formal system of distribution into the constitution. Thus territorial judicial precedent became the basis
of their system.[56]

"A right to water is a pleasing thing," observed one legal
commentator, "but it takes water in the laterals to raise the
crops." [57] Keeping water in the laterals was not an engineering
problem, but a legal one. To define rights in terms of priorities
was not sufficient; an administrative system of water distribution was needed to guarantee the execution of these rights. The
courts insisted that the state and national governments were
obligated to protect water rights, a philosophy that evolved
in Colorado from the Yunker case.[58] From the doctrine of
prior appropriation, a statewide system of public control of
water rights—the "Colorado System"—evolved, and by 1956
the codes of seventeen western states had been affected by this
unique legal development.[59] With Mississippi's recent adoption of the principle of prior appropriation, it can now be
argued that the influence of the Rocky Mountain territorial
courts has crossed to the east of the Mississippi River.[60]

The Colorado System (and others patterned after it) has

three basic functions.[61] First, it is a system of official ascertainment, determination, and recordation of all past rights. Second, it provides for state supervision and distribution—the establishment of rights "in action" as well as "on the books." Lastly, it involves the acquisition of new rights and their recordation. Though the keystone of the system can be found in Colorado's constitution, its basic statutory framework was constructed by the legislature in 1879. Today the administration of water rights in Colorado is still based largely on this framework.[62] Modified through the years, the state system involves seventy water districts—each with a commissioner—which are grouped into seven irrigation divisions. The seven divisions are administered by division engineers with a state engineer responsible for the entire network. While the influence of the Colorado System is widespread, the actual administrative procedure for determining priorities of water users varies from state to state.[63] In this century, water control has become an interstate concern, and water is divided among the states either by congressionally approved interstate compacts or by decree of the United States Supreme Court.[64]

In the area of public land policy, the territorial supreme court justices were unable to exercise the creativity which is evident in their mining and water law. The product of decades of struggle in the halls of Congress, land policy was dictated to a large extent by the national political climate, a reality which precluded major improvisation by the territorial judiciary. It must also be recognized that the pressures of litigation largely determine a court's opportunity to make law. While the territorial courts were jammed with lawsuits pertaining to water and mineral rights, the appellate courts under study here heard relatively few cases on other aspects of the public domain. Consequently, the territorial justices had less opportunity to shape land laws dramatically. The territories were split, as was the nation, in regard to the enforcement of land policy, especially when the open range was concerned. Each judge's attitude on range problems was apparently determined by his personal economic interests and the position of the national administration which he served.[65]

Today more than ever before, Wyoming proudly boasts of its leadership in the movement for women's suffrage. A visitor to the capitol building in Cheyenne is greeted by a statue of Esther Hobart Morris who was a proponent of the 1869 legislative act which granted equal rights to women. During their tours of the building, guide-ettes take advantage of present women's lib publicity and use every opportunity to sing the praises of Wyoming's own liberation movement of over a century ago. In April 1969, Representative John Wold of Wyoming introduced into the House of Representatives a resolution calling for national observance of the hundredth anniversary of the birth of women's suffrage. The first legislature of Wyoming Territory passed a bill, signed into law December 10, 1869, entitled "An Act to Grant to the Women of Wyoming Territory the Right of Suffrage and to Hold Office." [66] In relation to its length—only eight lines—more has probably been written about this act than any other in the nation's history, and for Wyoming's historians, its origins have been a favorite topic of research.[67]

What prompted the introduction of such a radical proposal in the Wyoming assembly and why did it receive enough support to assure its passage? William H. Bright, the author of the bill, never wavered in his claim that his motives were lofty, and historians have found no justification for doubting his sincerity.[68] But pure motives apparently ended with Bright. While it would be unfair to assume that none of the supporters of Wyoming's first women's suffrage law acted selflessly, most were influenced by political or economic considerations. The evidence for this is ample. Republican Governor John A. Campbell and the Democratic assembly were seldom in harmony, and the territory desperately needed immigrants, particularly the feminine variety. Justice John W. Kingman of the first territorial supreme court suggested that Bright's proposition was passed as a lark, either to harass the governor or for publicity. In a recent essay, Wyoming Supreme Court Justice Glenn Parker emphasized the "chamber of commerce zeal" of the early territorial residents.[69]

Two of Wyoming's justices, John W. Kingman and John H. Howe, were actively involved in the early phase of Wyoming's movement for women's suffrage. Howe professed he "had no agency in the enactment of the law," insisting that his sole interest was the fair administration of it. However, Kingman takes credit for persuading the governor to sign the law during a visit he made with Howe.[70] While both justices encouraged women to serve as jurors, Kingman evidently had stronger feelings about the movement than his associate did. The following is an excerpt from some remarks Kingman made to a leader of the American Women's Suffrage Association.

> A woman will not consent to be a butterfly when she can of her own choice become an eagle! Let her enjoy the ambitions of life; let her be able to secure its honors, its riches, its high places, and she will not be its toy or its simple ornament.[71]

Many of Wyoming Territory's settlers did not share Kingman's zeal for enlarging upon the privileges of the fairer sex, but the attempts of county officials to ridicule the legislation backfired. In the first term of district court in Laramie City, after the enactment of this revolutionary legislation, the venire was intentionally loaded with ladies in an attempt to cause confusion. But Kingman was able to turn the tables by convincing the women to serve.[72]

Though Justice Howe did not share Kingman's enthusiasm, he nevertheless insisted on enforcing the law and generally praised the performance of women jurors. He reassured those ladies who were apprehensive, promising to punish anyone who ridiculed or intimidated them. The chief justice vowed they would be protected "against everything which ought to offend the most refined, modest, and educated woman in any of the walks of life." Those who opposed the presence of women in the jury box must have been infuriated at Howe's endorsement of their service and his opinion that they exerted a "refining and humanizing influence"—their presence marked "a new and improved epoch in the administration of justice." [73]

The press's response to the use of women on juries varied, and it is hard to distinguish remarks offered in earnest from those made in jest. No accurate comparison exists of the number of convictions by juries with and without women, and the newspapers did play up the guilty verdicts of the mixed juries. The editor of the *Laramie Daily Sentinel* suggested that the bar's opposition to women jurors stemmed from the difficulty lawyers experienced in defending guilty parties before women. [74] Though Representative Wold expressed a great deal of pride in his recent attempt to get President Richard M. Nixon to proclaim a National Women's Suffrage and Equality State Month, it should be pointed out that the "flavoring of the jury with the distaff" did not continue in Wyoming after Justice Howe resigned in the fall of 1871. [75] Three-quarters of a century elapsed before women were again regularly used on juries in Wyoming. Nevertheless, the first Wyoming territorial supreme court participated actively in the women's suffrage movement in the West, and it must not be forgotten that Wyoming women have voted and held office for over a century.

The supreme courts of the Rocky Mountain territories under study here upheld the legislative extension of various legal rights of single and married women—*feme sole* and *feme covert*. In a number of cases, the courts affirmed the rights of women to own property, to enter into contracts, to suffer no disability before the courts, and to manage their own affairs. [76] The opinions reflect an amazingly modern viewpoint on the part of the judiciary. Moses Hallett observed that the law "clothes" women with the power "to manage her own affairs," and exhorted Colorado's women "to accept the responsibility which attends upon free agency." [77]

Recent investigation indicates that territorial judges, working in tandem with the legislatures, tended to limit the complexities of pleadings, making procedures simpler and faster
than in the East. Strong evidence has been presented to suggest that certain common law concepts—for example, those
relating to tenancy and mechanics' liens—were altered in the
territories of the Rockies.[78] Indeed, the importance of mining
and water law is so overwhelming that little attention has been
paid to the numerous procedural questions which resulted
from the fact that the territorial district courts had both
chancery (equity) and common law jurisdiction. The ability
of the justices to cut through procedural entanglements is
impressive. After some vacillation, the United States Supreme
Court ruled that under the Organic Acts, the territorial legislatures had the authority to mix, blend, or unite equity and
common law jurisdictions. It is worth noting that just a few
months before the high court ruled on the matter in 1873,
Hallett had written a Colorado opinion which anticipated the
ruling in Washington.[79]

While district court files shed considerable light on social
and economic conditions in the territories, they do not add
significantly to an understanding of the law made during the
judicial process. A large part of the docket in the lower courts
was comprised of commercial and criminal matters. Litigation
involving either important principles of law or sizable economic considerations were appealed to the territorial supreme
court. At this stage of the judicial process, the issues and
questions under examination were clarified; hence, the supreme court reports better reveal the legal contributions of the
justices.

In addition to the "making of law" through decisions and
practice, the territorial benches of Colorado, Montana, and
Wyoming afforded leadership in improving the operation of
the lower courts created by the territorial assemblies.[80] While
it is not within the scope of this study to itemize and illustrate
these modifications, credit is due the justices for their part in

these accomplishments, another example of the involvement of the justices in the process of development.

It is tempting to overstress the significance of the fact that territorial decisions were usually affirmed by the United States Supreme Court. Though this information is important, recognizing the contributions of the territorial bench to local jurisprudence is also necessary. Few lawyers will deny that each state has its own peculiar legal system. Though little has been included here about the accomplishments of the territorial bench in this realm, credit should be given to the early courts for laying the foundations of the jurisprudence of the various states. When the impact of the territorial supreme courts on national, regional, and state jurisprudence is kept in mind, it is hard to deny that the previously dominant "hanging judge" school of territorial history is myopic and inadequate.

The pleas of miners for qualified officials who would be familiar with their particular problems are fully understandable to anyone who has plodded through the early supreme court reports. After reading these records, even a confirmed skeptic would find it hard to condemn the judiciary as the weakest branch of a poor territorial government. The reader who has not studied the decisions may find such doctrines as prior appropriation and extralateral rights pedantic or academic. However, in reading the territorial opinions, these concepts take on substance. The gurgle of irrigation water can be heard, the heft of bullion felt. If for no other reason, the Rocky Mountain territorial supreme courts deserve a better place in history for their definition and refinement of mineral and water law.

The territorial opinions reveal an admirable balance— respect for precedent combined with common sense and prudence—and the record is hard to ignore. The United States Supreme Court often affirmed the judges' work, the state constitutional conventions generally endorsed it, and present state codes still reflect it. Partisan cries of corruption when the justices sat as an appellate body are not supported by statistics,

Call them what you like, but recognize that the territorial supreme court justices of Colorado, Montana, and Wyoming made law—law which permitted their territories to develop economically, law which was incorporated into the jurisprudence of the Rocky Mountain West and the nation.

10
"Send Us
a Civilizer"

The role of territorial supreme court justices was often ambivalent. One moment they performed as agents of the establishment, the next as fervent campaigners for territorial interests. It is doubtful that Montana's Governor Benjamin F. Potts fully recognized the implications of his remarks to the president when he suggested that "an able Judge has more power for good here than all the Federal officers put together." [1] Potts then implored his chief to "send us a Civilizer."

Of course, Potts had his own definition of a civilizer, and his motives for requesting another rotation on the bench probably had a political basis. Nevertheless, the governor's terminology was most appropriate. First, in their official capacities as well as in incidental ways, the justices were transmitters of the civilization of the East. Second, the judiciary acted as a civilizing force through its participation in the development process within the various territories. The sword of Potts's "Civilizers" indeed had two edges—external and internal.

Members of the bench sided surprisingly fast with the local constituency—even some of those justices about whom the residents have had little good to say down through the years. A good illustration is the involvement in the "Big Horn" expedition of Wyoming's first chief justice, John H. Howe, who left the territory after his resignation from the bench. The issue involved the settler's desire to penetrate into an area

allocated to the Indians by treaty.[2] During the winter of
1869–70, the excitement of the proposed armed mining expedition into the Big Horn Mountains dominated the attention of
Wyoming leaders, and all three justices orated in behalf of the
project at various public meetings. Chief Justice Howe was
selected by the territorial residents to present their appeal to
Washington because of his "ability, address, high character,
and social and political influence." [3] The governor, associate
justices, and United States attorney verified to the attorney
general that the people had chosen Justice Howe to represent
them, and Howe notified his superiors that he intended to
travel to Washington in response to their "en masse request." [4]
Howe indicated that in the past he had persistently refused
to represent Wyoming's people, but that he had decided that
he could best serve their interests by going to the capital. In
Washington, the judge may have encountered intimations
that his motivation was personal financial gain, for in a
lengthy letter he wrote in Washington to Attorney General
Ebenezer R. Hoar, Howe emphasized that he would gain no
personal or financial benefits from the expedition. He insisted
that his only interest was that of the territory, and he emphasized the orderly nature of the proposed project—led by
men who wished, above all, to avoid Indian trouble. In brief,
the justice explained that federal officials had a misconception
of the venture.[5] Permission for the expedition was granted,
provided that it remain west of the Big Horn Mountains and
east of the Shoshoni Reservation. The chief justice was show-
ered with praise for his work in Washington, but he paid a
price for it in terms of the Justice Department's reaction.
Howe's superiors there, after reading Wyoming newspaper
accounts of his report, felt that he had exaggerated conces-
sions made in Washington. But the judge was quick to set the
record straight.[6] In this incident, Howe, who was not widely
popular among lawyers because of his stern conduct on the
bench, revealed a genuine understanding of the mood of

frontiersmen with regard to the Indian question, and his part in the venture was played at the risk of his own security.[7]

As the Big Horn story illustrates, the territorial supreme court justices spent much of their time rendering services other than the hearing of cases and the writing of opinions. In most instances, the experiences of the jurists in one territory were duplicated in others. Like their colleagues in Wyoming, the Montana justices found themselves involved in nearly every aspect of Indian relations. A member of the first court represented the government as a special commissioner to the Gros Ventres, Piegan, and Blackfeet.[8] Those judges who dared enforce the United States restrictions on Indian trade found themselves dealing with a maze of malfeasance that extended from the territory all the way to Washington.[9] A few judges even bore arms in the Indian Wars. Justice Hiram Knowles of Montana wrote his wife a moving letter on the eve of his departure to the field against the Nez Perce; he enclosed his bankbooks and instructed her on actions to take "if anything not anticipated should happen." [10]

By virtue of their membership on the administration team, the justices sometimes acted as trusted assistants, delivering confidential messages and embarking on special assignments—in the role of today's ever-present troubleshooters.[11] Since the territories did not have an official comparable to an attorney general, throughout the territorial period supreme court justices responded to the requests of legislatures and governors for advice in formulating laws.[12] This assistance was rendered without remuneration. Similarly, the jurists often labored gratis on the codification of laws, although they were occasionally paid for their time. In either case, their work in codification was virtually invaluable to the jurisprudence of their respective territories, a fact little appreciated by most people who are not directly associated with the legal profession. While the contributions of Moses Hallett in Colorado and Decius S. Wade, Henry N. Blake, and Hiram Knowles in

Montana have been acknowledged previously, it must not be assumed that Wyoming's judges did not engage in the same work.[13]

There seems to be no end to the list of sundry duties performed by the justices in addition to their official responsibilities. They spent many extra days on the circuit covering the districts of absent associates, and as often happens, advantage was taken of the less selfish men. Judges were pressed into service as election officials, and their advice was frequently (though not often enough) sought in decisions on pardons since there was no parole board.[14] For many years the law profession was regulated by the supreme court which set standards for admission to the bar and established rules of practice.[15] Despite the many stories about frontier improvisations, the court took the regulation of the bar quite seriously. Hallett, for example, refused to recognize the election of a prosecuting attorney in his district because he was not a member of the bar. The attorney's supporters filed with the supreme court of the territory a petition for a writ of mandamus—an order directing Hallett to recognize the validity of the election. But the appellate court denied the petition.[16] A little-known justice, James B. Belford, took the occasion to write a truly brilliant treatise on the definition of an attorney and the necessity for a licensed bar in which he cited authorities as far back as the *Statutes of Henry IV*. As district judges, the justices were responsible for the supervision of grand juries, a task which involved them in controversies ranging from conditions of the "poor farm" to maintenance of public buildings. While territorial prisons were not directly their responsibility, the judges were affected by the myriad problems arising from the operation of these penitentiaries, and the effectiveness of the judges was undoubtedly hampered by inadequate prison facilities.[17] These varied and extensive unprescribed roles are seldom recognized in interpretive accounts of territorial operation. Evidently the day-by-day participation of the judiciary in territorial management has been obscured by overpublicized political feuds and the extreme visibility of the territorial chief executive.

As significant as these diverse activities, both official and voluntary, may have been in everyday territorial life, they were no more important in the developmental process than the participation of a number of the judges in the struggle for local control and statehood. Because Congress dominated territorial affairs, territorial residents were constantly angered by what they considered their second-class citizenship. Particularly in the late nineteenth century, an analogy was drawn between the abuses suffered by the American colonies and those inflicted upon the territories, and territorial objections were faithful to a theme which might be labeled domestic colonialism. In 1871, Montana's delegate protested in Congress "against the Territories being used by the Federal Government as the English uses its colonies." Two decades later, Delegate Joseph K. Toole, pleading for Montana statehood, compared the grievances cited in the Declaration of Independence with those endured by the territories. Legislative memorials were likewise loyal to the theme of domestic colonialism, alluding to "taxation without representation." [18] While these attitudes have been the subject of historical studies for years, to date little, if any, acknowledgment has been given to the manner in which territorial justices joined in the chorus. It is ironic that one of the strongest expressions of territorial resentment was offered by a Montana judge whose appointment certainly had strong political implications. Despite his political legacy, Decius S. Wade was an ardent advocate of home rule, and his treatise on self-government in the territories began with an ominous quotation by the famed jurist and legal commentator, James Kent, in which parallels were drawn between the mistakes of Great Britain a century before and conditions in the territories.[19] Wade hardly sounded like a carpetbagger as he focused on three arguments: the territories were not represented with a vote in Congress; the territories were not permitted to elect their own officials;

and the right of Congress to nullify territorial laws effectively deprived territorial citizens of making their own laws.

In Colorado, Montana, and Wyoming, residents sought control of their own affairs from the beginning of the organized existence of their territories, and the selection of their own judges was a matter of prime importance.[20] No better example can be found than the determination of Colorado's residents which finally paid dividends via the Hallett court. Settlers in Wyoming, harassed by a prolonged delay in organization, incessantly discussed the fact that none of their comrades were among the first appointees. When William T. Jones resigned from the bench in the middle of his first term, strong efforts were made to promote Joseph M. Carey to the court. Although he had lived in the territory only two years, he was offered as a local man.[21]

The campaign for appointment of territorial residents, which affected the justices deeply and in which many of them participated, resulted in the inclusion of statements favoring such a policy in the two major party platforms of 1884. The promises, however, were hollow. The House of Representatives tabled Delegate Toole's bill which would have made the appointment of bona fide residents to territorial offices a federal statute. The adverse committee report agreed in principle with the bill (HR 2883) but stated: "it would be unwise to require by statute that this should be done in all cases." As it happened, in the late 1870s and the 1880s more territorial residents were chosen.[22] Though appointing men of proven adaptability would have been the wise course, the naming of local candidates was not entirely foolproof. The highly factionalized political climate inevitably resulted in charges of partiality, even within the same party, when local men were picked. Besides, the local favorites were often Democrats, a prospect not inviting to the Republicans who were in control most of the time.[23]

It was very clear that the only redress from the abuses of territorial status was to become a state, and the arguments for that event were basically a replay of the territorial residents' complaints about being treated like inferior citizens. Both current and former members of the judiciary campaigned for statehood as vigorously as they worked in behalf of the appointment of local men to the court. Indeed, control of federal appointments, even after statehood was granted, was a major goal of local residents. This can be illustrated by Colorado Governor John Evans's reminder to President Lincoln that the president had agreed to consult with Colorado leaders should the first statehood movement be fruitful.[24] It is an interesting comment on Lincoln's character that he penned a note on the back of Evans's letter directing the attorney general to remind the president of this commitment.

In the drive for statehood, Judge Joseph M. Carey played a more dramatic role than any other justice or former member of the court. It was Judge Carey who steered the Wyoming statehood bill through Congress virtually unassisted.[25] Though his motives have been questioned, passage of the statehood legislation was Carey's most important achievement.[26] His correspondence with Willis Van Devanter indicates that he was not guided in this drive solely by the prospect of its beneficial effects on his political future, though there were undeniable partisan overtones to the movement, with the Republicans standing to profit politically by victory.[27] From Washington, Carey carefully directed the movements of local supporters down to the very details of the content of memorials and petitions. He was a bit perturbed, however, by the lack of enthusiasm among some members of his constituency, complaining that he was "receiving but little assistance from the people of Wyoming in the fight." Lewis L. Gould explains Carey's disappointment by suggesting that "politics operated in a vacuum for most citizens" who "watched with detached amusement the antics of their representatives." [28] There is little doubt that many citizens wanted to end their colonial status, but fears about the cost of independence probably dampened their spirits. Carey obviously commanded the allegiance of the territorial electorate as no other politician could, with the exception of Francis E. Warren. Regardless of the nature of his support at home, Carey successfully nurtured the bill for more than six months, and on July 10, 1890, President Benjamin Harrison signed the state of Wyoming into existence.

In the constitutional conventions of Colorado, Montana, and Wyoming, conspicuous roles were played by former members of the supreme court. Colorado's Ebenezer T. Wells, whose term had just expired, was an exceedingly active participant in the meeting; he chaired the Committee on Revisions and Adjustments and served on the Judiciary Committee. The initial draft presented to Wyoming's convention was the work of a former justice, Joseph W. Fisher. Asbury B. Conaway, who was appointed to the judiciary only several months prior to statehood, was among the leaders.[29] Conaway participated, in particular, in debates concerning water rights and administrative control. Of course, behind the scenes another member of the earlier court, Delegate Carey, made his presence strongly felt.

Regardless of the epithets these politicians accumulated during their careers, it cannot be denied that in the final analysis they ran the store. As Howard Lamar indicates in urging a functional view of territorial history, someone had to "develop the country industrially." [30] Just as the supreme court justices shared in the politics of development, they also played a part in economic development throughout the entire territorial period. Members of the judiciary, like other officials and practicing attorneys, were aware of financial opportunities and had connections with investors in the states.[31] Exploitive as it may appear today, the process was undeniably one of growth and development. The tremendous monetary value of the properties under litigation, especially in the mining areas, created a situation which was unusually tempting as well as conducive to accusations of venality—even when integrity prevailed. Except in situations in which the judge had a direct financial interest, there was, as is basically true today, no limitation on the private investments of the judges. In view of their low salaries, it can be assumed that all judges had outside income from investments either in their home areas or in the territories. A few may have been supported for short periods by their law firms, but it is unlikely that such an arrangement would have covered an extended period of time. While few justices were appointed from among the truly wealthy, Justice Department files indicate that a high percentage of them either had considerable property or married into a family of some means.[32]

Though Wyoming was not excluded from mining activity, it was in Colorado and Montana that the justices became deeply involved in mining ventures. The career of Moses Hallett of Colorado (see chap. 8) began in the gold fields and concluded with a brilliant tenure on the bench. Though other Colorado justices had mining interests, none apparently was as involved as Hallett. One of Montana's first justices, Hezekiah L. Hosmer (see chap. 6), was deeply involved in mining speculation as well as other ventures. Judging from the diversity of his interests and the size of the loans he made, his capital was considerable—its source is not known.[33] While the mining interests of later justices may not have been as strong, those who served on the supreme court at the end of the territorial period were still vitally involved in the basic industry. Jacob B. Blair, a three-term justice in Wyoming Territory, invested heavily in mining and became active in national mining associations after his retirement. The first territorial governor of Wyoming, John A. Campbell, dabbled in mineral stocks, and because of his unusually close association with members of the early bench, it is likely that they did also.[34]

The potential of the livestock industry stirred the imaginations of Wyoming's justices apparently as soon as they arrived in the territory, and by the time Wyoming was admitted to the Union, several members of the court had contributed substantially to the development of that part of the economy.

Though he was not one of the main livestock investors, Governor Campbell undoubtedly influenced his friends on the judiciary by recognizing the significance of ranching for the future of the territory.[35] Of the judges of Wyoming Territory, Joseph M. Carey became the biggest livestock operator.[36] Serving in Campbell's administration as a government attorney and a supreme court justice, Carey became a big-time operator by any standards. Guided by the example and advice of Colorado's pioneer cattleman, John W. Iliff, Carey convinced his brother, R. Davis Carey, to join him shortly after his own arrival, and the brothers engaged in land speculation and cattle grazing. In 1872 they trailed a herd from Texas to the range above Cheyenne, and by 1875 the J. M. Carey and Brother outfit boasted 6,000 head—a distinction that placed them at the top of the list of Wyoming ranchers with 1,000 or more head.[37] Two years later the herd numbered 8,000, and within a decade, company inventory showed 32,287 head of cattle and 436 horses, with an expected calf brand of nearly 8,000.[38] Carey valued his outfit at that time at $1,200,000. J. M. Carey and Brother was in operation for over three-quarters of a century. Considering his stature within the industry, it is not surprising that Carey was extremely active in the Wyoming Stock Growers' Association, serving as its president from 1884 through 1887 when it was at the peak of its political power.[39] As a member of the judiciary, and later as a delegate, Carey was criticized for his business interests. While he was on the bench in 1876, Delegate W. R. Steele and Governor John M. Thayer made an issue of his business interests in a complaint to the attorney general.

> Judge Carey is a young man of limited experience at the bar, is largely engaged in private business, which engrosses a very considerable portion of his time, almost the whole of it, thus preventing that undivided attention to his judicial duties, which is an absolute prerequisite to a good judicial officer.[40]

As a delegate from 1885 to 1890, Carey was painted by Democrats as the "kid-gloved representative" of the "cattle barons and dudes," but these accusations had no effect on his popularity at the polls; he handily won reelection in 1888.[41]

A member of the original Wyoming territorial supreme court, John W. Kingman, was another major figure in the early development of Wyoming's stock-growing industry. Kingman's enthusiasm for sheep was matched by his investment in them. In 1871 the *Laramie Daily Sentinel* reported Judge Kingman's receiving a "whole train load of sheep from the east." The shipment, which was driven from the train to the judge's ranch west of Laramie, was described as "between 3 and 4000" and as a "choice lot." Judge Kingman gained a wide reputation as an authority on sheep and was quoted as such in the *Report of the Secretary of the Interior*.[42] He addressed the annual meeting of the Wyoming Stock Graziers' Association on the future of sheep raising in the territory, going into great detail about the adaptability of various breeds to the soil, climate, and grass of the region.[43] Like Carey, Judge Kingman received some choice morsels of criticism for the attention he gave his stock raising. Only P. S. Posey, territorial "critic supreme," could have composed the following phrase: "and that Judge Kingman, instead of mounting armed chairs to frighten the souls of fearful lawyers, capers nimbly in an odorous sheepfold to the lascivious bawling of his rams." [44] Perhaps Posey intended a pun as he continued, "Besides he ranks much higher as a lawyer among sheep than he does among men."

The examples above are not meant to infer that the judges' investments were confined either to one segment of the economy or to one territory. And only a few of the most dramatic cases have been cited. Other judges invested in banks, farming, or land speculation, and some—Hosmer, for example—tried to get their fingers into every financial pie within reach. Hosmer's known interests included mines, roads, financing, ranches, and the manufacture of pottery and brick.[45] The financial affairs of Moses Hallett offer another excellent illustration of the diversity of economic activities in which judges could engage.

The legacies of the territorial court are viewed with feelings that range from gratitude to bitterness. Some manifested themselves early, others are still discernible. Nevertheless, from the judiciary came men who left rich mining and ranching heritages, and whose contributions to education were not minor. They often gave generously of both their influence and their money to establish colleges and historical societies. From a functional view of the political, social, and economic development of the territories, it cannot be denied that many of the justices were among those who kept the store— Governor Potts had not erred when he called them civilizers.

11
Conclusion

The varied roles of the supreme courts of the Colorado, Montana, and Wyoming territories provide a dramatic example of the fallacies of generalization. On the one hand the territorial justices were strong agents of the federal government and the national political parties. On the other, they reflected the impact of their environment so strongly that the temptation to isolate a territory and stress the local aspects of its development is easily understood. However, even though the peculiar needs of the region demanded new legal concepts, it becomes clear from the activities of the judiciary that isolating the territories in historical analysis is no longer valid.

While no amount of historiographical sorcery is going to convert scoundrels into heroes, it can now be recognized that villains were not as prevalent among the territorial judiciaries as has been believed. Nor is the carpetbagger stereotype any longer acceptable in reference to the majority of the group, for the parasites were matched by an equal, if not greater, number of builders. Historians have failed in describing territorial development because they have been more interested in motivation than in the answer to the question "what was done?" Accounts of the territories have been too moralistic at the expense of an accurate functional description, a fact which becomes more apparent when the behavior of territorial officials in the last third of the nineteenth century is compared to that of national leaders as a whole. The federal court system of that era was not a model of efficiency, nor was it devoid of politics. Recent attacks on members of, and designates to, the United States Supreme Court raise the question of whether a double standard has been applied in appraising the territorial bench.

Lacking sufficient financial support and operating within a restrictive and rigidly enforced congressional framework, the justices were instrumental in creating sorely needed organization in their respective territories. In the process, they played a major part in establishing law and order; they brought American society to the West—society as it was envisioned by the majority to the east. The territorial justices gave a hand in preserving the Union, particularly in Colorado, and in all three territories they endured the adverse financial, social, and political aftereffects of the struggle. They also created a workable system of mineral and water law that ensured the economic development of the Rocky Mountain region.

It was not by accident that the territorial supreme courts were political entities. The struggles of these courts reveal clearly both the magnitude of the national impact on the territories and their strong desire for local control. The extent of federal-local interplay becomes evident, a tug-of-war in which national power dominated. But the struggle proved that the force of the local thrust was considerable, and it was this collision of national and territorial forces that crushed some justices and tempered others.

Just as some of Frederick Jackson Turner's most avid disciples became obsessed with environmental factors, it is possible that scholars may overreact in their determination to accent the federal, national, or eastern influences on territorial development. An honest analysis of the territorial supreme courts should have a moderating effect on any such tendency. The men on those benches were in a difficult position. They were instruments of federal and national political power, and like William Goetzmann's explorers, they were programmed to be vehicles of acculturation. At the same time, however, the territorial justices were particularly sensitive to environmental pressures. Although the scholarship of

the past has to a large extent failed to recognize the ambivalence of their position, the judges' contemporaries praised
some of them as civilizers and others for their understanding
of the peculiar neeeds of their regions.

In the controversy over Judge William Ware Peck, the
federal-local struggle was clear. Peck was a transmitter of eastern morality but he failed because he was unable to adapt to
the territorial environment. At the other extreme was Moses
Hallett. Like Peck, he was also a vehicle of American culture,
but unlike his rigid colleague, he was a model of adaptability.
Modification and innovation in meeting environmental demands characterize his career. While the experiences of these
two highly capable men have been described in this work because of the dramatic contrast they afford, the careers of many
other judges could have been described with the same effect.
The ambivalence of the role of the territorial courts is also
accented by the judges' contributions to the political and economic growth of the territories. Another complicating factor
was the voice of the judiciary in the struggle for local control.

The nearly simultaneous appearance of studies producing
similar conclusions may point toward a new direction in interpretation. Six months after the first draft of this work had
been placed in the hands of the publisher, Gordon M. Bakken
completed a dissertation on Rocky Mountain constitution-
making in which many of the conclusions stated in the preceding chapters are affirmed. His statements about the contributions of territorial courts to mineral law and their impact
upon the modification of the common law are unequivocal.[1]
Bakken found that the constitutional conventions had confirmed and endorsed the work of Colorado's and Montana's
territorial benches, and, to a lesser extent, Wyoming's.[2] The
territorial executives, at least in terms of popular image, did
not fare as well as the judiciary.

When the distracting antics of some judges—antics which
have contributed to colorful but shallow narratives—are cast
aside, and when their functional role is examined, the positive

role of the judiciary becomes apparent. However, the implications of this study are much broader. Since the judiciary constituted a major part of each territorial administration, a more accurate assessment of their contributions sheds new light on the territorial history of Colorado, Montana, and Wyoming. Historians are now one step closer to placing the territories of the trans-Mississippi West in a new and proper perspective in American history.[3]

The territorial justices could not all have been of the carpetbagger ilk if the indisputable evidence of steady growth and development in the territories is viewed objectively. Similarly, the personal praise and recognition bestowed on many of the outstanding judges by their contemporaries as well as by historians cannot be discounted. That the period was one of difficult struggle and conflict, that national forces of great influence were loath to relinquish their power and control in the territories, that administrative positions were too frequently used as political payoffs and for selfish, financial opportunity, that the men appointed were often either too weak or too strong willed, that some served part or all of their appointments solely out of a sense of duty or missionary obligation with almost no personal involvement or identification with the people of the territory they served and left the area immediately thereafter, that some of the appointees were flagrantly immoral, unjust, and unscrupulous—these are facts which cannot be denied. These are the points that have heretofore received too much attention, along with the ludicrous tales of the wild informality of frontier justice. It has been the purpose of this study to place the territorial supreme courts of Colorado, Montana, and Wyoming in a more realistic perspective. The other side of the coin—the functional view—vindicates the jurists as a body, for they were civilizers, builders, and makers of law who contributed substantially to the territories and to the nation as a whole.

Appendix 1

To His Excellency, the President of the United States:

The people of the territory of Colorado, through their representatives in the legislative assembly, respectfully represent unto the president that many of the questions growing out of mining operations and concerning mining titles in this territory are novel and peculiar, while other questions, concerning the irrigation of lands, and growing out of the peculiar situation of the people, remote from all other communities, are almost unknown to the laws of the eastern states; and persons residing in the territory have acquired a knowledge of these questions, necessary to a correct understanding of them, which is not possessed by residents of eastern states; and for this reason, among others, the people of this territory, who are identified with the people and will attend to their public duties, should be appointed judges of the territory; therefore, the council and house of representatives of Colorado territory do most earnestly and respectfully pray that your Excellency will appoint Moses Hallett, a citizen of this territory, in whom we have confidence, to be chief justice of this territory.

Joint Memorial of the Colorado territorial legislature, February 8, 1866, citing needs of the region and calling for the appointment of Moses Hallett. *General Laws, Joint Resolutions, Memorials, and Private Acts, Passed at the Fifth Session of the Legislative Assembly of the Territory of Colorado* (Central City: David C. Collier, Miner's Register office), p. 181.

Appendix 2

Deer Lodge M. T.
March 6th 1870

Dear Sir

I received a letter by the last mail from Henry N. Blake Esq the U.S. Attorney for this Territory informing me somewhat of certain charges made against me in your department in relation to my official conduct in a cause tried before me about one year ago styled I believe John Carhart Adm^r of the Estate of Geo. Carhart dec^d *vs*. The Montana Minneral Land and Mining Co.—*et. al.* and also some things in relation to my political views and suggesting that I had better reply to them. It appears to me that the most satisfactory manner of doing so would be by sending you a transcript of the record with my reasons in full for my rulings. I am fearful however that this would be imposing upon you too arduous a duty especially if every man who should consider himself agrieved by the ruling of a Territorial Judge should instead of appealing to a higher Court to correct the errors assigned consider this a precedent and file charges in your department and succeed in putting the Judge on trial in lieu of his cause. For this reason I have decided to first write you my version of that trial and the circumstances attending it and afterward if you will permit or it will not be disagreeable to you to forward you a transcript of the record together with affidavits of the correctness of my statements.

A term of Court had been appointed in Beaverhead County before I reached the Territory for sometime in Oct. 1868 I believe. In Sept. as I was about to leave here to hold a term of Court in

---

Of the thousands of letters from and about supreme court justices in the National Archives, this letter from Montana Justice Hiram Knowles to Attorney General E. R. Hoar reveals better than most the numerous adversities which the territorial justices faced (Appointment Papers, Montana, Record Group 60, National Archives).

Missoula County I received a petition signed by all the attorneys save one of Beaverhead Co. together with all of the officers of the Court for that County requesting me not to hold that term of Court in that County as they had no business ready for a hearing but at the same time saying they would be ready with all their business by the 1st of Jan. following. The Attys. for the defts in the above action headed that petition, I believe. Their names I know were signed to it. About the same time I received a request from the bar of Helena, the largest city in the Territory, to come there and hold a term of court for them. A large docket had accumulated there. This was not in my district but I thought it best as there was then no Judge in the Territory for that district to hold a term of Court when one was desired and so granted the request of the petitioners of Beaverhead County. In the Dec. following, our Supreme Court convened. The duties imposed upon me by this Court occupied me until about the 1st of Feb. thereafter. The preceding Supreme Court had fixed the times for holding terms of the District Courts for the different counties of the Territory for the year 1868, but had appointed no terms for any period beyond that year. Some of the members of the legislature from Beaverhead County who knew nothing of the petition I had received complained that I had gone outside of my district to hold Courts and had slighted them. Sometime in Dec. we fixed the terms of Court for the different Counties. Owing to the above complaint it was thought I had better hold my first term of District Court at Bannock City in that County. So, a term of Court was fixed for there on the fourth Monday in Feb. The order fixing the terms of the district courts was published in every newspaper in the Territory in the last week of Dec. or in the first week of Jan. I have no files of any of those publications and hence cannot be precise. I wrote to the officers of that County that I would be there without fail at that time. Thus you will see they had two months notice of that term and as I before said the Attys. had written me that by the first of Jan. they would be ready with all their business. I rode on horseback one hundred and ten miles in Feb. crossing the main chain of the Rocky Mountains during severe stormy weather to fulfil my appointment. When Court convened this cause among others was called up for trial. It was about the oldest cause on the docket, if not the oldest one. As I have not the record here I cannnot tell how long it had been at issue but I think it must have been for at least one year and a half before the trial. It was an action of Ejectment and for damages to the mine in dispute on account of the unskillful working of the same and for the value of the quartz extracted therefrom. These can all be joined in one action under our Code. The pleadings were very poor but there were sufficient facts alleged to make out such a case. Mr. Phelps an attorney for the defense said that this cause could not be tried for the reason that all the parties deft. had not been served with summons. The Attys. for the plff. replied that Mr. Phelps and Hasford had appeared for all the parties deft. and had thereby waived any defect in the service of process and seemed surprised at the remarks of Mr. Phelps. Upon examining the papers it was found that Messrs Hasford and Phelps had signed and written some of their pleadings in such a way as to lead anyone to suppose that they did appear for all the defendants. Messrs Hasford and Phelps however said they never had received any authority to appear for any of the parties deft. but the Montana Mineral Land and Mining Co. and Mr. Clark. I believe I made some remarks to Messrs Hasford and Phelps for their carelessness but told the Attys. for plff. that as no judgment had been taken against these parties I would not consider them in Court. The Attys. for plff. then said they had been trying for a long time to get this cause tried and that with my permission they would dismiss the action as to those not served and proceed against those served. Mr. Phelps approved this on the ground that these persons were necessary parties. I ruled however that under our statute whatever estate the defendants might own in the mine in dispute they held as tenants in common and hence their estates were several and not joint and that in a mixed action of this character the plff. could undoubtedly proceed against the parties served. Mr. Phelps claimed to be surprised at the ruling of the Court.

I am quite confident that the records of that Court will show that no motion was made by the defendants at that term of Court for a Continuance. But I do not wish to cover up the slightest thing that was done or the smallest word said in the trial of that action. Mr. Hasford did say something to me about a Continuance on the ground of the absence of his client Mr. Clark for whom he especially appeared. He said he had some reason to believe that Mr. Clark might be on his way out and was probably at Salt Lake. I asked his grounds for such belief. He said that some time before he had written Mr. Clark that this case might come up for trial at this term. I asked if he had had any letter from him. He said no. I told him that to get a Continuance on the ground of absence of a party he must bring himself clearly within the rules of practice in such cases. No affidavit for Continuance was made or motion filed. During the trial Hasford disclaimed any title for Clark and as no damages had been proved against him I sustained his motion to dismiss the cause, as to him.

In the trial of the cause Mr. Phelps set up about the following defenses. The deft. the M.M.L. & M. Co. had a superior title to the plff. That about the time Geo. Carhart was murdered a man by the name of Henry Plummer who was afterward hung by the Vigilante Committee of this Territory as the head and leader of the band of highwaymen who had for some time infested it had taken out letters of administration upon the estate of the said Geo. Carhart in the miners court and under the authority conferred upon him by this court had sold the mine in dispute to certain parties of whom the deft. afterward purchased it. Here I must enter into an explanation. When what are termed the Bannock Mines were discovered the region of country in which they are situated was then a part of Idaho Territory. There were however no officers of the law in that portion of that Territory at that time; the miners finding disputes arising among their number convened and selected a man to act as judge pledging themselves to support his authority and enforce his judgments. They did not in any manner hamper his jurisdiction. This court was never recognized by the legislatures of Idaho or Montana and I hardly think under their organic acts they could have done so. This is the Miners Court which gave Plummer the authority to sell this mine. It is needless to add that none of Geo. Carharts estate was ever distributed to his heirs. I decided that a title derived from such a source was not valid. Again Mr. Phelps was surprised at the ruling of the Court. The second defense set up was the Statute of limitations. I decided that as this section had been incorporated with Montana Territory and as after this event the legislature of this Territory had enacted a statute of limitations taking the place of and repealing the Idaho Statute upon the subject the statute of limitations would not commence running until the enactment of the Montana Statute. Again Mr. Phelps was very

much surprised at the ruling of the Court. Considerable evidence
was aduced upon the subject of damages. And here let me say if I
committed any error on that trial it was in giving the plff. too large
a judgment for damages. I took notes of the evidence adduced in
the trial which were preserved by the Clerk. If I took down all the
evidence I undoubtedly committed an error but I have a very strong
impression that there was more evidence than I reduced to paper.
But if I did here commit an error I never had any power to correct
it. Under our statute when error is claimed in the findings of fact
by a jury or the Court the party assigning the error must make out
a statement of the evidence produced in the trial on the point in
which error is alleged. This statement must be agreed upon by the
Attys. in the cause and certified to be correct by the judge before
whom the cause was tried. Or, when the Attys. cannot agree upon
it, the statement must be settled before the judges court upon due
notice. Nothing of this kind was ever done. The error if it was such
occurred in this way. Twenty five hundred dollars damages were
claimed for unskillful working of the mine & twenty five hundred
for the value of quartz taken therefrom. There was a general prayer
in which a judgment for $5,000 was asked. My attention was not
directed to these, and there was sufficient evidence in warrenting
me in finding $5,000—or even $10,000—damages for the value of
quartz taken. I told Mr. Phelps that if this matter could be put into
such a shape I could properly rule on it I would require the plff. to
remit $2,500 of the damages or would grant him a new trial. This
was at the next term of Court. I do not think a judge can interfere
with the record he has made after the adjournment of the term
unless the matter is presented to him in a legal form.

There is another matter which came to my knowledge subsequent
to this trial which I wish to give them the benefit of. Mr. Phelps
informed me that the deft. claimed title to that mine from another
source. He said that a man by the name of Bigler, I believe, (I have
forgotten the name), at one time purchased this mine of Carhart:
that he had at one time been his partner. I asked where this man
was. Mr. Phelps said he did not know. I asked if he had been in
the Territory since the commencement of this action. He said he
had. "Did you know he was going to leave?" "Yes." "Why did you
not take his deposition?" Said Mr. Phelps "about that time I got
him into my office and wanted him to give us his deposition. Mr.

Bigler said that the M.M.L. & M. Co. had treated him badly and he would not give it unless they would pay him $1,500." Considering that this man was as he claimed a partner of Carhart's; that at the time Carhart was murdered his estate was administered upon and this mine publicly sold as his property; that there was no record of any conveyance from Carhart to this man; that Mr. Phelps did not know whether there ever had been any memoranda of this sale reduced to writing; that the amount Bigler claimed to have paid for it was small, at a time when the mine was considered very valuable; considering further that though old man Carhart, the father of the dec'd., had been in this country for about three years contending for this mine and the defts. had taken no steps to perfect this title, if they possessed it, and the suspicion will be inevitable to a man who has practiced law six or seven years in one of these mining Countries that this $1,500 was demanded as the price of perjury. Would Mr. Phelps bribe a man to do such a thing? I do not know. He has been publically accused in the town where he has lived five years of having accepted a bribe himself when a member of the legislature of this Territory. If all that Mr. Phelps said about this testimony was true, I think they were guilty of gross negligence in not procuring the testimony before or in not making an affidavit asking for time to procure this testimony or doing something to show that they ever expected to get it. I must confess if they had done these things I should not have felt like relaxing any of the rules of practice to allow them to get it.

About two months after this trial. Mr. Phelps came to this place and got me to issue an order staying the proceedings in this action pending a motion he had filed for a new trial and asking for time in which to prepare his record to support it. He had about five months in which to prepare this record. Nothing new was produced in regard to the title. I believe in Mr. Clark's affidavit there was something about which this man Bigler had told him, but I am quite confident it did not show that they knew where he was or had made any endeavor to find out or promised to ever procure his testimony. Mr. Phelps filed an affidavit the burden of which was his surprises at the rulings of this court. The largest number of affidavits were filed upon the point of the value of the quartz taken from the mine which they claimed newly discovered evidence. That mining co. had all the time the means of proving the exact value of that quartz. They had mined it and crushed it and emalgamated the ore in their mill. The agents of the Company who had done this were in New York, no longer residents of the Territory. Their depositions could have been procured at any time. But the records of the case do not show that they ever made a move to get the testimony of these men. These affidavits claimed that this quartz was not worth anything. The plff. produced quite a number of affidavits on this point and it was established that at that very time the man who was running this mill of the Company was paying $30 per cord for this very quartz and that some of the men who had made these affidavits that the quartz would not pay anything knew it, Mr. Clark among the number. The defendants did not seem to be satisfied with the record they had made themselves for they went about the streets of the little village telling what a wealthy man Mr. Bangs was, the principal owner of the Company; what great influence he had at Washington; what an eminent and experienced Washington lobbyist he was; what a great friend and how much influence he had with Senators Stewart and Nye who they claimed kept me in my present position. Finally Mr. Bangs himself stopped me when I was taking an evening walk and attempted to talk with me about the case. He said he wanted me to consider well my opinion. Finally Mr. Bangs told in a public saloon that unless I gave him a new trial he would go to Washington and have me removed. It was undoubtedly expected that I would hear all these things. So great an excitement did they create that about every man in that little dilapidated village assembled in their little dilapidated court room as I afterward learned "to see if the Judge would weaken to this wealthy, distinguished and experienced Washington lobbyist." I believe that the mother of the dec'd. was the adm^r. but his father who was the principal heir was managing the case. He had been a soldier in Gen. Cass' regiment during the War of 1812 and was very old and very poor. So poor he could not pay the clerk's fees or board at a hotel. The object of the defts. seems to have been to protract the litigation and try and wear out the old man. Sir, I believe I was uninfluenced by the threats of the rich and powerful or by the pleadings of the old and poor. I decided what I then thought the law to be and what after mature reflection I now think law. The next night after this decision, overruling their motion for a new trial, Mr. Bangs and his friends had a meeting at which it was agreed that Mr. Bangs should undertake my removal and Mr. Phelps should furnish the necessary affidavits. Mr. Phelps could not write an affidavit which could affect my character in any way in the county where he has lived five years. Mr. Phelps has occasion to feel that I am not altogether charitable in regard to some of his shortcomings. When I issued the order staying proceedings in this cause it was on the condition that defts. would give a bond in the sum of $5,000 to save the plff. harmless. Mr. Phelps, contrary to the rules of practice in this Territory, went on that bond himself and procured a Mr. Trask, a very respectable citizen, to go on it with him, promising him "to take his name off the bond" when Mr. Clark should arrive. And sure enough when Mr. Clark arrived he got the bond from the deputy clerk who was a friend of his after it had become a record of the court and erased Mr. Trask's name and inserted Mr. Clark's. I did not learn this until I was about to adjourn court when I took occasion to say to him that I considered his conduct very unprofessional, to say the least. Mr. Phelps may feel that he has some incentives to blacken my reputation as his own is somewhat at stake. If I remember correctly the judicial system of Massachusetts, you have presided over Nisi Prius Courts. Did you never meet a class of attys. whose innate stupidity was often the occasion of their clients loosing their causes and who seemed to think that there was no other way of preserving their own reputation than by declaring that it was the judge who was stupid who ruled against them? If you never met that class of lawyers I must exclaim that your judicial career must have been as happy and blessed as it was honorable and distinguished. Perhaps Mr. Bangs is not to blame for his opinion of me as his mind has been undoubtedly poisoned by Mr. Phelps.

I have never refused to sign any bill of exceptions presented to me by Mr. Phelps. I think I have given the defts. a fair hearing. There is one matter I had forgotten. I do not now remember that there was any affidavit filed in that motion for a new trial; that any deft. or witness had been stopped by the R.R. being blockaded by snow; that any of them had attempted to come and had been so prevented. If Mr. Clark had been so prevented a telegram would have reached his attys. There is a telegraphic office about seventy miles from Bannock to which a stage ran at that time as often as twice a week and I think three times. But at all events if Mr. Clark

could not have testified to more than was in his affidavit it would
not have changed the judgment a particle.

If I abused the discretion vested in me, that abuse of discretion can
be reviewed in a higher court. If I committed error in Law they
have their remedy. The case involves a sufficient amount to permit
them to appeal it to the Supreme Court of the United States where
old man Carhart is too poor to follow them. Any cause involving
over one thousand dollars can be carried to that Court from Territorial Courts.

In conclusion permit me to say that to a man of any sensitiveness
it is extremely annoying to know that a man with so poor a reputation as Mr. Phelps can go to Washington and secretly file charges in
one of the highest departments of the Government affecting his
reputation as an officer and his honor as a man and he not entitled
to any notice of them. If fortune favors him, as in my case, some
acquaintance who loves justice may accidentally learn them and
notify him.

In relation to the other charges I do not know whether I ought
to make any reply to them or not. Perhaps however as similar
charges were made against me last winter by a crowd of men, many
of whom I never saw and who knew nothing of me, I had better do
so. "I appointed a Democrat Clerk." True. I left to the bar which
had recommended me for this position the privilege of selecting a
clerk. They selected Mr. Newcomer, a Democrat, who already filled
the place. My predecessor, Judge Williston, had appointed him and
no one who knew the judge would doubt his Republicanism or honesty. "I removed him and appointed in his place Mr. O'Bannon who
had been removed by Pres. Grant from the place of Register of the
Land office for this Territory." True. I have known Mr. O'Bannon
for years. He is a Republican and as honest and upright a man as
there is in the whole Country. He is an educated man and fully
competent to fill the place, and you know that every man can't fill
the place of Clerk of a Court. Had Pres. Grant known him as long
as I have he would not have removed him, I believe. "I was a miner
when Pres. Johnson appointed me." This is false. But I have mined
in my time, and am rather proud of it. I mined in this county for
about four months in 1866, which is about the sum of all the
physical labor I ever performed. It gave me better health and I am
thankful. Before that time I had filled the place of district atty. in

Nevada and for a time a judicial position there. I had quite an extensive practice in Idaho and even while mining here attended to a few causes and formed the acquaintance of most of the members of this bar. Before that I had been recommended for the position of chief justice of Idaho. "I am not a sound Republican." I was born in the state of Maine. I never have traced my ancestry father back than to Cape Cod among the Pilgrims. My people ever since I can remember held anti-slavery views. I prepared for College at a little academy at Denmark, Iowa a place which was settled by a "Yankee Abolition Congregational Colony." I heard on the average while there three prayers a day for about two years and I don't think I ever heard one that there was not a petition something like this "that the Lord would arouse with his might and have his good right arm and strike the shackles from our poor oppressed bondbrothers in the South." What Collegiate education I possess I received at Antioch College, Ohio during the time Horace Mann was president of that institution. I studied law with Judge Miller a Kentucky Emancipationist. I graduated at the Cambridge Law School. I am a Unitarian in Religion and if with all these associations I have failed to turn out a Republican I think I can justly claim to be composed of unimpressible cast iron material and that it was preordained that I should be a Democrat—I never voted a Democratic ticket in my life nor my father nor my grandfather before me. I was one of the movers in organizing the first Grant club ever organized in Iowa. To the meeting, at which that club was organized, the letter of Mr. Wilson then Member of Congress from Iowa and chairman of the Judiciary Committee of the House of Representatives was read urging the nomination of Pres. Grant. I wrote the constitution of that club myself. The last political speech I ever made was to that Club urging the Election of Pres. Grant, and this was after I had been nominated for the position I now hold. How did it happen that with such a political record Pres. Johnson came to nominate me? Pres. Johnson did not know me. Mr. Cavanaugh the delegate in Congress from this Territory did not know me, but the bar of this county recommended me and upon this he secured my nomination. I never sought the position. I did not know I was to be nominated until I received a letter from my friend Mr. Clagett an atty. of this place informing [me] of that fact and requesting me to accept the position and use my influence to secure my confirmation as they wished a lawyer who understood something of this code practice and the class of litigation in this country. I was then practicing law at Keokuk, Iowa where my father resides. Judge Miller kindly telegraphed a recommendation of me to Senator Harlan who is a friend of some of my connections and I was confirmed. There are quite a number of persons at Washington who know my character for honesty and truth. Among them I will name Hon. Geo. W. McCrary who has been my intimate personal friend for years; Hon. I. B. Howell of the U.S. Senate who has known me for over twenty years; Judge Miller with whom I studied law and Gen. Belknap, Sec. of War. Understand me, I claim nothing as a politician. I have taken no part in politics in this Territory and don't propose to as long as I am a judge. I have held more terms of court and transacted more business during about the year and a half I have been on the bench in this Territory than any other judge who was ever in it in the same length of time. I do not know that an atty. save for Phelps has filed a charge against me. If you desire the record and affidavits please have me notified and I will forward them as soon as I can procure a transcript.

I beg your pardon for so long a letter. Not having the specific charges made I have written the whole history of the case as I now remember it. Mr. Blake wrote me what he could remember of the charges.

Yours truly,
Hiram Knowles

To
    The Hon. E. R. Hoar
        Atty. General of the United States
        Washington
            D.C.

Notes

Chapter 1: "Yesterday's Villains"

1 Howard R. Lamar, "Carpetbaggers Full of Dreams: A Functional View of the Arizona Pioneer Politician," *Arizona and the West* 7 (Autumn 1965) : 188.
2 The most concise and extensive commentary on trans-Mississippi territorial government is still Earl S. Pomeroy's *The Territories and the United States, 1861–1890*. Though Pomeroy recognized the adversities faced by the courts as well as the deficiencies of their design, he concluded that the judiciary was "one of the weakest parts" of territorial administration (p. 61). In the introduction to the 1969 edition (University of Washington Press), Pomeroy comments on recent territorial scholarship and discusses dimensions which he would add if he were writing the book now.
3 Richard N. Current, "Carpetbaggers Reconsidered," in *A Festschrift for Frederick B. Artz*, ed. David H. Pinckney and Theodore Ropp, pp. 156–57; idem, *Three Carpetbag Governors*, p. xi.
4 Lamar, "Carpetbaggers," p. 188.
5 Ibid.
6 William M. Neil, "The American Territorial System since the Civil War: A Summary Analysis," *Indiana Magazine of History* 60 (September 1964) : 219–40.
7 Earl S. Pomeroy, "Toward a Reorientation of Western History: Continuity and Environment," *Mississippi Valley Historical Review* 41 (March 1955) : 579–600. A decade earlier Pomeroy had described the territories as a "vehicle of American Institutions" and as areas of experimentation and modification in "The Territory as a Frontier Institution," *The Historian* 7 (Autumn 1944) : 41.
8 Pomeroy, "Toward a Reorientation of Western History," p. 583.
9 Ray A. Billington, "Introduction," in *The American West: An Appraisal*, edited by Robert G. Ferris, pp. 8–12.
10 Ray A. Billington, "The Frontier and I," *Western Historical Quarterly* 1 (January 1970) : 5–20.
11 Pomeroy, *The Territories*, p. 51.

12 The weaknesses of the system are outlined in Pomeroy, *The Territories,* pp. 151–56.

13 While a legal heritage within a family is properly a source of pride, this type of publication usually does not deal with the operational achievements of these men.

14 W. Turrentine Jackson, "Territorial Papers of Wyoming in the National Archives," *Annals of Wyoming* 16 (January 1944) : 45–55. Students of other territories of the same period would benefit by reading this analysis prior to planning their research.

15 Copies of the Executive Proceedings were rendered semiannually to the secretary of state. After 1873 the governor's "Annual Reports" were incorporated in the *Reports of the Secretary of the Interior.* But even more important are newspaper accounts and, in many instances, letterpress books of official correspondence.

16 Wilbur F. Stone, "History of the Appellate Courts of Colorado in Early Days" (An address before the Denver Bar Association, April 5 1905), *Colorado Reports* 34 : xxiv.

17 Richard B. Morris, "The Courts, the Law, and Social History," in *Essays in Legal History in Honor of Felix Frankfurter,* edited by Morris D. Forkosch, p. 409.

18 Kenneth N. Owens, "Research Opportunities in Western Territorial History," *Arizona and the West* 8 (Spring 1966) : 7–18.

19 Ibid.; Howard R. Lamar, *The Far Southwest 1846–1912: A Territorial History,* pp. 1–20.

20 Owens, "Research Opportunities," p. 8. The viewpoint of territorial residents is expressed by Decius S. Wade in "Self-Government in the Territories," *The International Review* 6 (1879) : 299–303. Wade was chief justice of the Montana Territorial Supreme Court when this article was published.

Chapter 2: "For Want of Judicial Organization"

1 Appropriate federal statutes are conveniently compiled in *Organic Acts for the Territories of the United States with Notes thereon, Compiled from Statutes at Large of the United States* (see bibliography for full citation).

2 Max Farrand, *The Legislation of Congress for the Government of the Organized Territories of the United States, 1789–1895,* p. 38. Farrand included a chronological summary of each act affecting the territories through 1895.

3 Ibid., pp. 39–45.

4 See the remarks of Senator Isaac P. Christiancy of Michigan, in *Congressional Record,* 45th Cong., 2d sess., 1878, 7, pt. 2 : 1204.

5 Senator Henry L. Dawes of Massachusetts, ibid., p. 1206.

6 *Organic Acts.* Colorado was established as a territory on February 28, 1861; Montana on May 26, 1864; and Wyoming on July 25, 1868.

7 The burden imposed on a court which heard cases in law as well as in equity is discussed in chap. 9.

8 Congress passed an act on March 2, 1867, which changed this procedure in Montana. See *Statutes at Large*, 14 : 426–27.

9 The characteristics and qualities of the men who served these courts are reviewed in chap. 6.

10 *Helena Daily Independent*, December 2, 1883.

11 The *Laramie Daily Sentinel* (January 29, 1878) praised Senator Roscoe Conkling's unsuccessful attempt to push through Congress legislation reforming the courts. See "Report of the Governor of Wyoming," in *Report of the Secretary of Interior*, Exec. Doc., House of Representatives, 46th Cong., 3d sess., 1880, Serial 1960, pp. 525–34; Memorial and Joint Resolution to the United States Congress, Wyoming Territory, *General Laws* (Sixth Session), pp. 159–60.

12 *Statutes at Large*, 24 : 138.

13 Supreme Court Opinions of Territory of Colorado, vol. 1, p. 4 (unpublished docket books), Colorado State Archives. Interesting anecdotes of early Colorado legal history can be found in Forbes Parkhill, *The Law Goes West.*

14 See Judge Henry N. Blake to Atty Gen. Charles Devens, January 23, 1880, in the Justice Department's Source-Chronological Files, Montana, Record Group 60, National Archives. (The Source-Chronological Files will hereafter be cited as S-C Files, followed by the abbreviation of the pertinent territory.) See also Schuyler Crosby to Major Martin Maginnis, March 8, 1884 (Maginnis Papers, Montana State Historical Society); and *Proceedings and Debates of the Constitutional Convention Held in Helena, Montana Territory, July 4, 1889–August 17, 1889* (Helena: State Publishing Co., 1921), pp. 286–87.

15 Curtis Nettels, "The Mississippi Valley and the Federal Judiciary, 1807–1837," *Mississippi Valley Historical Review* 12 (September 1925) : 202–26.

16 See *Organic Acts* and "Governor's Message to the 7th Legislative Assembly of Montana Territory," State Department Territorial Papers, Montana, Record Group 59, National Archives. (The Territorial Papers will hereafter be cited as SDTP, followed by the abbreviation of the pertinent territory.)

17 "Sagebrushing" was the gerrymandering of judicial districts. In chap. 5 the ramifications of this phenomenon are analyzed, and chap. 7 contains a detailed examination of one particular incident of sagebrushing.

18 *Statutes at Large,* 14 : 426.

19 Clark C. Spence, "The Territorial Bench in Montana: 1864–1889," *Montana the Magazine of Western History* 13 (January 1963) : 61. The innovations that were made despite this inflexibility are discussed in chap. 9.

20 Theodore Brantly, "Judicial Department," *Contributions to the Historical Society of Montana* 4 (1903) : 113.

21 Few histories of Colorado or Montana omit these courts. One of the briefest and most descriptive accounts of Miners' Courts is W. Y. Pemberton, "Montana's Pioneer Courts," *Contributions to the Historical Society of Montana* 8 (1917) : 99–104.

22 Gilpin to Atty Gen. Edward Bates, August 2, and October 8, 1861, Justice Department, Attorney General's Papers, Colorado, Record Group 60, National Archives. (The Attorney General's Papers will hereafter be cited as AGP, followed by the abbreviation of the pertinent territory.)

23 Weld to Seward, August 2, 1861, 2 letters (AGP Colo.). The secretary of state had general responsibility for the administration of the territories until March 1, 1873, when Congress transferred this trust to the secretary of interior.

24 See the following: Petition to President Andrew Johnson submitted by A. A. Paddock on July 21, 1868 (SDTP Wyo.); petition from Canon City and Pueblo City, no date (AGP Colo.); petition from Pueblo City, no date, Justice Department, Appointment Papers, Colorado, Record Group 60, National Archives. (The Appointment Papers will hereafter be cited as AP, followed by the abbreviation of the pertinent territory.)

25 *Message of Governor Campbell to the First Legislative Assembly of Wyoming Territory.*

26 T. A. Larson, *History of Wyoming,* pp. 64–71; Lewis L. Gould, *Wyoming: A Political History, 1868–1896,* pp. 1–8; *Congressional Globe,* January 5, 1865, 38th Cong., 2d sess., p. 116; *Statutes at Large,* 15 : 128–83.

27 *Cheyenne Daily Leader,* June 4, 1868.

28 E. P. Snow to Seward, August 8, 1868; O. T. B. Williams to Johnson, August 31, 1868; Sen. James Harlan of Iowa to Seward, September 25, 1868 (SDTP Wyo.).

29 *Rocky Mountain News* (Denver), July 8, 1861; ibid., July 9–27, 1861.

30 Howe to Atty Gen. E. R. Hoar, May 22, 1870 (AGP Wyo.).

31 Quoted from "Biographical Sketch of Hezekiah L. Hosmer," *Contributions to the Historical Society of Montana* 3 (1900) : 290.

32 Howe to Hoar, May 22, 1870 (AGP Wyo.).

33 See *Cheyenne Daily Leader,* July 20, September 8, October 15, 1869; and the Andrew J. Fisk Diary, April 1, 1869 (Montana State Historical Society).

34 The classic treatment of vigilantes (it appeared first as a newspaper series in 1865) is Thomas J. Dimsdale *The Vigilantes of Montana or Popular Justice in the Rocky Mountains.*

35 Munson to Atty Gen. James Speed, February 26, and March 6, 1866 (AGP Mont.).

36 *Laramie Daily Sentinel,* September 20, 1872; Munson to W. F. Sanders (Munson File, MSS Collection, Montana State Historical Society).

37 *Cheyenne Daily Leader,* December 15, 1869; Howe to Hoar, May 22, 1870 (AGP Wyo.).

38 *Laramie Daily Sentinel,* October 11, 1870.

39 *Report of the Secretary of Interior,* Exec. Doc., House of Representatives, 45th Cong., 3d sess., 1878, Serial 1850, p. 1175; see, for example, J. H. Triggs *History and Directory of Laramie City Wyoming Territory,* p. 15.

40 "Hezekiah L. Hosmer," pp. 292–95; "Honorable John W. Kingman," *Annals of Wyoming* 14 (July 1942) : 224.

41 "Hezekiah L. Hosmer," p. 291.

42 *Statutes at Large,* 12 : 172, 13 : 85, 15 : 178.

43 A more detailed account of the activities of Colorado's early territorial supreme court is in John D. W. Guice, "Colorado's Territorial Courts," *Colorado Magazine* 45 (Summer 1968) : 204–24.

44 *Weekly Commonwealth and Republican* (Denver), August 20, 1863. How the law evolved to meet Rocky Mountain conditions is discussed in chap. 9.

45 Spence, "The Territorial Bench in Montana," p. 26.

46 "Hezekiah L. Hosmer," pp. 292–93; Montana Territory, *General Laws* (First Session), p. 356; Montana Territory, Council Journal (First Session), p. 356; Montana Territory, Council Journal (First Session), pp. 17–18.

47 "Governor Green Clay Smith's Message," *Contributions to the Historical Society of Montana* 5 (1904) : 133; Montana Territory, *General Laws* (Fourth Session), pp. 136–233.

48 Literally hundreds of letters concerning court facilities are located in Record Group 60, National Archives. They are most abundant in the Justice Department's Source-Chronological Files.

49 John C. Friend, "Early History of Carbon County," *Annals of Wyoming* 15 (July 1943) : 283; Parkhill, *The Law Goes West,* pp. 11–31; *Rocky Mountain News* (Denver), July 9, 1861.

50 A. K. McClure, *Three Thousand Miles through the Rocky Mountains,* p. 332.

51 Kingman to Atty Gen. George H. Williams, no date (S-C Files Wyo.).

52 See chap. 4.

53 Judge W. J. Jones to Asst Sec. Int. W. T. Otto, September 25, 1869 (S-C Files Wyo.).

54 See, for example, U.S. Marshal Copeland Townshend to Sec. Int. C. B. Smith, May 18, 1862 (S-C Files Colo.). Townshend even enclosed a layout of the proposed facilities.

55 Leases dated September 15, and July 30, 1866, between William Thompson and the United States. See U.S. Marshal George W. Pinney to Sec. Int. James Harlan, March 17, 1866, and Comptroller R. W. Taylor to Otto, February 26, 1869 (S-C Files Mont.).

56 Potts to Sec. State Hamilton Fish, December 27, 1870 (SDTP Mont.); U.S. Marshal W. F. Wheeler to Atty Gen. Edwards Pierrepoint, November 10, 1875 (S-C Files Wyo.); Lt. Col. E. B. Carling, Depot Quartermaster at Fort D. A. Russell, to Otto, July 17, 1869 (S-C Files Wyo.); U.S. Marshal Church Howe to Sec. Int. (title only), July 7, 1869 (S-C Files Wyo.).

57 Messages concerning delays and leaves of absence comprise a high percentage of SDTP. See chap. 3.

58 Potts to Fish, February 27, 1871 (SDTP Mont.); Statement rendered to the United States by L. B. France, June 12, 1862, for services as special U.S. Atty, endorsed by Judge Hall (AGP Colo.); Hosmer to Henry Hamburg, October 8, 1866 (AGP Mont.).

59 Justice Decius S. Wade to Atty Gen. Benjamin H. Brewster, August 2, 1882 (S-C Files Mont.).

60 Hall to Atty Gen. Edward Bates, August 17, 1861 (AGP Colo.).

61 Edgerton to Johnson, March 27, 1866 (SDTP Mont.); U.S. Atty Edward B. Neally to W. F. Sanders in Bath, Maine, April 13, 1866 (Sanders Papers, Montana State Historical Society); "The Mining Law of Montana Territory," *Montana Radiator* (Helena), February 17, 1866.

62 Wyoming Territory, *Council Journal* (Fifth Session), pp. 16–17. Nearly a decade passed before Colorado's supreme court decisions were published in Moses Hallett, *Reports of Cases at Law and in Chancery Determined in the Supreme Court of Colorado Territory to the Present Time* (Albany, N.Y.: Weed, Parsons and Co., 1872).

63 Peter Wikoff, "The Bench and Bar of Colorado," *Magazine of Western History* 9 (March 1889): 606–07; Clerk W. D. Armstrong of the First District of Colorado Territory to Seward, April 14, 1863 (S-C Files Colo.); Joint Memorial to Congress, March 24, 1866 (Montana Territory, *General Laws* [Second Session], p. 47); Harlan to Sanders, April 19, 1866 (Sanders Papers).

64 Bids from major publishing houses with other pertinent correspondence are in the Interior Department Territorial Papers, Montana and Wyoming, Record Group 48, National Archives. Inventory signed by Wyoming Supreme Court Clerk J. W. Hutchinson, June 25, 1871 (ibid.); Wyoming Territory, *General Laws* (Sixth Session), p. 140.

65 *Report of the Secretary of Interior*, Exec. Doc., House of Representa-

tives, 49th Cong., 1st sess., 1885, Serial 2379, p. 1213; Wyoming Territory, *General Laws* (Ninth Session), p. 424.

Chapter 3: "The Juggle of Habeas Corpus"

1 Gilpin to Atty Gen. Edward Bates, October 8, 1861, and Gilpin to Sec. State William H. Seward, November 1, 1861 (AGP Colo.).

2 Paul H. Giddens, "Letters of S. Newton Pettis, Associate Justice of the Colorado Supreme Court, Written in 1861," *Colorado Magazine* 15 (January 1938) : 3–14; Hall to Seward, May 26, 1862 (SDTP Colo.).

3 Hall to Seward, October 30, 1861 (SDTP Colo.); *Rocky Mountain News* (hereafter cited as *RMN*), February 4, 1862.

4 Gilpin to Bates, October 8, 1861, and Gilpin to Seward, November 1, 1861 (AGP Colo.).

5 Gilpin to Hall, July 29, 1861 (SDTP Colo.).

6 Most Colorado territorial court records are in custody of the Records Management Service of the General Services Administration, Denver Federal Center. However, civil-case records for the First Judicial District as well as several volumes of territorial *Supreme Court Opinions* are in the Colorado State Archives.

7 Hall to Lincoln, October 9, 1861, in Colorado State Archives, Territorial Collection, photographic copies of items from the Lincoln Papers in the Library of Congress (hereafter cited as CSA-LP); Hall to Seward, October 30, 1861, and Hall to Seward, May 26, 1862 (SDTP Colo.); Hall to Bates May 24 1862 (AGP Colo.).

8 *RMN*, September 3, 1861. A typical report of one of these numerous arrests can be found in *RMN*, September 30, 1861.

9 Docket Folders 18–60, Records of the First Judicial District, 1861, Record Group 21, Denver Federal Records Center, Denver, Colorado.

10 Gilpin to Seward, November 1, 1861, and Gilpin to Bates, October 8, 1861 (AGP Colo.); Hall to Lincoln, September 13, 1861, and Hall to Gilpin, October 9, 1861 (CSA-LP).

11 Hall to Bates, July 22, and November 14, 1862, and July 2, 1863 (AGP Colo.); Hall to Bates, May 20, 1863 (CSA-LP); Hall to Seward, October 30, 1861, and Hall to Seward, April 25 1862 (SDTP Colo.); Hall to Bates, November 20, 1861 (AGP Colo.).

12 Hall to Lincoln, October 9, 1861 (CSA-LP).

13 SDTP, vol. 1., fol. 60.

14 Bates to George A. Caffery, U.S. Atty, Eastern District of Pa., June 4, 1861 (Atty Gen. Letter Book No. B-2, 744, Record Group 60, National Archives); Hall to Seward, May 26, 1862 (SDTP Colo.).

15 *Weekly Commonwealth and Republican* (Denver), August 20, 1863.

16 Gilpin to Bates, November 1, 1861 (AGP Colo.).

17 Executive order, Lewis L. Weld, February 5, 1862, and related documents (AGP Colo.).

18 Armour to Bates, February 8, 1862 (AGP Colo.).

19 Hall to Seward, October 30, 1861 (SDTP Colo.).

20 Hall to Lincoln, October 9, 1861 (CSA-LP), Hall to Seward, November 1, 1861 (AGP Colo.).

21 *RMN*, November 1, 1861.

22 The balance of the Armour affair is covered in chaps. 5 and 6. See the poster by James M. Cavanaugh, dated September 22, 1863 (Western Historical Collection, Norlin Library, University of Colorado).

23 *RMN*, June 14, October 25 and 30, December 17, 1861; Pettis to Lincoln, May 31 1862 (AGP Colo.); Register of Territorial Accounts no. 1, Colo., 1–2, Record Group 60, National Archives.

24 See Giddens, "Letters of S. Newton Pettis" and the biographical synopsis compiled for the Colorado State Historical Society by the Pennsylvania State Library, March 26, 1936, Biographical Cross Index, Colorado State Historical Society.

25 Pettis to Lincoln, May 31, 1862 (AGP Colo.); *RMN*, June 14, and July 3, 1861.

26 *RMN*, December 7, 1861.

27 Letter signed "H" (Denver, November 27, 1861), to Messrs. Knapp and Peck. This letter had been printed in Auburn's *Daily Journal and Union* on December 10, 1861, and was reprinted with editorial comment by *RMN* on May 15, 1862.

28 *RMN*, May 30, 1862.

29 Petitions for removal dated July 14, 1863 (AP Colo.).

30 These topics are discussed fully in later chapters.

31 Hall to Bates, August 17, and October 27, 1861 (AGP Colo.).

32 Atty Gen. Benjamin H. Brewster to Justice E. J. Conger, January 18, 1884 (Judges and Clerks Letters Sent, II, 272, Record Group 60, National Archives); Justice Hezekiah L. Hosmer to Atty Gen. James Speed, May 29, 1865 (AGP Mont.).

33 Gould, *Wyoming*, p. 43.

34 W. Y. Pemberton, "Changing the Names of Edgerton County," *Contributions to the Historical Society of Montana* 8 (1917) : 326.

35 Robert Edwin Albright, "The Relations of Montana with the Federal Government, 1864–1889" (Ph.D. diss., Stanford University, 1933), pp. 55–57.

36 Charles S. Ashley "Governor Ashley's Biography and Messages," *Contributions to the Historical Society of Montana* 6 (1907) : 191; Albright, "The Relations of Montana," p. 52.

37 McClure, *Three Thousand Miles*, p. 380.

38 "Governor Edgerton's First Message to the First Legislative Assembly

of the Territory of Montana," *Contributions to the Historical Society of Montana* 3 (1900) : 347–48; *Statutes at Large,* 14 : 426–27.

39 Albright, "The Relations of Montana," p. 78.

40 "Honorable John W. Kingman," p. 224; Campbell to W. A. Carter, December 1, 1869 (Campbell Letterbook, 242, Wyoming State Archives and Historical Department, Cheyenne, Wyoming); Petition of March 22, 1890, to President Harrison (AP Wyo.).

41 *Frontier Index* (Green River City), August 11 and 18, 1868.

42 Ibid., August 11, 1868.

Chapter 4: "Making Bricks Without Straw"

1 Territorial finances are summarized in Pomeroy, *The Territories,* pp. 28–50.

2 Chief Justice Benjamin F. Hall to Atty Gen. Edward Bates, August 17, 1861 (AGP Colo.).

3 *Statutes at Large,* 12 : 172, 13 : 85, 15 : 178.

4 Ibid., 14 : 426–27, 16 : 152.

5 Ibid., 15 : 178, 313.

6 Ibid., 16 : 152.

7 Meagher to Johnson, January 20, 1866 (Johnson Papers, Library of Congress). Treasury Department records indicate Meagher was not entirely accurate. Hezekiah L. Hosmer, first chief justice of Montana's territorial supreme court, was paid for all of 1864–65 (Miscellaneous Treasury Report No. 154578, *Register of Territorial Accounts,* Montana, Record Group 217, National Archives).

8 Hall to Bates, January 9, 1863 (AGP Colo.); Hall to Sec. State William H. Seward, January 19, 1863 (SDTP Colo.); Justice William H. Gale to Atty Gen. James Speed, February 10, 1866 (AGP Colo.).

9 *Statutes at Large,* 19 : 309, 21 : 225.

10 Resolutions are found in the official proceedings of the three legislative assemblies.

11 *Congressional Globe,* 41st Cong., 2d sess., 1870, p. 1336; ibid., 42d Cong., 3d sess. 1873 p. 412; *Helena Weekly Herald* December 5, 1867.

12 Montana Territory, *General Laws* (First Session), p. 716.

13 Hall to Seward, April 25, 1862 (SDTP Colo.). For examples of prices see Colin B. Goodykoontz, "Colorado as Seen by a Home Missionary, 1863–1868," *Colorado Magazine* 12 (March 1935) : 60–69. Hall to Bates, October 27, 1861, and Hall to Seward, October 27, 1861 (AGP Colo.).

14 Hosmer to Sanders, January 24, 1867 (Sanders Papers, Montana State Historical Society). Though newspaper advertisements reveal the cost of living, conditions are concisely summarized in J. R. Boyce, *Facts about Montana Territory and the Way to Get There.*

15 Moonlight to Lamar, November 11, 1887 (Moonlight Letterpress Book, Wyoming State Archives and Historical Department).

16 Hosmer to Atty Gen. Henry Stanbery, October 8, 1866 (AGP Mont.).

17 *Helena Weekly Herald,* November 28, 1867.

18 "Report of the Governor of Wyoming," in *Report of the Secretary of Interior,* Exec. Doc., House of Representatives, 46th Cong., 3d sess., 1880, Serial 1960 p. 534; *Congressional Globe,* 41st Cong., 2d sess., 1870, p. 1336.

19 McLeary to Cleveland, February 13, 1888 (AP Mont.).

20 *Laramie Daily Sentinel,* June 7, 1870.

21 Montana Territory, *General Laws* (First Session), p. 391; ibid. (Second Session), p. 3. The political implications of this act are discussed in chap. 5.

22 Gov. Benjamin F. Potts to Lyman Trumbull, February 17, 1871 (Potts Letter Books, 1870–73, Montana State Historical Society).

23 *Congressional Globe,* 41st Cong., 3d sess., 1871, p. 971.

24 The first session voted increased compensation, but the second repealed it (Wyoming Territory, *General Laws* [First Session], p. 415; ibid. [Second Session], p. 120; ibid. [Ninth Session], p. 425; ibid. [Tenth Session], p. 207). "Governor's Message to the Seventh Legislative Assembly" (SDTP Mont.). Potts is quoted in Pomeroy, *The Territories,* p. 49.

25 *Statutes at Large,* 2 : 788.

26 Gale to Acting Atty Gen. J. H. Ashton, July 19, 1866 (AGP Colo.); *RMN,* May 12, 1866.

27 Servis to President Grant, July 15, 1875 (S-C Files Mont.).

28 U.S. Marshal William F. Wheeler to Devens, April 6, 1878 (ibid.).

29 In reality it was difficult to apportion expenses. The federal government was to operate the district courts when they sat as United States courts, but the territories were to pay for the expenses of cases in their jurisdictions.

30 Gould, *Wyoming,* p. 264.

31 Hall to Bates, August 17, 1861; Edgerton to President Andrew Johnson, March 27, 1866 (SDTP Mont.).

32 Atty Gen. George H. Williams to U.S. Marshal M. A. Shaffanburg, February 19, 1873, Attorney General's Instruction Book, No. C, p. 629, Record Group 60, National Archives. (The Attorney General's Instruction Books will hereafter be cited as AGIB.) Williams to Wheeler, January 10, 1873 (AGIB No. C, p. 574).

33 Acting Atty Gen. B. H. Bristow to U.S. Atty E. P. Johnson, April 29, 1872 (AGIB No. C, p. 287); U.S. Marshal A. G. Botkin to Devens, February 24, 1880 (S-C Files Mont.).

34 Bristow to Wheeler, January 7, 1871 (AGIB No. B1, p. 250); "Governor

Green Clay Smith's Message," p. 134; U.S. Marshal Copeland Townshend to Sec. Int. C. B. Smith, September 12, 1861 (S-C Files Colo.).

35 First Comptroller R. W. Taylor to Sec. Int. James Harlan, March 16, 1866 (S-C Files Mont.); U.S. Marshal George W. Pinney to Harlan, March 17, 1866 (ibid.).

36 Justice Hiram Knowles to Devens, February 15, 1878 (S-C Files Mont.).

37 *Statutes at Large*, 10 : 167–68, 16 : 363, 21 : 43.

38 S-C Files for Colo., Mont., and Wyo.

39 Grand jury report of April 10, 1876, enclosed in letter from Knowles to Atty Gen. Edwards Pierrepont, April 13, 1876 (S-C Files Mont.).

40 U.S. Atty M. C. Brown to Atty Gen. Benjamin H. Brewster, December 30, 1882 (S-C Files Wyo.).

41 *Statutes at Large*, 12 : 172, 13 : 85, 15 : 178.

42 Montana Territory, *General Laws* (Third Session), p. 49.

43 "Governor's Message," Wyoming Territory, *Council Journal*, pp. 22–23. A similar attitude was displayed by Governor Benjamin F. Potts of Montana; see Potts to Sec. Int. Columbus Delano, April 1, 1873, Interior Department Territorial Papers, Mont., Record Group 48, National Archives. (The Interior Department's Territorial Papers will hereafter be cited as IDTP.) Brown to Brewster, December 30, 1882 (S-C Files Wyo.); *RMN*, June 18, 1866.

44 Pomeroy, *The Territories*, p. 31.

45 Veto message of Governor Potts to the Council of the Territory of Montana on the return of Council Bill No. 29, February 21, 1879 (IDTP Mont.).

Chapter 5: "Meanness, Political Chicanery, &
Rotten Machinations"

1 *Statutes at Large*, 12 : 172, 13 : 85, 15 : 178. The nature of territorial courts and judicial tenure are analyzed in considerable detail in John Welling Smurr, "Territorial Constitutions: A Legal History of the Frontier Governments Erected by Congress in the American West. 1787–1900" (Ph.D. diss., Indiana University, 1960).

2 Gould, *Wyoming*.

3 AP for Colo., Mont., and Wyo.

4 Giddens, "Letters of S. Newton Pettis," pp. 3–4.

5 Spence, "The Territorial Bench in Montana," p. 28; *The National Cyclopedia of American Biography* (New York: James T. White and Co., 1906), 13 : 24.

6 Christian Eyster to Edgar Cowan, U.S. Senate, Pennsylvania, July 27, 1866 (AP Colo.).

7 Thomas S. Kane to President Grant, August 17, 1871 (AP Wyo.).

8 Wade, "Self-Government," p. 306.

9 W. E. Cullen, Chairman of the Montana Democratic Territorial Committee, to Atty Gen. A. H. Garland, November 7, 1885 (AP Mont.); Coburn to Garland, December 5, 1885 (ibid.); Petitions from Yellowstone, Dawson, and Custer Counties (ibid.).

10 Chief Justice J. S. Fisher to Atty Gen. George H. Williams, September 23, 1872 (S-C Files Wyo.).

11 Ibid.; J. H. Platt, Jr., Secretary of the Union Republican Congressional Executive Committee, to Hamilton Fish, October 13, 1870 (SDTP Wyo.).

12 Judge A. C. Campbell, "Fading Memories," *Annals of Wyoming* 15 (January 1943) : 43.

13 Helen Fitzgerald Sanders, *A History of Montana,* 1 : 592; Spence, "The Territorial Bench in Montana," p. 61.

14 Bangs to Atty Gen. E. R. Hoar, January 28, 1870 (AP Mont.).

15 Christian Mead to Knowles, March 31, 1870 (ibid.).

16 Knowles to Hoar, March 6, 1870 (ibid.). This letter, a classic account of the many problems encountered by the judiciary, appears as app. 2.

17 Ibid. Affidavits of attorneys Sample Orr and Christian Mead, March 30 and 31, 1870 (AP Mont.).

18 McCrary to Hoar, December 14, 1869 (ibid.).

19 Potts to Williams, October 20, 1874 (S-C Files Mont.).

20 Sanders, *History of Montana,* 1 : 595-96; Knowles to Williams, November 4, 1874 (S-C Files Mont.); petition enclosed in letter, Knowles to Williams, November 23, 1874 (ibid.); petitions in letter, Delegate Martin Maginnis to Williams, January 8, 1875 (AP Mont.).

21 *Helena Weekly Independent,* November 20, 1874; Joaquin Miller, *An Illustrated History of the State of Montana,* p. 69.

22 W. L. Hull to Horace Maynard, Congressman from Tennessee, January 22, 1872; James L. Fisk to Maynard, March 21, 1872 (AP Mont.).

23 AP Mont.

24 Fisk to H. G. Brownlow and Maynard, March 20, 1872 (AP Mont.).

25 S-C Files Wyo.

26 Chief Justice John H. Howe to Acting Atty Gen., September 29, 1871 (S-C Files Wyo.); Wilson to Edwards Pierrepont, November 13 and 24, 1875 (AP Wyo.).

27 Undated clipping enclosed in letter, Wilson to Williams, May 5, 1873 (S-C Files Wyo.).

28 Albright, "The Relations of Montana," pp. 98–99. Albright's analysis of early territorial politics in Montana (pp. 50–102) is excellent.

29 The involvement of the judiciary in Wyoming's territorial politics is recognized by Gould.

30 Diaries of John A. Campbell, Wyoming State Archives and Historical Department (hereafter cited as Campbell Diary), June 9, 1869.

31 Campbell to Jones, May 13, 1870 (John A. Campbell Papers, Wyoming State Archives and Historical Department); Gould, *Wyoming*, pp. 32–33. The governor gave campaign expense money to Jones on August 15, and September 2, 6, and 12, 1870 (Campbell Diary).

32 July 20, 1874, Campbell Diary.

33 Larson, *History of Wyoming*, p. 123.

34 Howe to Atty Gen. A. T. Akerman, August 13, 1870 (AGP Wyo.); Kingman to Williams, September 28, 1872 (S-C Files Wyo.).

35 *Cheyenne Daily Leader*, May 18, 1871.

36 Gould, *Wyoming*, pp. 38–48.

37 Thayer to Grant, December 4, 1875 (quoted in Gould, *Wyoming*, pp. 51–52).

38 Michael A. Leeson, ed., *History of Montana, 1739–1885*, p. 320; Masonic correspondence, April 28, 1879; W. C. Clark to Knowles September 11, 1878 (Hiram Knowles Papers, Montana State Historical Society).

39 J. J. Humphrey, "The Political and Social Influences of Freemasonry in Territorial Wyoming, 1870–1885" (M.A. thesis, University of Wyoming, 1964). The first United States attorney, Carey, was a dominant figure in Wyoming's territorial politics both as a justice and as a delegate.

40 December 21, 1869, Campbell Diary; "Honorable John W. Kingman," p. 226.

41 Potts to Fish, September 2, 1870; Akerman to Fish, October 24, 1870 (SDTP Mont.); Potts to Governor John A. Campbell, November 4, 1870 (John A. Campbell Papers, Wyoming State Archives and Historical Department).

42 Potts to Fish, October 11, 1870 (SDTP Mont.).

43 *Statutes at Large*, 13 : 87.

44 Robert G. Athearn, *Thomas Francis Meagher: An Irish Revolutionary in America*.

45 *Montana Post* (Virginia City), December 22, 1866.

46 Ibid., *Statutes at Large*, 14 : 426–27.

47 Meagher to Sec. State William H. Seward, March 12, 1866 (AGP Mont.); *Montana Post* (Virginia City), March 9, 1867.

48 Hosmer to Wilbur F. Sanders, January 24, 1867 (Wilbur F. Sanders Papers, Montana State Historical Society); *Montana Democrat* (Virginia City), August 30, and September 6, 1866; Albright, "The Relations of Montana," p. 99.

49 Montana Territory, *General Laws* (Third Session), p. 45.

50 *Statutes at Large*, 14 : 426–27.

51 For an account of Colorado's most interesting act of sagebrushing, see Guice, "Colorado's Territorial Courts," p. 220. The most celebrated incident in Wyoming Territory is related in chap. 7.

Chapter 6: Judicial Derelicts?

1 Clark C. Spence, "The Territorial Officers of Montana, 1864–1889," *Pacific Historical Review* 30 (May 1961) : 128; see also table 2.

2 Guice, "Colorado's Territorial Courts," pp. 223–24.

3 The most accurate list of territorial justices for Colorado, Montana, and Wyoming appears in app. 1 of Pomeroy's *The Territories.*

4 Bach (initials unidentified) to Alfred C. Harmer, Congressman from Pennsylvania (Territorial Appointment Papers, 1857–1873, Record Group 60, National Archives).

5 Western Historical Collection, Norlin Library, University of Colorado.

6 A vagabond himself, Democrat Cavanaugh was a fortune hunter whose career became part of the territorial history of Minnesota, Colorado, and Montana.

7 Delegate Allen A. Bradford to President Lincoln, August 18, 1862 (AP Colo.).

8 Stone, "The Appellate Courts of Colorado," p. xxv.

9. Unidentified newspaper clipping in Dawson Scrapbooks, 35 : 7, Colorado State Historical Society.

10 Ibid.

11 AP Colo.

12 Committee Report appended to Memorial of the House of Representatives of the Colorado Territorial Assembly, August 14, 1862 (AP Colo.).

13 Petition, Central City, July 25, 1862 (AP Colo.); Evans to Lincoln, August 18, 1862 (ibid.).

14 Stephen S. Harding to Lincoln, July 18, 1864 (CSA-LP).

15 Stone, "The Appellate Courts of Colorado," p. xxv.

16 Parkhill, *The Law Goes West,* endsheets.

17 *The National Cyclopedia of American Biography* (New York: James T. White and Company, 1907), 5 : 515

18 Samuel Bowles, *Across the Continent: A Summer's Journey to the Rocky Mountains, the Mormons, and the Pacific States, with Speaker Colfax,* pp. 60–61.

19 Harding to Lincoln, July 18, 1864.

20 Copy of the grand jury report, including transcripts of the testimony presented to the jury (AP Colo.).

21 Transcript of the proceedings of the People v. Charles F. Holly (AP Colo.); *RMN,* July 25, 1866.

22 Holly to Atty Gen. Henry Stanbery, July 25, 1866, and April 21, 1867 (AGP Colo.); Holly to Stanbery, July 30, 1866 (AP Colo.); Hallett to Stanbery, October 5, 1866 (AGP Colo.).

23 T. C. Everts to Hezekiah L. Hosmer, January 6, 1865, Hezekiah Lord Hosmer MSS, Western Americana Collection, Yale University (hereafter cited as Hosmer MSS).

24 Everts to Hosmer, January 12, 1865 (Hosmer MSS).

25 Giddings to Hosmer, May 5, 1865 (Hosmer MSS).

26 Everts to Hosmer, January 12, 1865 (Hosmer MSS).

27 *Biographical Directory of the American Congress 1774–1961* (Washington: Government Printing Office, 1961), p. 492.

28 "Hezekiah L. Hosmer," pp. 288-89; *Helena Herald,* November 1, 1893; Hezekiah L. Hosmer Papers, Montana State Historical Society.

29 Larson, *History of Wyoming,* p. 70; Hubert H. Bancroft, *History of Washington, Idaho, and Montana, 1845–1889,* p. 654.

30 Merrill G. Burlingame, *The Montana Frontier,* p. 162; Llewellyn L. Callaway, "Something about the Territorial Judges," *Montana Law Review* 4 (Spring 1943) : 9–10.

31 Miller, *History of the State of Montana,* pp. 71–72; *The Montanian* (Virginia City), August 26, 1875.

32 Henry N. Blake, "The First Newspaper of Montana," *Contributions to the Historical Society of Montana* 5 (1904): 253.

33 *Montana Reports,* 1 : 250–72.

34 See Blake's "Historical Address," *Contributions to the Historical Society of Montana* 2 (1896) : 76–87, and his "Tales of an Old Harvard Soldier," *Harvard Alumni Bulletin,* June 16, 1927, pp. 1058–60. Blake edited vol. 1 of *Montana Reports* and was co-editor of vols. 2 and 3.

35 Affidavit, Alexander M. Woolfolk, November 21, 1879 (AP Mont.); E. S. Wilkerson, *Rocky Mountain Gazette* (Helena), to Martin Maginnis, July 15, 1873 (Maginnis Papers, Montana State Historical Society).

36 *The Montanian* (Virginia City), August 26, 1875.

37 Allen A. Bradford, "History of Colorado" (Bancroft Manuscript File, Colorado State Historical Society); William S. Speer and John Henry Brown, eds., *The Encyclopedia of the New West,* pp. 44–45.

38 Dawson Scrapbooks, 7 : 13, 8 : 511, 35 : 7; George Rex Buckman, "An Historical Rocky Mountain Outpost," *The Trail* 7 (April 1915) : 5–16.

39 E. H. Sears to James Harlan, March 12, 1861 (AP Colo.).

40 See Gould, *Wyoming,* and Larson, *History of Wyoming.*

41 That the effectiveness of the well-intentioned was not always great is illustrated in chap. 7, an account of the judicial career of William Ware Peck of Wyoming.

42 Edward L. Munson, "Lyman Ezra Munson," *Contributions to the Historical Society of Montana* 7 (1910) : 199–202; "Editor's Note," ibid., pp. 5, 200; Giddings to Hosmer, May 5, 1865 (Hosmer MSS).

43 *Helena Weekly Herald,* August 6 and 13, 1868.

44 Woolfolk to Atty Gen. Benjamin H. Brewster, February (no day), 1883 (AP Mont.); Wilkerson to Maginnis, July 15, 1873 (Maginnis Papers).

45 Munson to Atty Gen. James Speed, July 19, 1866 (AGP Mont.); *Helena Republican* quoted by the *Montana Post* (Virginia City), October 6, 1866.

46 Munson to Sec. State Hamilton Fish, May 22, 1869 (Appointment Papers, Department of State, Record Group 59, National Archives).

47 *Evening Leader* (New Haven) cited in the *Helena Independent*, March 1, 1908.

48 February 19, 1908.

49 Sanders, *History of Montana*, 1 : 590.

50 Miller, *History of the State of Montana*, p. 69; Sanders, *History of Montana*, 1 : 609; *Helena Independent*, April 7, 1911; Knowles Papers; AP Mont.; Callaway, "Something about the Territorial Judges," pp. 8–9.

51 Freeman Knowles to Hiram Knowles, October 17, 1859 (Knowles Papers).

52 Knowles Papers.

53 Knowles to Angus McDonald, November 20, 1879 (Knowles Papers).

54 AP Mont.

55 William H. Todd to Knowles, July 26, 1909 (Knowles Papers). Todd's descriptions of the effects of Valley Tan deserve repeating. Anyone who had too much contracted "rheumatism of the hair" and had "heads on 'em like pizened pups"—they had to reach "out at arm's length to scratch their ear."

56 *Helena Independent*, April 7, 1911.

57 Sanders, *History of Montana*, 1 : 413, 605; AP Mont.; *Ashtabula County Sentinel* (Jefferson, Ohio), August 17, 1905 (Wade file, Montana State Historical Society).

58 Wade to Knowles, April 27, 1871 (Knowles Papers).

59 Edward D. Russell, *Proceedings of the Montana Bar Association from Its Origin, January 8, 1885, to January 14*, n.d., p. 320.

60 Wade, "Self-Government"; *Clare Lincoln: A Novel* (Cambridge, Mass.: Riverside Press, 1876). According to some biographers, the novel was "widely read." See Sanders, *History of Montana*, 1 : 413, 605.

61 AP Mont.

62 Report of Peter C. Shannon, July 19, 1883 (S-C Files Mont.).

63 Ibid.

64 Telegram, Arthur to Conger, March 31, 1883 (Judges and Clerks Letters Sent, 2 : 198); Brewster to Conger, January 18, 1884 (ibid., p. 272).

65 Conger to Arthur, January 25, 1884 (AP Mont.).

66 Bowles, *Across the Continent*, p. 60.

67 *Congressional Record,* 45th Cong., 2d sess., 1878, 7, pt. 2 : 1203.
68 Bowles, *Across the Continent* p. 60.
69 Campbell Diary, December 6, 1869.
70 Ibid., June 22, 1869.
71 Ibid., June 2, 1869.
72 U.S. Atty M. C. Page to Atty Gen. Charles Devens, May 12, 1877 (S-C Files Mont.).
73 W. F. Chadwick to Delegate Martin Maginnis, December 28, 1873 (Maginnis Papers). An *Indian Ring* was a term denoting a group of men engaged in illicit traffic of various sorts among the Indians.
74 Wade to Knowles, April 27, 1871.
75 Teller to Atty Gen. George H. Williams, February 10, 1875 (S-C Files Colo.).

Chapter 7: William Ware Peck

1 Wyoming Territory, *General Laws* (Fifth Session), pp. 34–35.
2 Governor John M. Thayer to Delegate W. W. Corlett, January 3, 1878 (AP Wyo.). Thayer's figures were provided by the county treasurer. Some of Peck's adversaries rashly charged that court expenses increased tenfold.
3 Larson, *History of Wyoming,* p. 129.
4 White and Davis, Attorneys, to James Proctor Knott, Congressman from Kentucky, March 10, 1878, Record of the U.S. Senate Committee on the Judiciary File No. Senate 45A-E9, Record Group 46, National Archives (hereafter cited as Sen. Jud. Com.).
5 Ibid.; Alfred G. Lee to President Hayes, December 6, 1877 (AP Wyo.).
6 *Congressional Record,* 45th Cong., 2d sess., 1878, 7, pt. 2 : 1207.
7 The recommendations in Peck's file indicate high professional attainment, and they are distinguished by the absence of a strong political flavor (AP Wyo.).
8 *Congressional Record,* 45 Cong., 2d sess., 1878, 7, pt. 2 : 1171, 1204.
9 Lee to Hayes, December 6, 1877 (AP Wyo.).
10 *Congressional Record,* 45th Cong., 2d sess., 1878, 7, pt. 2 : 1206.
11 Ibid., p. 1204.
12 Campbell "Fading Memories," p. 42.
13 Peck to Hayes, October 17, 1877; Peck to President Grover Cleveland, December 27, 1887 (AP Wyo.).
14 AP Wyo.
15 Peck to Hayes, October 17, 1877 (AP Wyo.).
16 *Congressional Record,* 45th Cong., 2d sess., 1878, 7, pt. 2 : 1204; *Cheyenne Daily Sun,* December 4, 1884.

17 William R. Steele, addressee unknown (most likely the Atty Gen.), February 10, 1879 (AP Wyo.).
18 Lee to Hayes, December 6, 1877 (AP Wyo.); Affidavit, J. W. Kingman, December 27, 1877 (Sen. Jud. Com.).
19 Wyoming Territory *General Laws* (Fifth Session), pp. 34–35.
20 The most valuable single compilation of data regarding the Wyoming Territorial Supreme Court (including maps of the districts) is Marie H. Erwin's, *Wyoming Historical Blue Book: A Legal and Political History of Wyoming, 1868–1943,* pp. 185–210.
21 Wyoming Territory, *General Laws* (Fifth Session), pp. 34–35.
22 Ibid., pp. 29–35; *Congressional Record,* 45th Cong., 2d sess., 1878, 7, pt. 2 : 1170.
23 Thayer to Corlett, January 3, 1878 (AP Wyo.).
24 Francis E. Warren to Corlett, March 25, 1878 (quoted in Gould, *Wyoming,* p. 55).
25 Affidavits, Mary Anne Blackburn, January 9, 1878, and A. H. Davis, January 18, 1878 (Sen. Jud. Com.); Peck to Atty Gen. Charles Devens, January 7, 1878 (AP Wyo.).
26 *Congressional Record,* 45th Cong., 2d sess., 1878, 7, pt. 1 : 973, pt. 2 : 1210, 1236; *Cheyenne Daily Leader,* March 6, 1878.
27 *Congressional Record,* 45th Cong., 2d sess., 1878, 7, pt. 2 : 1169–71, 1201, 1210.
28 Ibid., p. 1210.
29 Steele, February 10, 1879 (AP Wyo.).
30 Campbell, "Fading Memories," p. 40; George H. Peck, brother of Justice Peck, to President Chester A. Arthur, October 24, 1882 (AP Wyo.).
31 Petition to the House of Representatives, April 23, 1878 (Sen. Jud. Com.).
32 Ibid.
33 Corlett to Devens, January 27, 1879 (AP Wyo.).
34 Resolution of the Wyoming Territorial Republican Convention signed by E. A. Thomas (AP Wyo.).
35 Steele, February 10, 1879 (AP Wyo.).
36 T. A. Larson, "Exiling a Wyoming Judge," *Wyoming Law Journal* 10 (Spring 1956) : 171–79.
37 F. L. Arnold to Hayes, December 10, 1877 (AP Wyo.).
38 AP Wyo.
39 Steele, February 10, 1879; Steele to Devens, November 1, 1877 (AP Wyo.).
40 J. W. Kingman to Hayes, October 20, 1879 (AP Wyo.); *Laramie Weekly Sentinel,* March 11, 1878; *Cheyenne Daily Leader,* March 25, 1880.
41 *Laramie Weekly Sentinel,* March 11 and 9, 1878.

42 *Congressional Record,* 45th Cong., 2d sess., 1878, 7, pt. 2 : 1202.

43 Petition to Senator George F. Edmunds, October 13, 1877 (Sen. Jud. Com.); Petition to George F. Edmunds, October 23, 1877 (AP Wyo.); Affidavit, Charles M. White, January 4, 1878 (Sen. Jud. Com.).

44 Petition to the Senate Judiciary Committee, the Senate, and the President, n.d. (AP Wyo.).

45 Affidavit, Samuel H. Stevenson, December 14, 1877 (Sen. Jud. Com.).

46 Steele, February 10, 1879 (AP Wyo.).

47 Ibid.; *Laramie Weekly Sentinel,* November 11, 1878.

48 Peck to Devens, September 25, 1878 and January 13, 1879 (S-C Files Wyo).

49 White and Davis to Knott, March 10, 1878; Affidavit, J. W. Kingman, December 27, 1877; Blair to Devens, December 29, 1877 (S-C Files Wyo.).

50 *Cheyenne Daily Leader,* April 18, September 13, November 19 and 20, 1878.

51 Governor John W. Hoyt to Hayes, November 16, 1879 (AP Wyo.).

52 Hoyt to Peck, December 20, 1879 (John W. Hoyt Letterbook, Wyoming State Archives and Historical Department); *Cheyenne Daily Leader,* November 22, 1878; Lee to Hayes, August 24, 1879 (AP Wyo.).

53 Kingman to Hayes, October 29, 1879 (AP Wyo.).

54 Larson, "Exiling a Wyoming Judge," p. 176.

55 Ibid., p. 179.

56 Smurr, "Territorial Constitutions," pp. 355–56, 422–23. The case in point is *McCann v. United States,* 2 Wyo. 274 (1880).

57 *Union Pacific Railway Co. v. Ryan,* 2 Wyo. 408 (1881).

58 Peck to Hayes, July 7, 1877 (AP Wyo.).

59 Peck to Hayes, October 15 and November 9, 1879 (AP Wyo.); Peck to Devens, March 14, 1880 (S-C Files Wyo.).

60 *Cheyenne Daily Leader,* March 25, 1880.

61 Benjamin H. Brewster to Chief Justice James B. Sener, January 26, 1882 (Judges and Clerks, Letters Sent, 2 : 93–94). AP Wyo.

62 Larson, "Exiling a Wyoming Judge," pp. 178–79; W. Turrentine Jackson, "The Governorship of Wyoming, 1885–1889: A Study in Territorial Politics," *Pacific Historical Review* 13 (March 1944) : 4–5

63 Lee to W. R. Rogers, October 13, 1877 (AP Wyo.); *Congressional Record,* 45th Con., 2d sess., 1878, 7, pt. 2 : 1207.

64 *Cheyenne Daily Leader,* September 15, 1878, quoting the (Chicago) *Inter-Ocean.*

65 *Cheyenne Daily Leader* April 27, 1878, citing the *Washington Republican; Cheyenne Daily Leader,* December 11, 1877, citing the (Chicago) *Times.*

Chapter 8: Moses Hallett

1 Colorado Territory, *General Laws* (Fifth Session), p. 181. See app. 1.
2 Bowles, *Across the Continent*, p. 60.
3 Petition, July 14, 1863, bearing the attest of Governor John Evans to the character of the attorneys on the list (AP Colo.); Minutes of July 6, 1863, Colorado Territorial Bar Association, Benjamin F. Hall File (ibid.).
4 Petition, October 17, 1863 (AP Colo.); Evans to Lincoln, July 15, 1863 (ibid.); Evans to Lincoln, March 6, 1865 (CSA-LP).
5 Bradford to President Andrew Johnson, July 8, 1865 (AP Colo.).
6 The most reliable biographical sketches can be found in *Dictionary of American Biography*, 8 : 155–56, and *Portrait and Biographical Record of Denver and Vicinity, Colorado*, pp. 171–72.
7 James Philip MacCarthy, *Political Portraits by Fitz-Mac*, p. 214.
8 Dawson Scrapbooks, 4 : 121, *Denver Post*, n.d., Colorado Historical Society.
9 Wikoff, "The Bench and Bar of Colorado," pp. 606–07.
10 Ebenezer T. Wells, an address before the Colorado State Bar, *Colorado Bar Association Report* 9 (1906) : 15.
11 *RMN*, July 12, 1861.
12 Colorado State Archives.
13 Hallett to Teller and Johnson, June 30, 1862 (Teller Papers, 1 : 54, Western Historical Collection, Norlin Library, University of Colorado).
14 Advertisements for Hallett and Sayre appear in *RMN* from January 3, 1865, at least through January 2, 1866; Wilbur Fisk Stone, ed., *History of Colorado*, 1 : 743.
15 *RMN*, September 30, 1865; March 31, April 7, 1866.
16 Hallett to Teller and Johnson, July 28, 1863 (Teller Papers, 1 : 54).
17 Evelyn Bradley, "The Story of a Colorado Pioneer: Mrs. Charles A. Finding," *Colorado Magazine* 2 (January 1925) : 50.
18 *RMN*, December 5, 1865.
19 Teller to George H. Williams; Teller to President Ulysses S. Grant, February 23, 1874 (AP Colo.).
20 Robert B. Murray, "The Supreme Court of Colorado Territory," *Colorado Magazine* 44 (Winter 1967) : 24–27.
21 Colorado State Archives.
22 Wells, in his address before the Colorado State Bar, pp. 9, 10.
23 Ibid., p. 16.
24 *RMN*, March 19, 1874.
25 Numerous citations of Hallett's railroad decisions can be found in Robert G. Athearn's *Rebel of the Rockies*.

26 *RMN,* June 29, 1866, and June 4, 1867.

27 *RMN,* February 6, April 13, 1867, and June 1, 1868.

28 Thompson to Chief Clerk, War Department, *Journal of the Colorado Territorial Secretary, 1861–75,* reel no. 2, "Colorado Executive Records," Microcopy from National Archives, 32.

29 Richard Peete, ed., *Anecdotes of the Jealous Mistress: Selections from the Gustave Ornauer Collection (Rocky Mountain Law Review,* University of Colorado, 1959). Forty-nine separate items refer to Moses Hallett in this anthology of newspaper clippings, many more references to him than to any other single member of the bar.

30 Ray H. Cooper, "Early History of San Juan County," *Colorado Magazine* 22 (September 1945) : 212.

31 Dawson Scrapbooks, 33 : 7.

32 Parkhill, *The Law Goes West,* p. 25.

33 Warrant, October 30, 1868 (Box 13, Records of the Third Judicial District, Pueblo, Record Group 21, Denver Federal Records Center, Denver, Colorado); *US v. Refenberg,* GD 185 (ibid.).

34 George Q Richmond, "The Men with Whom I've Smiled," *Colorado Magazine* 1 (May 1924) : 146–47.

35 *Crary v. Barber,* 1 Colo. 172 (1869). Hallett also insisted on adherence to due process in *Palmer v. Cowdrey,* 2 Colo. 1 (1873).

36 *Sullivan v. Hense,* 2 Colo. 424, 434 (1874).

37 Territorial Secretary Frank Hall to Hallett, February 21, 1872 (*Journal of the Colorado Territorial Secretary, 1861–1875,* p. 111).

38 Hall to Hallett, January 20, 1873 (ibid., p. 147); E. M. McCook to Hallett, August 31, 1869 (ibid., p. 390).

39 George W. Jenkins to Hallett, January 9, 1875 (ibid., p. 427).

40 F. Hall to Hallett, July 9, 1866 (ibid., p. 262).

41 *Forms of Oaths for the District Court of the First Judicial District of Colorado Territory,* Edward F. Bishop, Clerk.

42 MacCarthy, *Political Portraits,* p. 214.

43 Letter from William K. Alderfer, Illinois State Historian, to the author; a reference report on Hallett's father was included, March 29, 1968.

44 Hallett to H. A. Johnson (Teller and Johnson), August 27, 1862 (Teller Papers, 1 : 54); *The Legislative Manual of the State of Colorado,* 1st ed. (Denver: Denver Times Publishing House and Bindery, 1877), pp. 214–15.

45 Ann W. and LeRoy R. Hafen, "The Beginnings of Denver University," *Colorado Magazine* 24 (March 1947) : 64–66.

46 *RMN,* September 1, September 4, and October 31, 1865.

47 Evans to Lincoln, March 6, 1865 (CSA-LP).

48 *RMN,* March 12, 1867; Lamar, *The Far Southwest,* p. 100.

49 *RMN,* February 4, 1874.

50 MacCarthy, *Political Portraits*, p. 214; *D.A.B.*, 7 : 493, 15 : 402. Rawlins was a native of Galena, and Grant lived there briefly before the Civil War, clerking in a leather goods store.
51 Teller Letters, Western History Department, Denver Public Library
52 Hallett to Teller, Teller Letters, pp. 417, 418, 419, 236.
53 Ibid., p. 418.
54 D.A.B. 8 : 155; Dawson Scrapbooks, 65 : 15; *The Graphic* 7 (April 15, 1898) : 253 (Western Historical Collection, Norlin Library, University of Colorado).
55 *Magazine of Western History* 12 (1891–92), Western History Department, Denver Public Library.
56 *Statutes at Large*, 12 : 172–76, 14 : 426–27, 16 : 152.
57 Illinois State Historical Society Reference Report, March 29, 1968.
58 Certificate of Incorporation, Colorado State Archives.
59 *RMN*, February 26, June 11, 1874.
60 Hallett to Atty Gen. Stanbery, May 1, 1867; Hallett to Atty Gen. E. R. Hoar, January 17, 1870 (AGP Colo.).
61 John G. Canfield, ed., *Mines and Mining Men of Colorado*, p. 32; Stone, *History of Colorado*, p. 402; Clyde Lyndon King, *The History of the Government of Denver with Special Reference to its Relations with Public Service Corporations*, p. 202.
62 The diaries of George W. Clayton are in the possession of the Clayton College for Boys in Denver, Colorado; they were read with the permission of the institution's governing board through the courtesy of Richard Stare, Director.
63 Inheritance tax appraisals and receipts, Denver County Court (presently known as Probate Court), file no. 15889.
64 *Denver Post*, November 8, 1909, 1 : 4.

Chapter 9: Making Law

1 Justice Oliver Wendell Holmes quoted by Morris D. Forkosch, "What is Legal History?" in *Essays in Legal History in Honor of Felix Frankfurter*, edited by Morris D. Forkosch, p. 4.
2 Colorado Territory, *General Laws* (First Session), p. 35. The assemblies of the Montana and Wyoming territories also adopted the common law.
3 Walter Prescott Webb, *The Great Plains*, pp. 385–452.
4 Walter Prescott Webb, *The Great Frontier* (Cambridge: The Riverside Press, 1952).
5 The most recent and comprehensive treatment of the sources and evolution of American mining law is included in a five-volume work

compiled by 51 attorneys and law professors, *The American Law of Mining,* edited by the Rocky Mountain Mineral Law Foundation (hereafter cited as *ALM*); Rodman W. Paul, *California Gold: The Beginning of Mining in the Far West,* pp. 210–39.

6 Paul, *California Gold,* pp. 224, 225.

7 *ALM,* 1 : 24.

8 *Statutes at Large,* 14 : 251 (1866); amended to include placer claims, *Statutes at Large,* 16 : 217 (1870).

9 Its limitations are discussed in *ALM,* 1 : 45.

10 *Statutes at Large,* 17 : 91 (1872); summarized in *ALM,* 1 : 53–54.

11 Petitions for the removal of Benjamin F. Hall and Charles Lee Armour, July 14, 1863 (AP Colo.); Henry M. Teller to Atty Gen. George H. Williams, April 27, 1874 (S-C Files Colo.); Montana Territory, *General Laws* (Third Session), p. 94.

12 The message of Governor John A. Campbell to the first session of the territorial assembly directed attention to the need for mining codes in Wyoming as well.

13 *Helena Weekly Herald,* November 20, 1870, see, for example, *The New North-West* (Deer Lodge), May 9, 1874.

14 Numerous petitions of 1883 (AP Mont.).

15 H. A. Clark, Chairman of the Montana Territorial Democratic Central Committee, to Solicitor General George A. Jenks, May 3, 1887 (AP Mont.).

16 Rodman W. Paul, "Colorado as a Pioneer of Science in the Mining West," *Mississippi Valley Historical Review* 47 (June 1960) : 34–50.

17 The terms *lode, vein,* and *quartz* are used interchangeably in this context.

18 *Del Monte M. and M. Co. v. Last Chance M. and M. Co.,* 171 US 55, 67 (1897).

19 R. S. Morrison, *Mining Rights in Colorado,* 7th ed., pp. 1–13; Charles Howard Shinn, *Mining Camps: A Study in American Frontier Government;* Percy Stanley Fritz, "The Constitutions and Laws of Early Mining Districts in Boulder County, Colorado," *The University of Colorado Studies* 21 (March 1934) : 127–48.

20 Shinn, *Mining Camps,* p. 277.

21 *Sullivan v. Hense,* 2 Colo., 424 (1874).

22 Shinn, *Mining Camps,* pp. 27–28.

23 *King v. Edwards,* 1 Mont. 235 (1870); local custom for lode mining was likewise accepted in *Carrhart v. Montana Mineral Land and Mine Co.,* 1 Mont. 245 (1870).

24 *Lincoln v. Edwards,* 1 Mont. 217, 222 (1870).

25 *Belk v. Meagher,* 3 Mont. 65 (1878), 104 US 279 (1881). Cited as controlling in *Garfield v. Hammer,* 130 US 191, 301 (1888); cited in 25

different sections by Curtis H. Lindley, *A Treatise On the American Law Relating to Mines and Mineral Lands;* appears often in *ALM* and is included in latest student case books.

26 *Garfield M. and M. Co. v. Hammer,* 6 Mont. 53 (1886), 130 US 291 (1888). Record of affirmations by the U.S. Supreme Court is in table 3. Clyde O. Martz, ed., *Cases and Materials on the Law of Natural Resources,* pp. 575–77.

27 *Silver Bow M and M. Co. v. Clark,* 5 Mont. 378 (1885); affirmed in *Talbott v. King,* 6 Mont. 76 (1886).

28 *Butte City Smokehouse Lode Cases,* 6 Mont. 397 (1887); filed individually in appeal and dismissed. First dismissal, *Beal v. Murray,* 140 US 671 (1891).

29 *Foote v. National Mining Co.,* 2 Mont. 402 (1876).

30 Extralateral rights are summarized in *ALM,* 2 : 33–34.

31 Side lines parallel the course of the vein; end lines are crosswise to it.

32 *Larkin v. Upton,* 7 Mont. 449 (1888), 144 US 19 (1891); *ALM,* 1 : 660, 2 : 49.

33 *Montana Co. v. Clark,* 42 Fed. 626 (1890).

34 *Davis's Administrator v. Weibold,* 139 US 507, 530 (1890); Colorado's former territorial chief justice, Moses Hallett, ruled similarly from the U.S. District Court in *Elgin M. and M. Co. v. Iron Silver Mining Co.,* 117 US 196 (1882).

35 *Colorado Bar Association Report* 16 (1913) : 311.

36 *Iron Silver Mining Co. v. Cheeseman,* 8 Fed. 297, 301 (1881), 116 US 529 (1885).

37 *ALM,* 2 : 40–42.

38 *Del Monte M. and M. Co. v. Last Chance M. and M. Co.,* 171 US 55 (1897).

39 This development is summarized in terms that can be readily understood by the layman in Albert T. Frantz, "The Law Mirrors History," in Forkosch's *Essays in Legal History,* pp. 77–85.

40 The following comparison of riparian rights and prior appropriation is based largely on Jean S. Breitenstein, "Some Elements of Colorado Water Law," *Rocky Mountain Law Review* 22 (June 1950) : 343–56.

41 *Yunker v. Nichols,* 1 Colo. 551 (1872); Samuel C. Wiel, "Public Policy in Western Water Decisions," *California Law Review* 1 (1912–13) : 21; Clesson S. Kinney, *A Treatise on the Law of Irrigation and Water Rights,* 2d ed., 4 vols. (San Francisco: Bender-Moss Company, 1912), p. 21. The Yunker case is cited by Kinney 15 times.

42 1 Colo. 551, 553. Hallett's opinion was only three pages long.

43 Ibid., pp. 554, 555.

44 Ibid., p. 567.

45 Ibid., p. 570.

46 *Atchison v. Peterson*, 1 Mont. 561 (1872), 87 US 507 (1874); Callaway, "Something about the Territorial Judges," p. 35.

47 1 Mont. 561, 569 (1872).

48 *Taylor v. Stewart, Helena Weekly Herald,* December 26, 1867.

49 1 Mont. 651 (1872).

50 1 Mont. 457 (1872).

51 1 Mont. 651, 170 (1872).

52 *Caruthers v. Pemberton,* 1 Mont. 111 (1869); *Shepard's Montana Citations,* 2d ed. (Colorado Springs: Shepard's Citations, Inc., 1960), p. 21.

53 1 Mont. 544 (1872).

54 *Constitution of the State of Colorado,* art. 16, sec. 5.

55 *Journal and Debates of the Constitutional Convention of the State of Wyoming,* pp. 289–92, 497–503.

56 Gordon M. Bakken, "Rocky Mountain Constitution-Making, 1850–1912" (Ph.D. diss., University of Wisconsin, 1970), pp. 323–26. Water as a constitutional issue in the Rocky Mountains is discussed on pp. 314–33.

57 Moses Lasky, "From Prior Appropriation to Economic Distribution of Water by the State—via Irrigation Administration," *Rocky Mountain Law Review* 1 (April 1929) : 174.

58 *Coffin v. Left Hand Ditch Co.,* 6 Colo. 443 (1882) is a landmark water case used in two sections of Martz's *Cases and Materials,* pp. 71–74, 148–55. It cited as controlling *Schilling v. Rominger,* 4 Colo. 100 (1878), which cited *Yunker v. Nichols* as controlling.

59 William J. Burke, "Western Water Law," *Wyoming Law Journal* 10 (Spring 1956) : 180; idem, "The Origin, Growth, and Function of the Law of Water Use," *Wyoming Law Journal* 10 (Winter 1956) : 97. Lasky ("From Prior Appropriation, pp. 161–62) refers to the "Colorado System" as "a thing *sui generis.*"

60 William M. Champion, "Prior Appropriation in Mississippi—A Statutory Analysis," *Mississippi Law Journal* 39 (December 1967) : 1–38.

61 Lasky, "From Prior Appropriation," p. 174.

62 Philip A. Danielson, "Water Administration in Colorado—Higher-ority or Priority," *Rocky Mountain Law Review* 30 (April 1958) : 293–314.

63 Martz, *Cases and Materials,* pp. 279–300.

64 Breitenstein, "Some Elements of Colorado Water Law," p. 345.

65 Larson, *History of Wyoming,* pp. 181, 183. Justice Department files reveal the various pressures on the court from factions involved in range controversies.

66 *RMN,* April 4, 1869; Wyoming Territory, *General Laws* (First Session), p. 371.

67 Larson, *History of Wyoming,* pp. 89–94; idem, "Woman Suffrage in Western America," *Utah Historical Quarterly* 38 (Winter 1970) : 7–19.

68 Larson, "Woman Suffrage," pp. 12–16. This article contains an excel-

lent summary of the factors which influenced the Wyoming assembly.

69 "Honorable John W. Kingman," pp. 224–25; Glenn Parker, "Historia Legis in Terra Lata," in Forkosch's *Essays in Legal History,* p. 120.

70 Howe to Mrs. Myra Bradwell, April 4, 1870 (quoted in Elizabeth C. Stanton, Susan B. Anthony, and Matilda J. Gage, eds., *History of Woman Suffrage,* vol. 3, p. 736); "Honorable John W. Kingman," pp. 224–25.

71 Kingman to Mrs. Lucy Stone, September 22, 1874 (Stanton et al., *History of Woman Suffrage,* p. 836).

72 "Honorable John W. Kingman," p. 225.

73 *Laramie Daily Sentinel,* March 6 and 16, 1871.

74 Ibid., March 9 and 10, and February 27, 1871.

75 Parker, "Historia Legis in Terra Lata," p. 120.

76 *Allen v. Eldridge,* 1 Colo. 287 (1871); *Holladay v. Daily,* 1 Colo. 460 (1872); *Griswold v. Boley,* 1 Mont. 545 (1872); *Granger v. Lewis Bros.,* 2 Wyo. 231 (1880); *Manton v. Tyler,* 4 Mont. 364 (1882); *Palmer v. Murray,* 6 Mont. 169 (1886).

77 *Mills v. Angela,* 1 Colo. 334 (1871).

78 Gordon M. Bakken, "The English Common Law in the Rocky Mountain West," *Arizona and the West* 11 (Summer 1969) : 114.

79 *Hornbuckle v. Toombs,* 85 US 648 (1873); *Palmer v. Cowdrey,* 2 Colo. 1 (1873)—here Hallett also insisted that process must be personally served when the defendant is within the jurisdiction, an important modern rule.

80 See Spence, "The Territorial Bench in Montana," p. 61.

Chapter 10: "Send Us a Civilizer"

1 Potts to President Ulysses S. Grant, November 25, 1870 (AP Mont.).

2 Larson, *History of Wyoming,* pp. 95–96.

3 *Cheyenne Daily Leader,* March 25 and 26, 1870.

4 Governor John A. Campbell, Justice William T. Jones, Justice Joseph W. Kingman, U.S. Atty Joseph M. Carey to Atty Gen. E. R. Hoar, received April 1, 1870; Howe to Hoar, March 28, 1870 (AGP Wyo.).

5 Howe to Hoar, April 11, 1870 (AGP Wyo.).

6 *Cheyenne Daily Leader,* April 15 and 26, 1870; Kingman to Hoar, May 9, 1870; Howe to Hoar, May 9 and 10, 1870 (AGP Wyo.).

7 Howe to Hoar, May 10, 1870 (AGP Wyo.).

8 Munson, "Lyman Ezra Munson," pp. 200–01.

9 Albright, "The Relations of Montana," pp. 179–82; Clerk of the First District Court of Montana Territory to Delegate Martin Maginnis,

April 12, 1876 (AP Mont.); Potts to Sec. Int. Columbus Delano (SDTP Mont.).

10 Knowles to Mrs. Hiram Knowles, July 28, 1877 (Knowles Papers).

11 Gov. William Hale to Justice Samuel C. Parks, September 12, 1884 (IDTP Wyo.); Campbell to Kingman, October 8, 1869 (John A. Campbell Letterpress Book).

12 Legislative summary, *Cheyenne Daily Leader*, October 23, 1869; Governor's Message to the Fifth Legislative Assembly, *Cheyenne Daily Leader*, November 18, 1877.

13 Supreme Court of Colorado Territory to Atty Gen. Benjamin H. Brewster, March 20, 1882 (S-C Files Wyo.).

14 Proclamation of the Governor of Wyoming Territory, June 3, 1889 (IDTP Wyo.); Gov. Francis E. Warren to Jacob B. Blair, January 4, 1886 (ibid.).

15 *RMN*, September 10, 1861; Montana Territory, *General Laws* (First Session).

16 *Baxter v. Hallett*, 1 Colo. 352 (1871).

17 *Avant Weekly Courier* (Bozeman), June 21, 1883; *Laramie Daily Sentinel*, February 8, 1878; Spence, "The Territorial Bench in Montana," p. 57; Larson, *History of Wyoming*, p. 146.

18 *Congressional Globe*, 41st Cong., 3d sess., 1871, p. 970; *Congressional Record*, 50th Cong., 2d sess., 1889, 20, pt. 1 : 821 (the Toole oration is one of the most exhaustive and colorful statements ever made of territorial resentments); Wyoming Territory, *General Laws* (Second Session), p. 138.

19 Wade, "Self-Government," pp. 299–308.

20 Coloradans in vain presented a four-foot-long petition to President Lincoln to impress him with their impatience for the appointment of Jacob Downing from Colorado (AP Colo.).

21 *Cheyenne Daily Leader*, January 6 and 25, and April 3, 1869; Campbell to Grant, September 23, 1871; Petition to Delegate Jones (AP Wyo.).

22 *Congressional Record*, 49th Cong., 1st sess., 1886, 17, pt. 1 : 529; ibid., pt. 5 : 4891; House Committee on the Territories, *Report to Accompany Bill HR 2883*, Report No. 2581, 49th Cong., 1st sess., 1885–86, serial 2443.

23 Atty J. J. Davis to Atty Gen. Charles Devens, November 17, 1879 (AP Mont.); Albright, "The Relations of Montana," p. 392.

24 Evans to Lincoln, December 22, 1863 (AP Colo.).

25 Based largely on the Willis Van Devanter Papers, the best account of Carey's contribution to the statehood movement is Lewis L. Gould, "Joseph M. Carey and Wyoming Statehood," *Annals of Wyoming* 37 (October 1965) : 157–69.

26 Larson, *History of Wyoming,* p. 237.

27 Carey to Van Devanter (quoted by Gould, "Joseph M. Carey," pp. 161–62).

28 Gould, "Joseph M. Carey," pp. 164, 160.

29 *Proceedings of the Constitutional Convention Held in Denver, December 20, 1875,* pp. 36–37; Larson, *History of Wyoming,* pp. 245–50.

30 Howard R. Lamar, "Carpetbaggers," p. 206.

31 Lewis Atherton, "The Mining Promoter in the Trans-Mississippi West," *The Western Historical Quarterly* 1 (January 1970) : 35–50.

32 Justice John H. Howe, Wyoming, to Atty Gen. A. T. Akerman, March 24, 1871 (S-C Files Wyo.); many similar letters can be found in the Appointment Papers.

33 T. C. Everts to Hosmer, January 6 and 12, 1865 (Hosmer MSS); there is a note in the amount of $6,000 signed by S. C. Johnson in favor of Hosmer and Everts (May 25, 1865) in the Hosmer Papers.

34 Campbell, "Fading Memories," p. 40; Francis E. Warren to Blair, November 6, 1889 (IDTP Wyo.); Campbell Diary, April 16, 1874.

35 Campbell Diary, September 20 and 29, 1873. His awareness of the cattle industry's potential was also clearly expressed in his first address to the legislature, *Message of Governor Campbell to the First Legislative Assembly of Wyoming Territory.*

36 Maurice Frink, W. Turrentine Jackson, and Agnes Wright Spring, *When Grass Was King,* pp. 392–93; Larson, *History of Wyoming,* 163–94.

37 *Cheyenne Daily Leader,* September 20, 1875.

38 Frink et al., *When Grass Was King,* p. 393.

39 Larson, *History of Wyoming,* p. 172; W. Turrentine Jackson, "The Wyoming Stock Growers' Association: Political Power in Wyoming Territory, 1873–1890," *Mississippi Valley Historical Review* 33 (March 1947) : 571–94. Interpretations stressing the political muscle of the Wyoming Stock Growers' Association are challenged by Gould, *Wyoming,* p. 70.

40 Steele and Thayer to Edwards Pierrepont, January 13, 1876 (AP Wyo.). Though he was only 24 when he went to Wyoming, Carey had a most impressive set of recommendations.

41 Larson, *History of Wyoming,* p. 239.

42 *Laramie Daily Sentinel,* July 24, 1871; Kingman to Silas Reed, Surveyor General of Wyoming Territory, in *Report of the Secretary of the Interior,* Exec. Doc. 1, House of Representatives, 42d Cong., 2d sess., 1871, Serial 1505, pp. 296–98.

43 *Laramie Daily Sentinel,* November 20, 1871.

44 Posey to Atty Gen. George H. Williams, November 27, 1872 (S-C Files Wyo.).

45 U.S. Atty M. C. Page to Atty Gen. Charles Devens, May 12, 1877 (S-C Files Mont.); Thomas J. [Larry] to Gov. B. F. Potts, February 24, 1872 (AP Wyo.); Everts to Hosmer, January 6 and 12, 1865 (Hosmer MSS).

Chapter 11: Conclusion

1 Bakken, "Rocky Mountain Constitution-Making," pp. 81–83. Bakken's research of codes, reports, and convention journals was exhaustive.
2 Ibid., pp. 233–38, 250–51, 300.
3 A recent reinterpretation of the frontier lawyer of the old Northwest which will interest legal historians is Elizabeth Gaspar Brown's "The Bar on a Frontier: Wayne County, 1796–1831," *The American Journal of Legal History* 14 (April 1970) : 136–56.

Bibliography

Manuscripts

Bancroft Manuscripts. Copies of manuscript material gathered by Hubert Howe Bancroft, Colorado State Historical Society. Western Historical Collection, Norlin Library, Univerisity of Colorado.

Clara J. Blake Manuscript. Manuscript entitled "A Honeymoon of Long Ago," n.d. Montana State Historical Society, Helena.

John A. Campbell Diaries, 1869–73. Wyoming State Archives and · Historical Department, Cheyenne.

John A. Campbell Letterpress Book, 1869–75. Wyoming State Archives and Historical Department, Cheyenne. Of the letterpress books of the governors, Campbell's is the most revealing.

John A. Campbell Papers. Incoming correspondence, 1869–75. Wyoming State Archives and Historical Department, Cheyenne.

James M. Cavanaugh Poster. Poster printed in Central City in 1863, concerning Justice Charles Lee Armour. Western Historical Collection, Norlin Library, University of Colorado.

Chumasero and Chadwick Letterbook. Letters of attorneys William Chumasero and W. F. Chadwick, 1869–86. Montana State Historical Society, Helena.

George W. Clayton Diaries, 1852–78. Clayton College for Boys, Denver. Read with the permission of the institution's governing board obtained through Richard Stare, Director.

T. F. Dawson Scrapbooks. Eighty volumes collected by T. F. Dawson, private secretary to Henry M. Teller. Colorado State Historical Society. These scrapbooks of clippings are indexed and extremely useful.

District Court Records, Colorado Territory. Record Group 21, Denver Federal Records Center, Denver. Early records of the First Judicial District are in custody of the Colorado State Historical Society in Denver.

Andrew J. Fisk Diary, 1864–70. Montana State Historical Society, Helena.

William Hale Letterpress Books, 1882–85. Wyoming State Archives and Historical Department, Cheyenne.

Hezekiah Lord Hosmer Letters. Nine letters from 1865. Montana State Historical Society, Helena.

Hezekiah Lord Hosmer Manuscripts. Xerox copies of selected letters from this collection were obtained with permission for their use from the Western Americana Collection, Yale University, New Haven, Connecticut. Items are listed in Mary C. Withington catalog.

John W. Hoyt Letterpress Book, 1878–80. Wyoming State Archives and Historical Department, Cheyenne. These copies are barely legible.

Interior Department Territorial Papers of Colorado, Montana, and Wyoming Territories. Papers of the Patents and Miscellaneous Division, executive proceedings and official correspondence of territorial officials, papers of the Appointments Division, appointments files of territorial officials. Record Group 48, National Archives.

Justice Department Appointment Papers. Appointment files of the territorial officials of Colorado, Montana, and Wyoming. Record Group 60, National Archives. On the whole, the files are arranged alphabetically by territory. However, at the end of the series there are several boxes of miscellaneous appointment papers. These files contain much information which is unavailable in state historical society collections.

Justice Department, Attorney General's Instruction Books and Attorney General's Letterbooks. Outgoing letters from the attorney general to state and territorial officials under his jurisdiction. Record Group 60, National Archives. Mainly routine matters appear here.

Justice Department, Attorney General's Papers. Letters received by the attorney general, filed by title of office under state and territorial names. Record Group 60, National Archives. Conditions in the territories are vividly described in these letters.

Justice Department, Judges and Clerks Letters Sent. Correspondence from the Justice Department to judges and clerks of the states and territories. Record Group 60, National Archives. Routine policy and instructions are the main subjects of this correspondence.

Justice Department, Source-Chronological Files. Letters received from Colorado, Montana, and Wyoming Territories. Record Group 60, National Archives. Only the appointment files are more revealing than these records.

Hiram Knowles Papers. Montana State Historical Society, Helena. This collection is very limited.

Lincoln Papers. Photographic copies of items from the Lincoln Papers in the Library of Congress. Colorado State Archives, Territorial Collection, Denver.

Martin Maginnis Clipping File, Papers, and Scrap Book. Montana State Historical Society, Helena.

Thomas Moonlight Letterpress Book, 1887–89. Wyoming State Archives and Historical Department, Cheyenne.

Probate Records. Denver County Court (Probate Court), File No. 15889, relative to the estate of Moses Hallett.

Silas Reed Papers. Xerox copies of selected letters from this collection were obtained with permission for their use from the Western Americana Collection, Yale University, New Haven, Connecticut. See Mary C. Withington catalog.

Wilbur F. Sanders Papers. Montana State Historical Society, Helena.

Senate Territorial Papers of Colorado, Montana, and Wyoming. Records of the United States Senate relating to territorial affairs. Record Group 46, National Archives.

State Department Appointment Papers. Appointment files of territorial officials. Record Group 59, National Archives. Most of the correspondence has evidently been transferred to the Justice Department, but a few pertinent files remain in the State Department Appointment Papers.

State Department Domestic Letters. Correspondence from the State Department to officials in the United States under State Department jurisdiction. Record Group 59, National Archives.

State Department Territorial Papers of Colorado, Montana, and Wyoming Territories. Letters from governors and secretaries of the territories to the president or the secretary of state, journals of executive proceedings, acts of territorial legislatures, and some miscellaneous correspondence from other territorial officials. Record Group 59, National Archives.

Henry M. Teller Letterbooks. Western History Department, Denver Public Library, Denver.

Henry M. Teller Papers. Western Historical Collection, Norlin Library, University of Colorado.

Francis E. Warren Papers. Western History Research Center, University of Wyoming, Laramie.

Unpublished Material and Interviews

Albright, Robert Edwin. "The Relations of Montana with the Federal Government, 1864–1889." Ph.D. dissertation, Stanford University, 1933.

Alderfer, William K., Illinois State Historian. Letter to the author including reference report on Moses Hallett's father, March 29, 1968.

Anderson, Albert G., Jr. "The Political Career of Senator Clarence D. Clark." M.A. thesis, University of Wyoming, 1953.

Bakken, Gordon M. "Rocky Mountain Constitution-Making, 1850–1912." Ph.D. dissertation, University of Wisconsin, 1970.

Barnhill, Kenneth, attorney and lecturer on natural resources, University of Colorado Law School, Boulder. Interview, June 29, 1970.

Breitenstein, Judge Jean S., United States Tenth Court of Appeals, Denver, Colorado. Interview, July 23, 1970. Prior to his appointment, Judge Breitenstein represented Colorado in extensive interstate litigation over water rights before the United States Supreme Court.

Erwin, Marie H. "Index of the Historical Material concerning the State of Wyoming as Found in the Congressional Documents." Wyoming State Library, Cheyenne, 1937.

Humphrey, J. J. "The Political and Social Influences of Freemasonry in Territorial Wyoming, 1870–1885." M.A. thesis, University of Wyoming, 1964.

Kelsey, Harry Edwards, Jr. "John Evans." Ph.D. dissertation, Denver University, 1965.

Nelson, Mildred E. "Subject Index of the Cheyenne Daily Leader, 1867–1890." Unpublished manuscript.

Samuels, Cindy, and Guice, William Lee, III. Analysis of territorial

opinions, June 1970. Miss Samuels and Mr. Guice, honor law students at Tulane University and members of the Tulane Law
Review, were impressed with the reason, documentation, prag-
matism, and literary quality evident in so many opinions. Neither
of the researchers was aware of the author's thesis until their reports were filed.

Spiegel, Sydney B. "History of Laramie County, Wyoming, to 1890."
M.A. thesis, University of Wyoming, 1961.

Smurr, John Welling. "Territorial Constitutions: A Legal History
of the Frontier Governments Erected by Congress in the American
West, 1787–1900." Ph.D. dissertation, Indiana University, 1960.

Trelease, Frank J., Dean of School of Law, University of Wyoming,
Laramie. Interview, July 31, 1970.

Government Documents

United States:

Congressional Globe. 38th Cong., 2d sess.; 41st Cong., 2d sess.; 41st
Cong., 3d sess.; 42 Cong., 3d sess.

Congressional Record. Vols. 7, 17, 20.

House of Representatives, Committee on the Territories. *Additional
Associate Justice of the Supreme Court of Wyoming.* Report No.
231. 51st Cong., 1st sess., 1890, Serial 2807.

———. *Federal Officials in the Territories.* Report No. 2581. 49th
Cong., 1st sess., 1886, Serial 2443.

———. *A Joint Resolution of the Legislature of Colorado Territory.*
House of Representatives Miscellaneous Document No. 24. 37th
Cong., 2d sess., 1861, Serial 1141.

———. *Supreme Court of the Territory of Wyoming.* Report No.
4013. 50th Cong., 2d sess., 1889, Serial 2674.

———. *Report of the Secretary of Interior.* 1871–86.

Senate. *Organic Acts for the Territories of the United States with
Notes thereon, Compiled from Statutes at Large of the United
States.* Senate Document No. 148. 56th Cong., 1st sess., 1900, Serial
3852.

Statutes at Large. Vols. 2, 5, 10–16, 21, 24.

Treasury Department. *Register of Territorial Accounts.* Montana.
Record Group 217, National Archives.

Colorado Territory:

Colorado Reports. Vols. 1–3.
Forms of Oaths for the District Court of the First Judicial District of Colorado Territory. Edward F. Bishop, Clerk. Denver: Daily Evening Times Printing House, 1875.
General Laws. First-Fifth Sessions.
Proceedings of the Constitutional Convention Held in Denver, December 20, 1875. Denver: Smith-Brooks Press, State Printers, 1907.
Records of Incorporation. Colorado State Archives.

Montana Territory:

General Laws. First-Sixth Sessions.
House Journal. Fourth-Fifth Sessions of the Legislative Assembly of the Territory of Montana.
Montana Reports. Vols. 1–9.

Wyoming Territory:

Council Journal. Second-Fifth Sessions.
General Laws. First-Eleventh Sessions.
Journal and Debates of the Constitutional Convention of the State of Wyoming. Cheyenne: *The Daily Sun* Book and Job Printing, 1893.
Message of Governor Campbell to the First Legislative Assembly of Wyoming Territory. Cheyenne: *Daily Argus* Office, 1869.
Message of Governor Thayer to the Fourth Legislative Assembly of Wyoming Territory. Cheyenne: H. Glafcke, Printer, *Daily Leader,* 1875.
Message of the Governor of Wyoming, Transmitted to the Sixth Legislative Assembly. Cheyenne, Wyoming Territory: n.p., 1879.

Newspapers

Avant Weekly Courier (Bozeman, Montana).
Cheyenne Daily Leader.
Daily Press (Miles City, Montana).
Frontier Index (Green River City, Wyoming).
Helena Daily Independent.
Helena Weekly Herald.

Helena Weekly Independent.
Laramie Daily Sentinel.
Montana Post (Virginia City and Helena).
Montana Democrat (Virginia City).
Montana Radiator (Helena).
New North-West (Deer Lodge, Montana).
Rocky Mountain Gazette (Helena).
Rocky Mountain News (Denver).
Tri-Weekly Republican (Helena).
Weekly Commonwealth and Republican (Denver).
Weekly Independent (Helena).

Books

Athearn, Robert G. *High Country Empire.* New York: McGraw-Hill, 1960.

———. *Rebel of the Rockies.* New Haven: Yale University Press, 1962.

———. *Thomas Francis Meagher: An Irish Revolutionary in America.* University of Colorado Studies Series in History, no. 1. Boulder: University of Colorado Press, 1949.

———, and Ubbelohde, Carl. *Centennial Colorado.* Denver: E. L. Chambers, 1959.

Bancroft, Hubert Howe. *History of Nevada, Colorado, and Wyoming, 1540–1888.* San Francisco: The History Company, 1890.

———. *History of Washington, Idaho, and Montana, 1845–1889.* San Francisco: The History Company, 1890.

Beale, Howard K., ed. *The Diary of Edward Bates, 1859–1866.* Washington, D.C.: United States Government Printing Office, 1933.

Beard, Frances Birkhead, ed. *Wyoming from Territorial Days to the Present.* 3 vols. Chicago: The American Historical Service, Inc., 1933.

Bothwell, Samuel C. *A Sketch of the Life of the Honorable James Harvey MacLeary.* [Puerto Rico] 1912.

Bowles, Samuel. *Across the Continent: A Summer's Journey to the Rocky Mountains, the Mormons, and the Pacific States, with Speaker Colfax.* Springfield, Mass.: Samuel Bowles and Co., 1865.

Boyce, J. R., Sr. *Facts about Montana Territory and the Way to Get There.* Helena: Rocky Mountain Gazette, 1872.

Burlingame, Merrill G. *The Montana Frontier.* Helena: State Publishing Company, 1942.

Canfield, John G., ed. *Mines and Mining Men of Colorado.* Denver: John G. Canfield, 1893.

Carey, Joseph M. "State of Wyoming." In *The Province and the States,* edited by W. A. Goodspeed. Madison, Wis.: The Western Historical Association, 1904.

Carpenter, M. B. *Mining Code.* Denver: Stone and Company, 1879.

Carter, Clarence E., ed. *The Territorial Papers of the United States.* Vol. 1. Washington, D.C.: United States Government Printing Office, 1934.

Clark, Robert Emmet. *Waters and Water Rights.* 4 Vols. Indianapolis: The Allen Smith Company, 1967.

Clough, Wilson O. *A History of the University of Wyoming: 1887–1964.* Laramie: n.p., 1965.

Current, Richard N. *Three Carpetbag Governors.* Baton Rouge: Louisiana State University Press, 1967.

————. "Carpetbaggers Reconsidered." In *A Festschrift for Frederick B. Artz,* edited by David H. Pinkney and Theodore Ropp. Durham: Duke University Press, 1964.

Dimsdale, Thomas J. *The Vigilantes of Montana, or Popular Justice in the Rocky Mountains.* Norman: University of Oklahoma Press, 1953.

Erwin, Marie H. *Wyoming Historical Blue Book: A Legal and Political History of Wyoming, 1868–1943.* Denver: Bradford-Robinson Printing Co., 1946.

Farrand, Max, ed. *The Legislation of Congress for the Government of the Organized Territories of the United States, 1789–1895.* Newark, N.J.: William A. Baker, Printer, 1896.

Ferris, Robert G., ed. *The American West: An Appraisal.* Santa Fe: Museum of New Mexico Press, 1963.

Forkosch, Morris D., ed. *Essays in Legal History in Honor of Felix Frankfurter.* New York: Bobbs-Merrill Co., Inc., 1966.

Frink, Maurice. *Cow Country Cavalcade.* Denver: The Old West Publishing Co., 1954.

————; Jackson, W. Turrentine; and Spring, Agnes Wright. *When Grass Was King.* Boulder: University of Colorado Press, 1956.

Goetzman, William H. *Exploration and Empire*. New York: Alfred A. Knopf, 1966.

Gould, Lewis L. *Wyoming: A Political History, 1868–1896*. New Haven: Yale University Press, 1968.

Gressley, Gene M. *Bankers and Cattlemen*. New York: Alfred A. Knopf, 1966.

Hafen, LeRoy R., ed. *Colorado and Its People: A Narrative and Topical History of the Centennial State*. 4 vols. New York: Lewis Historical Publishing Company, Inc., 1948.

Hall, Frank. *History of the State of Colorado*. 4 vols. Chicago: The Blakely Printing Company, 1889–1895.

Hicks, Frederick C. *Materials and Methods of Legal Research*. 3d ed. Rochester, N.Y.: The Lawyers Co-operative Publishing Company, 1942.

Hicks, John D. *The Constitutions of the Northwest States*. The Studies of the University of Nebraska, vol. 23, nos. 1–2. Lincoln: University of Nebraska Press, 1924.

Jacobstein, J. Myron, and Mersky, Roy M. *Water Law Bibliography, 1847–1965*. Silver Springs, Md.: Jefferson Law Book Company, 1966.

Kennedy, Joseph C. G., comp. *Population of the United States in 1860: Compiled from the Original Returns of the Eighth Census, under the Direction of the Secretary of the Interior*. Washington, D.C.: The United States Government Printing Office, 1864.

King, Clyde Lyndon. *The History of the Government of Denver with Special Reference to Its Relations with Public School Corporations*. Denver: The Fisher Book Company, 1911.

Kinney, Clesson S. *A Treatise on the Law of Irrigation Including the Law of Water Rights and the Doctrine of Appropriation of Waters, as the Same are Construed and Applied in the States and Territories of the Arid and Semi-Humid Regions of the United States*. Washington, D.C.: W. H. Loudermilk, 1894.

Kraenzel, Carl F. *The Great Plains in Transition*. Norman: University of Oklahoma Press, 1955.

Lamar, Howard R. *Dakota Territory, 1861–1889*. New Haven: Yale University Press, 1956.

———. *The Far Southwest, 1846–1912: A Territorial History*. New Haven: Yale University Press, 1966.

Langeluttig, Albert George. *The Department of Justice of the United States.* Baltimore: Johns Hopkins Press, 1927.

Larson, T. A. *History of Wyoming.* Lincoln: University of Nebraska Press, 1965.

Leeson, Michael A., ed. *History of Montana, 1739–1885.* Chicago: Warner, Beers and Company, 1885.

Lindley, Curtis Holbrook. *A Treatise on the American Law Relative to Mines and Mineral Lands within the Public Land States and Territories and Governing the Acquisition and Enjoyment of Mining Rights in Lands of the Public Domain.* 3 vols. 3d ed. San Francisco: Bancroft-Whitney, 1914.

MacCarthy, James Philip. *Political Portraits by Fitz-Mac.* Colorado Springs: The Gazette Publishing Co., 1888.

McClure, A. K. *Three Thousand Miles through the Rocky Mountains.* Philadelphia: J. B. Lippincott and Company, 1869.

Malone, Rose Mary. *Wyomingana: Two Bibliographies.* Denver: University of Denver Press, 1950.

Martz, Clyde O., ed. *Cases and Materials on the Law of Natural Resources.* St. Paul, Minn.: West Publishing Company, 1951.

Miller, Joaquin. *An Illustrated History of the State of Montana.* Chicago: Lewis Publishing Co., 1894.

Morris, Richard B. "The Courts, the Law, and Social History." In *Essays in Legal History in Honor of Felix Frankfurter,* edited by Morris D. Forkosch. New York: Bobbs-Merrill Co., Inc., 1966.

Morrison, R. S. *Mining Reports.* 22 vols. Chicago: Callaghan and Company, 1883–1906.

———. *Mining Rights in Colorado.* 7th ed. Denver: Chain and Hardy Co., 1892.

Parker, David W., ed. *Calendar of Papers in Washington Archives Relating to the Territories of the United States (to 1873).* Washington, D.C.: Carnegie Institution of Washington, 1911.

Parkhill, Forbes. *The Law Goes West.* Denver: Sage Books, 1956.

Paul, Rodman Wilson. *California Gold: The Beginning of Mining in the Far West.* Cambridge, Mass.: Harvard University Press, 1947.

———. *Mining Frontiers of the Far West, 1848–1880.* New York: Holt, Rinehart & Winston, 1963.

Phillips, Paul C., ed. *Forty Years on the Frontier as Seen in the*

Journals and Reminiscences of Granville Stuart. 2 vols. Cleveland: Arthur H. Clark Company, 1925.

Pollack, Ervin H. *Fundamentals of Legal Research.* 3d ed. Brooklyn: The Foundation Press, Inc., 1967.

Pomeroy, Earl S. *The Territories and the United States, 1861–1890.* Philadelphia: University of Pennsylvania Press for the American Historical Association, 1947.

Porter, Kirk H., and Johnson, Donald Bruce, eds. *National Party Platforms, 1840–1964.* Urbana: University of Illinois Press, 1966.

Portrait and Biographical Record of Denver and Vicinity, Colorado. Chicago: Chapman Publishing Co., 1898.

Riegel, Robert E., and Athearn, Robert G. *America Moves West.* 4th ed. New York: Holt, Rinehart & Winston, Inc., 1964.

Rocky Mountain Mineral Law Foundation, University of Colorado, ed. *The American Law of Mining.* 5 vols. New York: Matthew Bender, 1969.

Russell, Edward C., ed. *Proceedings of the Montana Bar Association from Its Origin, January 8, 1885, to January 14, 1902.* Helena: State Publishing Company, n.d.

Sanders, Helen Fitzgerald. *A History of Montana.* 3 vols. Chicago: The Lewis Publishing Co., 1913.

Shinn, Charles Howard. *Land Laws of Mining Districts.* Johns Hopkins University Studies in History and Political Science, ser. 2, no. 12. Baltimore: Johns Hopkins University Press, 1884.

———. *Mining Camps: A Study in American Frontier Government.* New York: Charles Scribner's Sons, 1885.

Smurr, J. W., and Toole, K. Ross, eds. *Historical Essays on Montana and the Northwest.* Helena: Historical Society of Montana, 1957.

Speer, William S., and Brown, John Henry, eds. *The Encyclopedia of the New West.* Marshall, Texas: The United States Biographical Publishing Co., 1881.

Stanton, Elizabeth C.; Anthony, Susan B.; and Gage, Matilda J., eds. *History of Woman Suffrage.* Vol. 3. Rochester, N.Y.: Charles Mann Printing Company for Susan B. Anthony, 1886.

Stone, Wilbur Fisk, ed. *History of Colorado.* Vol. 1. Chicago: S. J. Clark Publishing Co., 1919.

Toole, K. Ross. *Montana: An Uncommon Land.* Norman: University of Oklahoma Press, 1959.

Trelease, Frank J.; Bloomenthal, Harold S.; and Geraud, Joseph R.,
eds. *Cases and Materials on Natural Resources*. St. Paul, Minn.:
West Publishing Company, 1965.

Triggs, J. H. *History and Directory of Laramie City, Wyoming
Territory*. Laramie City: Daily Sentinel Printing, 1875.

Ubbelohde, Carl. *A Colorado History*. Boulder: Pruett Press, 1965.

Wade, Decius S. *Necessity for Codification*. Helena: Williams and
Sons for the Helena Bar Association, 1894.

Webb, Walter Prescott. *The Great Plains*. Boston: Ginn and Company, 1931.

Wiel, Samuel C. *Water Rights in the Western States*. 2 vols. 3d ed.
San Francisco: Bancroft-Whitney, 1911.

Articles

Albright, Robert Edwin. "Politics and Public Opinion in the Western Statehood Movement of the 1880's." *The Pacific Historical
Review* 3 (1934) : 297–306.

Ashley, Charles S. "Governor Ashley's Biography and Messages."
Contributions to the Historical Society of Montana 6 (1907) :
143–290.

Atherton, Lewis. "The Mining Promoter in the Trans-Mississippi
West." *The Western Historical Quarterly* 1 (January 1970) : 35–50.

Bakken, Gordon M. "The English Common Law in the Rocky
Mountain West." *Arizona and the West* 11 (Summer 1969) : 109–
28.

"Biographical Sketch of Hezekiah L. Hosmer." *Contributions to the
Historical Society of Montana* 3 (1900) : 288–99.

Blake, Henry N. "The First Newspaper of Montana." *Contributions
to the Historical Society of Montana* 5 (1904) : 253–72.

———. "Historical Address." *Contributions to the Historical Society of Montana* 2 (1896) : 76–87.

———. "The Rise of the Territories of the United States" (An address before the Montana Bar Association Meeting, July 13,
1887). *Montana Reports* 1 : 250–72.

———. "Tales of an Old Harvard Soldier." *Harvard Alumni Bulletin*, June 16, 1927, pp. 1058–60.

Bradley, Evelyn. "The Story of a Colorado Pioneer: Mrs. Charles A.
Finding." *Colorado Magazine* 2 (January 1925) : 50–51.

Brantly, Theodore. "Judicial Department." *Contributions to the Historical Society of Montana* 4 (1903) : 109–21.

Breitenstein, Jean S. "Some Elements of Colorado Water Law." *Rocky Mountain Law Review* 22 (June 1950) : 343–56.

Buckman, George Rex. "An Historical Rocky Mountain Outpost." *The Trail* 7 (April 1915) : 5–16.

Burke, William J. "The Origin, Growth, and Function of the Law of Water Use." *Wyoming Law Journal* 10 (Winter 1956) : 95–111.

———. "Western Water Law." *Wyoming Law Journal* 10 (Spring 1956), 180–87.

Callaway, Llewellyn L. "Justices of the Supreme Court of the State of Montana." *Montana Law Review* 5 (Spring 1944) : 34–52.

———. "Something about the Territorial Judges." *Montana Law Review* 4 (Spring 1943) : 5–13.

Campbell, Judge A. C. "Fading Memories" (An address before the Natrona County Bar Association in Casper, n.d.). *Annals of Wyoming* 15 (January 1943) : 39–49.

Ceremonies attending the retirement of Judge Moses Hallett, and the introduction into the office of Judge Rovert E. Lewis, at Denver, Colorado, May 1, 1906. *Colorado Bar Association Report* 9 (1906) : 1–38.

Champion, William M. "Prior Appropriation in Mississippi—a Statutory Analysis." *Mississippi Law Journal* 39 (December 1967) : 1–38.

Coutant, C. G. "History of Wyoming." *Annals of Wyoming* 13 (January 1941) : 74–80.

Danielson, Philip A. "Water Administration in Colorado—Higherority or Priority." *Rocky Mountain Law Review* 30 (April 1958) : 293–314.

Dunbar, Robert G. "The Origins of the Colorado System of Water-Right Control." *Colorado Magazine* 27 (October 1950) : 241–62.

———. "Water Conflicts and Controls in Colorado." *Agricultural History* 22 (July 1948) : 180–86.

Friend, John C. "Early History of Carbon County." *Annals of Wyoming* 15 (July 1943) : 280–86.

Fritz, Percy Stanley. "The Constitutions and Laws of Early Mining Districts in Boulder County, Colorado." *The University of Colorado Studies* 21 (March 1934) : 127–48.

Goodykoontz, Colin B. "Colorado as Seen by a Home Missionary, 1863–1868." *Colorado Magazine* 12 (March 1935) : 60–69.

Gould, Lewis L. "Joseph M. Carey and Wyoming Statehood." *Annals of Wyoming* 37 (October 1965) : 157–69.

"Governor Green Clay Smith's Message." *Contributions to the Historical Society of Montana* 5 (1904) : 128–39.

Hansen, Anne Carolyn. "The Congressional Career of Senator Francis E. Warren, 1890–1902." *Annals of Wyoming* 20 (January 1948) : 3–49.

Heman, Howard W. "Water Rights under the Law." *Montana Law Review* 10 (Spring 1949) : 13–34.

Henderson, Harry B. "Governors of the State of Wyoming." *Annals of Wyoming* 12 (April 1940) : 121–30.

Hill, Burton S. "Frontier Lawyer, T. P. Hill." *Annals of Wyoming* 34 (April 1962) : 43–49.

Hill, Walter B. "The Federal Judicial System." *Report of the Twelfth Meeting of the American Bar Association,* 1889, pp. 289–324.

Holmes, Oliver W., ed. "James A. Garfield's Diary of a Trip to Montana in 1872." *Frontier and Midland* 15 (Winter 1934–35) : 159–68.

Holsinger, M. Paul. "Willis Van Devanter: Wyoming Leader, 1884–1897." *Annals of Wyoming* 37 October 1965) : 170–206.

"Honorable John W. Kingman." *Annals of Wyoming* 14 (July 1942) : 220–27.

Humphries, Abram. "Removal of Territorial Judges." *American Law Review* 26 (1892) : 470–71.

Jackson, W. Turrentine. "The Administration of Thomas Moonlight: 1887–1889." *Annals of Wyoming* 18 (July 1946) : 139–62.

———. "The Governorship of Wyoming, 1885–1889: A Study in Territorial Politics." *Pacific Historical Review* 13 (March 1944) : 1–11.

———. "Railroad Relations of the Wyoming Stock Growers' Association." *Annals of Wyoming* 19 (January 1947) : 3–24.

———. "Territorial Papers of Wyoming in the National Archives." *Annals of Wyoming* 16 (January 1944) : 45–55.

———. "The Wyoming Stock Growers' Association: Political Power in Wyoming Territory, 1873–1890." *Mississippi Valley Historical Review* 33 (March 1947) : 571–94.

Lamar, Howard R. "Carpetbaggers Full of Dreams: A Functional View of the Arizona Pioneer Politician." *Arizona and the West* 7 (Autumn 1965) : 187–206.

Larson, T. Alfred. "Exiling a Wyoming Judge." *Wyoming Law Journal* 10 (Spring 1956): 171–79.

———. "Woman Suffrage in Western America." *Utah Historical Quarterly* 38 (Winter 1970) : 7–19.

———. "Wyoming Statehood." *Annals of Wyoming* 37 (April 1965) : 5–29.

Lasky, Moses. "From Prior Appropriation to Economic Distribution of Water by the State—via Irrigation Administration." *Rocky Mountain Law Review* 1 (April 1929): 161–216, 1 (June 1929) : 284–70, 2 (November 1929) : 35–58.

McDermott, John Dishon. "Fort Laramie's Iron Bridge." *Annals of Wyoming* 34 (October 1962) : 138–44.

"A Memorial to the Members of the Constitutional Convention of Wyoming." *Annals of Wyoming* 12 (October 1940) : 273–94.

Munson, Lyman E. "Pioneer Life in Montana." *Contributions to the Historical Society of Montana* 5 (1904) : 200–34.

Munson, Major Edward L. "Lyman Ezra Munson." *Contributions to the Historical Society of Montana* 7 (1910) : 199–202.

Murray, Robert B. "The Supreme Court of Colorado Territory." *Colorado Magazine* 44 (Winter 1967) : 20–34.

Neil, William M. "The American Territorial System since the Civil War: A Summary Analysis." *Indiana Magazine of History* 60 (September 1964) : 219–40.

Nettels, Curtis. "The Mississippi Valley and the Federal Judiciary, 1807–1837." *Mississippi Valley Historical Review* 12 (September 1925) : 202–26.

"Our State Universities." *The Graphic* 7 (April 15, 1898): 250–54. Western Historical Collection, Norlin Library.

Owens, Kenneth N. "Research Opportunities in Western Territorial History." *Arizona and the West* 8 (Spring 1966) : 7–18.

Paul, Rodman Wilson. "Colorado as a Pioneer of Science in the Mining West." *Mississippi Valley Historical Review* 47 (June 1960) : 34–50.

Pemberton, W. Y. "Changing the Name of Edgerton County." *Contributions to the Historical Society of Montana* 8 (1917) : 321–27.

Pomeroy, Earl S. "Carpetbaggers in the Territories, 1861–1890." *The Historian* 2 (Winter 1939) : 53–65.

———. "The Territory as a Frontier Institution." *The Historian* 7 (Autumn 1944) : 29–41.

————. "Toward a Reorientation of Western History: Continuity and Environment." *Mississippi Valley Historical Review* 41 (March 1955) : 579–600.

"Portrait of Honorable J. M. Carey is Presented to the University of Wyoming." *Annals of Wyoming* 3 (January 1926) : 176.

Richmond, George Q. "The Men with Whom I've Smiled." *Colorado Magazine* 1 (May 1924) : 145–51.

Riner, William A. "Honorable Moses Hallett." *Wyoming Law Journal* 4 (Fall 1949) : 86–95.

Shields, Alice. "Edwin J. Smalley, One of Cheyenne's First Native Sons." *Annals of Wyoming* 13 (January 1941) : 58–72.

Spence, Clark C. "Spoilsman in Montana: James M. Ashley." *Montana the Magazine of Western History* 18 (April 1968) : 24–35.

————. "The Territorial Bench in Montana: 1864–1889." *Montana the Magazine of Western History* 13 (January 1963) : 25–65.

————. "The Territorial Officers of Montana: 1864–1889." *Pacific Historical Review* 30 (May 1961) : 123–36.

Stanton, Irving W. "Reminiscences of the Bench and Bar of Colorado in Early Days." *Colorado Bar Association Report* 16 (1913) : 205–18.

Stone, Albert W. "Are There Any Adjudicated Streams in Montana?" *Montana Law Review* 19 (Fall 1957) : 19–31.

Stone, Wilbur Fisk. "History of the Appellate Courts of Colorado in Early Days" (An address before the Denver Bar Association, April 5, 1905). *Colorado Reports* 34 : xxiii–xxxiii.

Teetor, Henry Dudley. "Honorable Moses Hallett." *Magazine of Western History* 9 (March 1889) : 613–14.

Wade, Decius S. "Self-Government in the Territories." *The International Review* 6 (1879) : 299–308.

Wiel, Samuel C. "Public Policy in Western Water Decisions." *California Law Review* 1 (1912–13) : 11–31.

————. "Theories of Water Law." *Harvard Law Review* 27 (April 1914) : 530–44.

Wikoff, Peter. "The Bench and Bar of Colorado." *Magazine of Western History* 9 (March 1889) : 605–13.

Younger, Richard D. "The Grand Jury on the Trans-Mississippi." *The Southwestern Social Science Quarterly* 36 (September 1955) : 148–59.

Index